The Encyclopedia of
Knitting and Crochet
Stitch Patterns

The Encyclopedia of
Knitting and Crochet Stitch Patterns

by Linda Mariano

Service Communications, Ltd.

VAN NOSTRAND REINHOLD COMPANY

NEW YORK   CINCINNATI   TORONTO   LONDON   MELBOURNE

Copyright © 1976 by Service Communications, Ltd.

Library of Congress Catalog Card Number 76-29142

ISBN 0-442-25117-3

Printed in the U.S.A.

Published in 1977 by Service Communications, Ltd. and
Van Nostrand Reinhold Company
A division of Litton Educational Publishing, Inc.
450 West 33rd Street, New York, NY 10001, U.S.A.

Van Nostrand Reinhold Limited
1410 Birchmount Road, Scarborough, Ontario M1P 2E7, Canada

Van Nostrand Reinhold Australia Pty. Limited
17 Queen Street, Mitcham, Victoria 3132, Australia

Van Nostrand Reinhold Company Limited
Molly Millars Lane, Wokingham, Berkshire, England

Library of Congress Cataloging In Publication Data (CIP)
Mariano, Linda.
   The encyclopedia of knitting and crochet stitch patterns.

   1. Knitting—Patterns.   2. Crocheting—Patterns.
I. Title.
TT825.M27   746.4'3   76-29142
ISBN 0-442-25117-3

Credits

Color photography	Alfreda Bromberg
Illustrations	Joseph Mariano
Diagrams	Mary E. Kornblum

Designs by Judith Glassman: Rainbow Hat and Scarf, Zig Zag Scarf, Professor's Delight, Crocheted Bath Mat, Knit Place Mat, Rattail Chokers, Crocheted Belts, Boy's Fisherman Sweater, Lacy Skimmer Dress, Angora Cardigan, Textured Pullover, Pink Bumpy Stitch Sweater, Green and Yellow Basket. Materials used in garments not available locally—Frederick J.Fawcett, Inc., 129 South Street, Boston, MA 02111; Fibre Yarn Co., Inc., 840 Sixth Avenue, New York, NY 10001; Golden Fleece Imports, P.O. Box 1142, Radio City Station, New York, NY 10019; Mexiskeins, P.O. Box 1624, Missoula, MT 59801; School Products Co., 1201 Broadway, New York, NY 10001. Equipment displayed on Page 34 courtesy of Coulter Studios, 118 East 59 Street, New York, NY 10022.

Contents

Introduction

Knitting and crocheting are fun and practical arts. Best of all, the design and stitch variations of these crafts are virtually limitless. Once you've mastered the few basic stitch steps, you're free to stow away instructions and let your creative instincts take over. And once you get the knack of blending colors, types of materials and stitches into your designs, you will be amazed at the visual and textural combinations you can create with your hooks and needles!

Instructions and swatch illustrations are given for over 600 knitting and crochet stitches—more than enough design ideas to last a lifetime. Along with this invaluable stitch compendium are knitting and crochet projects including detailed instructions and color illustrations for a collection of fashion and home furnishing projects, from baby wear to wall hangings. Use the project ideas to pique and inspire your needlecraft imagination. Spend time stitch browsing, and experiment with decorative effects and ornaments. In no time at all, you will be working intricate designs which are unique reflections of your own personal taste and imagination.

Basics and Techniques

History of Knitting

The name *knitting* comes from an Anglo-Saxon word *cnyttan* which means to tie or to knot. Knitting is the making of a non-woven elastic fabric from yarn with special kinds of needles. The fabric consists of a series of interlaced loops which hang from each other, something like a chain.

The earliest fabric ever discovered was a pair of hand-knitted woolen socks, found in a tomb in Egypt which was built some time in the 4th century B.C.

Other fabrics found at later periods were made of grass knotted into nets, mats and baskets. Many traces of knitted fabrics may be found on the surface designs of statues; they display a quality of knitted clothing or knitted sacks. Some of these reliefs are dated 2750-2625 B.C.

The first knitting needle found is on display in the Corinium Museum, Cirencester, Gloucestershire, in England. It is a bronze rod, broken and bent, dating from the early Iron Age.

Later, hand knitting was done on the four fingers of the left hand, or on a series of pegs arranged in a row or circle. The craft of knitting really became popular in the 14th and 15th centuries in Scotland and England. Wool was the major source for these fabrics.

All knitting was done by hand until 1589, when an English clergyman named William Lee invented a machine that could knit stockings. Queen Elizabeth refused a patent at that time on the grounds that it would put the hand knitters out of work. However, the machine was sold in other countries.

Today, knitting by hand and by machine flourishes in every country of the world.

Basics of Knitting

Tools

Needles: The size knitting needle you use is very important. It produces the gauge and thus affects the finished product and the final measurements.

Straight Single-Pointed Needles are made of bone, aluminum or plastic. They come in 7-, 10-, 12-, 14-, and 18-inch lengths. Sizes range from 0 (the smallest) to 15 (largest).

Circular and Long Flexible Needles have points at each end. They are made of nylon or steel. Lengths vary from 11, 16, 24, 29, to 36 inches. Sizes are the same as for straight needles. Use a circular needle when you have too many stitches to handle on straight needles, or use it to make articles without seams.

Double-Pointed Needles are made of steel, aluminum or plastic. The aluminum and plastic ones are sized the same as single-pointed needles. The steel needles are sized in reverse: size 15 (the smallest) to size 10 (the largest). Pointed at each end, they are primarily used to knit seamless items such as socks, skirts, mittens.

The size of knitting needles varies in England and Canada. The following is a comparison guide:

Size Chart of Knitting Needles

American	0	1	2	3	4	5	6	7	8	9	10	10½	11	13	15
British	13	12	11	10	9	8	7	6	5	4	3	2	1	00	000
Millimeters	2¼	2½	3	3¼	3½	4	4½	5	5½	6	6½	7	7½	8½	9

Knitting Abbreviations

k	knit
p	purl
oz. (s)	ounce (s)
tog	together
pat	pattern
st (s)	stitch (es)
dpn	double-pointed needle
sp	space
beg	beginning
sl st	slip stitch
psso	pass slip stitch over
pc	popcorn stitch
inc	increase
dec	decrease
rnd	round
yo	yarn over
rem	remaining
MC	Main Color
CC	Contrasting Color
lp	loop
rep	repeat
St st	stockinette stitch
skn (s)	skein (s)
dble	double
dk	dark
doz	dozen
gr	gram
lt	light
sk	skip
in. (s)	inch (es)
Skp	sl 1, k 1, psso
yib	yarn in back—yarn is carried behind the stitch
yif	yarn in front—yarn is carried in front of the stitch

Cable Stitch Holders keep the stitches in front or back of your work until you need them. They come in many shapes and sizes. A simple pin or a small double-pointed needle can be substituted when a cable stitch holder is required.

Markers are small plastic rings which can be slipped onto the work to designate a particular place. You can substitute a safety pin, or make your own marker by using a small circle of yarn of another color, putting it on needle where indicated in instructions, and slipping marker from left to right needle without knitting it.

Tapestry Needle: A blunt-end needle used to sew knitted or crocheted articles together; also used for duplicate stitch. They are made of steel and come in an assortment of sizes. The needles are made with a large eye for easy threading. The recommended size is 18.

Crochet Hook: Available in many sizes and lengths. Most crochet hooks are made of plastic, bone, aluminum or steel. Wooden hooks are also available.

Yarn Bobbin: Make your own yarn bobbin. Just cut a small piece of cardboard about 2 or 3 inches long and about an inch wide. Simply wind yarn around this cardboard; wind enough yarn on bobbin to complete several rows. Yarn bobbins are used when several colors are being worked at the same time. These may also be purchased at your local shop. They are made of plastic.

Pins: Purchase a bunch of rust-proof straight pins; they come in handy when sewing articles together. You may also want to use them when blocking or steaming.

Tape Measure: This is a must! Most tape measures are made of plastic or cloth. Always use a tape measure for accurate results. Don't leave a chest measurement to the imagination.

Foundation Stitches

Casting on

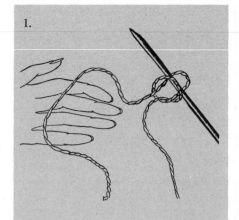

1. Make a slip knot on one needle about 2 yards from the end of your yarn. Allow approximately 1 inch for each stitch to be cast on.

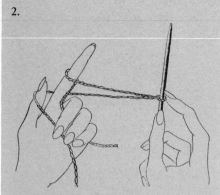

2. Needle is held in right hand. Hold both strands of yarn in the palm of left hand. Loop the free end of yarn around left thumb and the other end around left forefinger. Hold firmly.

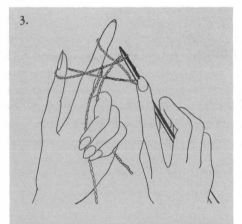

3. Slip the tip of the needle in right hand under the strand on left thumb. Pull toward the strand of yarn on forefinger.

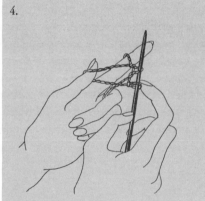

4. Catch the yarn on your forefinger, pass needle under it and pull it through the loop on thumb onto needle. Pull to tighten.

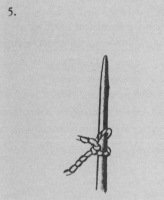

5. One stitch has been cast on. Repeat steps 2-4 until you have cast on the desired amount of stitches.

Knitting

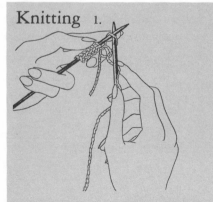

1. Yarn is held in back of work. Holding needle with cast-on stitches in left hand, place point of other needle from left to right into the first stitch (point is under left needle).

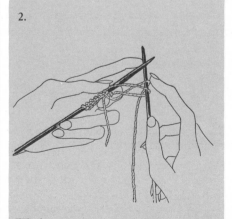

2. Wind yarn in right hand under and over the point of right hand needle and draw yarn toward you through stitch.

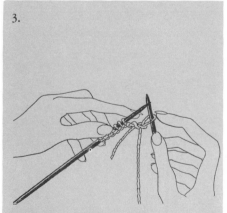

3. Slip stitch just made off left needle. One stitch has been made. Repeat steps 1-3 until all stitches on left needle have been worked. One row will be completed.

Purling

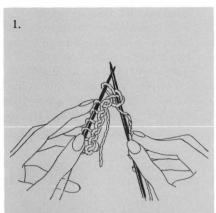

1.

Hold needle in same manner as if to knit a stitch—this time hold yarn in front of work. Slip right needle into front of first stitch, from right to left. Wind yarn around point.

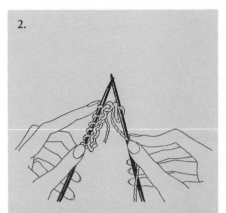

2.

Pull yarn back through stitch. This will complete the purl stitch. Slip stitch off left needle onto right needle. Repeat steps 1 and 2 across row until all stitches have been worked.

More Knitting Stitches and Techniques

Stockinette Stitch: Alternating one knit row and one purl row. The knit side (this is called "reverse stockinette") is the smooth side, the purl side is rough.

Garter Stitch: When every row is knitted. Both sides look the same.

Seed or Moss Stitch: Work this on an even number of stitches. Row 1: * K 1, p 1, repeat from * across row, end p 1. Repeat this pattern for every row.

Cable Stitch: Slip the number of stitches required in your instructions onto a cable stitch holder, work the next number of stitches, then work the stitches remaining on the cable holder.

Duplicate Stitch: Embroidery over a knitted surface. It is not knitted in the work. It is used when an additional color or perhaps a small design is desired. This stitch actually duplicates the knitted work. It is made by using a contrasting color. Thread yarn through a tapestry needle, insert needle into the center of a stitch and follow the directions for the knitted piece according to the design you are following (see Alphabet Chart).

Ribbing: This type of knitting is often used for sleeve cuffs and sweater edges. Working with an even number of stitches, knit one, purl one across row. Repeat this pattern for every row. Variations: K 2, p 2, across row, or K 3, p 3, across row.

To Increase: Add stitches to work.
  Method 1: Knit a stitch in the usual way, but do not slip it off the left needle. Knit the same stitch again, inserting needle into back of stitch. Now slip the completed stitch off left needle. Increasing when purling is done in a similar manner, inserting needle into front of stitch.
  Method 2: Knit between stitches. Knit the strand of yarn between 2 stitches, going into the back of the strand.

To Decrease: Reduce the number of stitches. A decrease is usually made at the beginning or middle of a row.
  1. Middle of row: Knit or purl 2 stitches together by inserting needle through the loops of 2 stitches on left needle at the same time.
  2. End of row: Slip one stitch to right needle, knit next stitch, pass the slipped stitch over the knitted stitch and off the needle.

Binding Off: Getting the stitches off the needle, to hold them securely in place. This is done when you have finished knitting a piece. Always bind off in established pattern. It sometimes helps to use a larger size needle. This keeps the edges from becoming too tight. Knit or purl the first two stitches loosely. Insert left needle from left to right into front of first stitch, lift and pass the stitch over the second stitch and off top of right needle. The first stitch has been bound off. Knit one more stitch loosely and repeat the passing over method. Work across row until one stitch remains. Cut yarn and pull through last stitch. Tighten.

Reading and Understanding Knitting Directions

Slip a Stitch (Sl st): Slip a stitch from left needle to right needle— do not knit or purl this stitch.

Pass slip stitch over (Psso): Slip a stitch, knit a stitch, pass the slipped stitch over the knit stitch just made. This method is often used for decreasing.

Yarn Over (Yo): This method is used to form an extra stitch in your work. For knitting, draw yarn under needle to front and over needle to back. For purling, bring yarn around the right needle once.

Asterisk (*): Directions immediately following it are to be repeated the given number of times.

Parentheses (   ): Directions within the parentheses are to be repeated as often as indicated.

Even: Work in established pattern stitch without increasing or decreasing.

Knit 2 together (k 2 tog): Knit 2 stitches together at the same time.

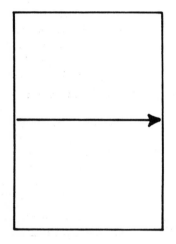

1. Width

Purl 2 together (p 2 tog): Purl 2 stitches together at the same time.

Multiple: The number of stitches required to make one particular design or motif. For example, if the number of stitches needed for a particular pattern is 8, the number of stitches to be cast on should be divisible by 8. Cast on 16, 24, 32, and so on. *Another example:* If your pattern is a multiple of 8 plus 3, cast on a number which is divisible by 8, and cast on 3 extra stitches for the plus 3.

Motif: Design or pattern.

Ply: The number of strands in a piece of yarn. For example, if the wrapper on your yarn reads 2 ply it means that 2 strands of yarn are twisted together for this type of yarn.

Tension: The tightness or looseness with which you knit. Your tension should be kept as even as possible to insure a properly fitting garment and the correct gauge.

Swatch: A small sample of the pattern stitch used to check a gauge. The swatch is usually about 4 inches square.

Measuring Work: Place article on a smooth flat surface. Use a tape measure. First measure the width, then measure length from center of work to the edges.

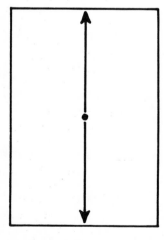

2. Length

Joining Yarns: Always join additional yarn at the outer edge of your work. Join by making a slip knot with the other strand going around the working strand. Move the slip knot to edge of work and tighten. Weave ends into the piece by weaving with a tapestry needle. Weave for about 3 inches. Joining the new yarn at the edge rather than in the center prevents holes from forming in your work.

"Ripping": If you spot an error in your work or your tension is not even, you "rip"—remove work from needles and pull on yarn gently; work carefully to desired spot. Correct mistake, replace stitches on needle and work in the usual manner.

Picking up Dropped Stitches: Insert a crochet hook into loop of dropped stitch. From front to back, pull thread of the row above through loop (new loop made) and place dropped stitch on needle. *If purling:* Insert crochet hook into loop of the dropped stitch from back to front. When working in a pattern stitch pick up dropped stitch in established pattern.

Picking up Stitches along Edges: With right side facing, insert needle into knitting a short distance from edge, place yarn around needle as to knit and draw a loop through piece. Continue in this manner across edge, spacing stitches evenly.

Reversible Pattern (R.P.): Most patterns have a "right" side and a "wrong" side. It can be interesting to use a "wrong" side sometimes to create a very unusual design. The patterns marked R.P. are recommended for such a purpose.

Crochet

History

Unlike knitting the art of crochet does not have an exact birthday. The earliest we know of its existence is in 16th century Europe. However, crochet first became popular at the end of the 18th century.

Crochet is actually a development of tambour work, which is embroidery worked in a chain stitch with a small hook. Crochet eliminated the use of background material as used in tambour or embroidery and became a craft in its own right. Simply, crochet is a series of loops and chains worked with a hook which draws the thread or yarn through intertwined loops and chains.

During a period of extreme poverty in the late 1840s crochet became a means of support for many women in Ireland. This country quickly became the focal point for what is now one of the greatest international handcrafts.

Women and children were able to make garments and yield a profit for their crocheted work. At a convent in Ireland nuns taught children the art of crochet and were able to sell these simple garments for support of the church.

An early craft pioneer in that country was Mrs. Susannah Meredith who in 1847 began a school for the formal education on the subject of crochet. The earliest instruction books recorded on crochet date back to 1820. Equally constructive in these early beginnings was Mrs. W.C. Roberts who taught poverty-stricken women and children to crochet for a living. Boys quickly learned to crochet as well as their mothers and little sisters. Skilled crocheters were in great demand at this time; as a result the best crocheters traveled throughout Ireland and taught their skill.

Several types of crochet were developed at this time. *Plain crochet* consisted of small articles worked in just one piece, and *edgings* trimmed tablecloths and curtains. As crochet developed separate motifs were joined together with twisted threads or bars creating a very delicate effect.

Other techniques were used in different parts of Ireland. *Guipure* was made with heavy linen or silk or cord. This technique was composed of crocheted bars closely arranged with a few motifs intermittently worked in the design. *Knotted Guipure* was somewhat more complex in design, as was *Lifted Guipure* in which the threads were knotted as the garment was worked. This last method was more expensive and the most difficult to execute. Two other types of crochet at this time were *"Spanish lace"* and *"Jesuit lace."*

Crochet was very popular until the 1850s. Circumstances changed and so did crochet. People were no longer interested in quality but needed to make simple garments quickly and with the least expense; thus, standards dropped to a level of very poor quality.

The years after brought competition from machine-made laces. But at the same time crocheted work improved, and the standards were maintained and have remained so until the present time.

Basics of Crochet

Crochet Abbreviations

These abbreviations are commonly used in crocheting instructions:

ch	chain
sl st	slip stitch
sc	single crochet
dc	double crochet
hdc	half double crochet
tr	treble crochet
dtr	double treble crochet
tr tr	triple treble
st(s)	stitch(es)
beg	beginning
cl	cluster
sk	skip
inc	increase
dec	decrease
rnd(s)	round(s)
sp	space
p	picot
bl	block
lp(s)	loop(s)
yo	yarn over
pat	pattern
thru	through

These abbreviations are not as frequently used, but you may run across them:

oz.(s)	ounce(s)
incl	inclusive
rem	remaining
pc	picot
CC	contrasting color
MC	main color
rep	repeat
skn(s)	skein(s)
gr(s)	gram(s)
doz	dozen
dk	dark
lt	light

Hooks: Each crochet hook has been specially designed to use with a particular size yarn or thread. The materials for the first hooks used were made of tortoise shell and bone. Most crochet hooks used today are made of plastic and aluminum and steel. Wooden crochet hooks are used for jiffy crochets.

Hooks come in a variety of sizes. Steel hooks which are used for delicate cotton work come in size 14 (very fine) to 00 (large). They are approximately 5 inches long.

Other hooks of plastic, bone, aluminum are slightly longer and are lettered from B (fine) to K (large). Afghan hooks come in sizes 1-10 and F to J. The wooden hooks come in sizes 10-15.

The size of hooks is not the same in England and Canada as in the United States. Here is a comparison guide:

American	1	2	3	4	5	6	7	8	9	10	11	12	13	14
British	0	1	1½	2	2½	3	3½	4	4½	5	5½	6	6½	7

Symbols and Terms

[ ] Brackets: What is enclosed in brackets is worked number of times following brackets.

* Asterisk: Repeat directions following * as many times as directed.

( ) Parentheses: Used to show repetition, work directions in parentheses as many times as directed.

Work even: Work same stitch without any changes.

Multiple: Number of stitches required for the pattern. The number of stitches used should be evenly divisible by the multiple.

Picot: Ch 3, sc or sl st in first stitch of chain.

Even: Work rows without increasing or decreasing.

Triple treble: Yarn over the hook 4 times.

Double treble: Yarn over hook 3 times.

Treble crochet: Yarn is wrapped around hook twice, then yarn over and through 2 loops, yarn over and through 2 loops, yarn over hook and through 2 loops.

To Increase: Work 2 stitches in one stitch.

To Decrease: Draw up loop in each of 2 stitches, yarn over and draw through all loops on hook.

To Add a Row: Make number of chains as directed, turn, work 1 single crochet in 2nd chain from hook, 1 single crochet in each stitch across to end of ch, work in pattern to end of row.

To Omit Stitches: Slip stitch in the number of stitches stated in directions, work to last stitch as directed, chain, turn.

To Turn Work: When turning work specific number of stitches is required to work on the reverse side. This chart lists the number of chains according to the stitch being worked to turn work, unless otherwise stated in directions.

Stitch You Are Working

	Chains to make for turn:
Single crochet	Chain 1
Half Double crochet	Chain 2
Double crochet	Chain 3
Treble crochet	Chain 4
Double Treble crochet	Chain 5
Triple Treble crochet	Chain 6

How to Crochet

These are the basic crochet stitches and all you need to know to create the most complex of designs.

Foundation Chain

In learning to crochet the very first step is to make a Foundation Chain. All you do is...

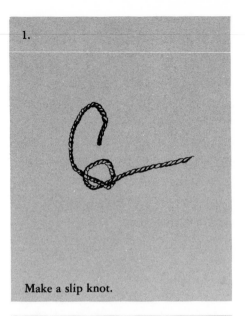

1.

Make a slip knot.

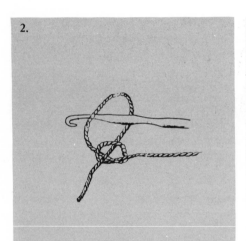

2.

Loop several inches of yarn over hook and through knot.

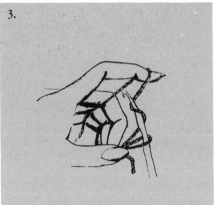

3.

Tighten knot and place between thumb and third finger of left hand. Thread yarn through left hand as shown. Loop yarn over hook, held by right hand.

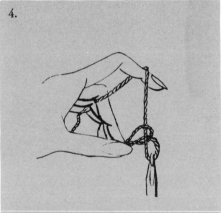

4.

Catch yarn with hook and pull through loop. This completes the first chain. To add chains just repeat.

5.

Yarn over hook.

6.

Pull through loop. It's that easy!

7.

Repeat Figures 5 and 6 to work foundation chain.

Single Crochet (sc)

After you have learned the fundamental chain, the next stitch is the single crochet.

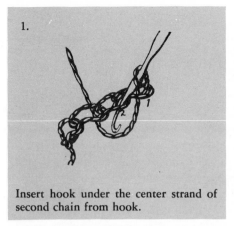

1.

Insert hook under the center strand of second chain from hook.

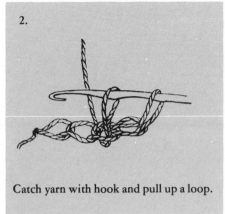

2.

Catch yarn with hook and pull up a loop.

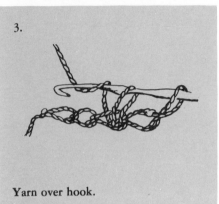

3.

Yarn over hook.

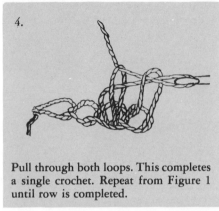

4.

Pull through both loops. This completes a single crochet. Repeat from Figure 1 until row is completed.

Half Double Crochet (hdc)

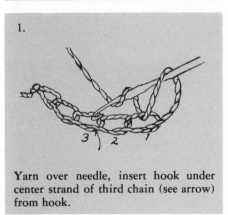

1.

Yarn over needle, insert hook under center strand of third chain (see arrow) from hook.

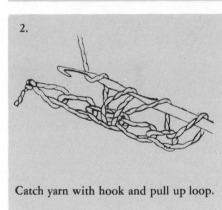

2.

Catch yarn with hook and pull up loop.

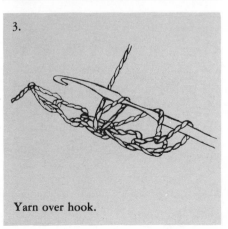

3.

Yarn over hook.

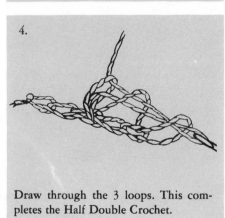

4.

Draw through the 3 loops. This completes the Half Double Crochet.

Double Crochet (dc)

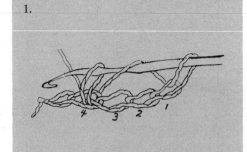

1.

Yarn over hook, insert hook under center strand of 4th chain from hook and pull up a loop.

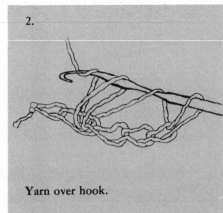

2.

Yarn over hook.

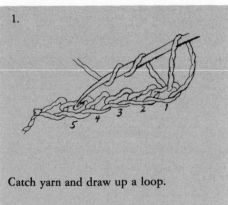

3.

Draw through first 2 loops on hook.

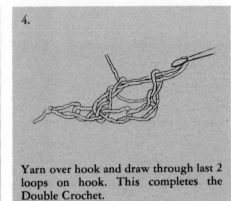

4.

Yarn over hook and draw through last 2 loops on hook. This completes the Double Crochet.

Treble Crochet (tr)

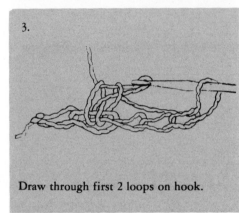

1.

Catch yarn and draw up a loop.

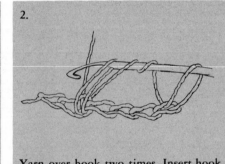

2.

Yarn over hook two times. Insert hook under center strands of fifth chain from hook.

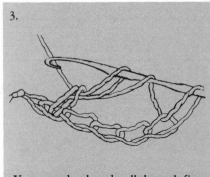

3.

Yarn over hook and pull through first 2 loops.

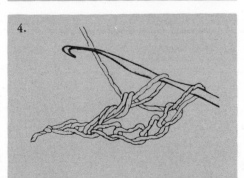

4.

Yarn over hook and pull through the next 2 loops.

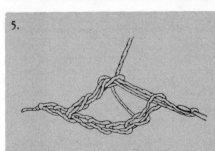

5.

Yarn over hook and pull through the remaining 2 loops to complete stitch.

Slip Stitch (sl st)

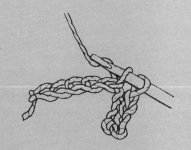

Make a foundation chain of desired length. * Insert hook under top strands of second chain from hook. Catch yarn and pull up a loop through both chain and loop on hook. Repeat from * across row.

Double Treble (dtr)

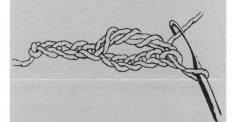

Yarn over hook 3 times. Place hook under center strand of sixth ch from hook, catch yarn and pull up loop. * Yarn over hook and pull through 2 loops, repeat from * 4 times. This completes the stitch.

Triple Treble (tr tr)

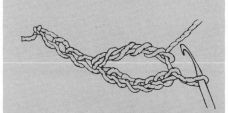

Yarn over hook 4 times. Place hook under center strand of seventh chain from hook, catch yarn and pull up loop. * Yarn over hook and pull through 2 loops, repeat from * 5 times more to complete stitch.

Afghan Stitch 1.

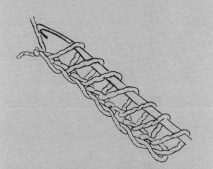

Make a foundation chain of desired length. Draw up a loop in second chain from hook and in each chain across row. Keep all loops on hook.

2.

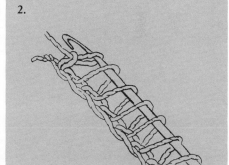

To work off loops, yarn over hook and draw through the first loop.

3.

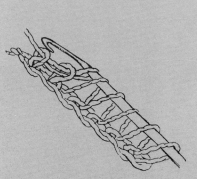

* Yarn over hook and draw through next 2 loops, repeat from * across row until 1 loop remains. This loop will be the first stitch of next row.

4.

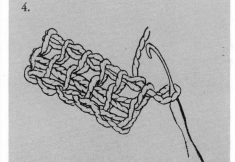

Skip first vertical bar, place hook in front of next vertical bar and pull up a loop, pull up a loop in each remaining vertical bar across row. Work off loops as previously stated. Edge Stitch (keeps edges even): In last stitch place hook into double loop and draw up a loop.

How to Read a Chart

If you've never seen an instruction chart before, you might mistake it for a random and unsuccessful tic-tac-toe game. It's really a pictorial chart showing you how to create special motifs and designs into your work. Whether you are creating decorative flower motifs or fashioning an intricate afghan rug, learning the simple chart lingo is essential to your work.

Each block should be read as one separate stitch. Depending on the chart you are following, each symbol (which will be fully explained on an accompanying legend) will represent a particular color or type of stitch to be knitted or crocheted.

To prevent confusion, cross out rows as they are completed. This way you always know where you are.

Begin at lower right-hand corner and work across row, making necessary changes as instructed in chart. * Work from left to right across next row, work from right to left across next row, repeat from * until pattern is completed.

Example Chart: **Rows** 1-3: Work in one color all the way across rows.

Row 4: Work across 5 sts in main color, next stitch with Yellow, next 8 stitches with Black, next st in Yellow, next 5 stitches in main color.

Rows

Taking Measurements

Our table of body measurements is based on the standard body measurements recommended by the Pattern Fashion Industry. This table corresponds to the standard measurements used in the ready-to-wear industry. Before starting your garment use the table on the following page for accurate sizing.

Caution: Taking the correct body measurement, carefully measure the person to determine the size you should make.

Now compare your measurements with those in the table and locate the measurement closest to yours. Directly above this measurement is the proper size to make.

If your measurement differs from the measurements given in the table, adjustments can be made in the blocking and finishing. Be sure and note that childrens' sizes are determined by chest measurements, not the age of the child.

Standard Body Measurements
(All measurements in inches)

Misses

Size	Bust	Waist	Hip
6	30½	22	32½
8	31½	23	33½
10	32½	24	34½
12	34	25½	36
14	36	27	38
16	38	29	40
18	40	31	42

Women

Size	Bust	Waist	Hip
38	42	34	44
40	44	36	46
42	46	38	48
44	48	40½	50
46	50	43	52
48	52	45½	54
50	54	48	56

Juniors

Size	Bust	Waist	Hips
5	30	21½	32
7	31	22½	33
9	32	23½	34
11	33½	24½	35½
13	35	26	37
15	37	28	39

Teens

Size	Bust	Waist	Hip
5-6	28	22	31
7-8	29	23	32
9-10	30½	24	33½
11-12	32	25	35
13-14	33½	26	36½
15-16	35	27	38

Pre-Teens

Size	Chest	Waist	Hips
8	28	23	31
10	29	24	32
12	31	25	34
14	33	26	36

Men

Size	Chest	Waist
34	34	30
36	36	32
38	38	34
40	40	36
42	42	38
44	44	40
46	46	42
48	48	44

Girls

Size	Bust	Waist	Hip
6	24	22	26
8	27	23½	28
10	28½	24½	30
12	30	25½	32
14	32	26½	34

Boys

Size	Chest	Waist	Hip
6	24	22	25
8	26	23	27
10	28	24	29
12	30	25½	31
14	32	27	33
16	34	29	35½

Infants & Toddlers

Size	Chest	Waist
6 mos.	19	19
1	20	19½
2	21	20½
3	22	20½
4	23	21

To change the size of any garment add or subtract the number of stitches equal to 1 inch to both back and front of article for each size larger or smaller than the size given in the pattern instructions you are following. For a pattern stitch add or subtract the number of stitches for one or more multiples of a pattern.

Girls', Boys' and Infants and Toddlers

Height—Measure from back of neck to floor (with shoes)
Hip—Fullest part of hips
Arm length—Underarm to wrist

Women's and Misses'—Juniors and Teens

Bust—Measure the largest part
Waist—Measure natural waistline
Hip—7 inches below waist
Arm length—Measure from underarm to wrist

Men's

Chest—Measures across largest part
Arm length—Underarm to wrist

Basics for Fitting and Finishing

Before You Begin

Read the Directions Carefully. Read each paragraph as a whole. Watch for special instructions such as "9 times more" or "change to hook size J." Be sure you have the correct materials and enough yarn to complete your article. Be specific about the size you are following and underline or circle the size you are going to make.

Checking for the Correct Size. Please refer to the standard table measurements.

Changing Size. If the pattern and style are relatively simple, it is possible to vary the size and make adjustments where necessary. For each size add or subtract about 2 inches in total measurements for adults and approximately 1 inch for children. If there are special shapings such as raglan sleeve or diagonal patterns we do not suggest converting the size. These patterns do not always adapt well. Sometimes the size can be altered simply by using smaller or larger size hook.

Length can be altered by knitting or crocheting more or less rows before making the hip, the armhole or the neck shaping.

Check Your Stitch Gauge. This is the most important aspect of knitting and crocheting. The gauge will determine the size and fit of your garment. Gauge is the number of stitches per inch crocheted or knit with a particular size hook or needle with the specified yarn used in the instructions you use. Now using the hook or needle and yarn recommended, make a swatch about 4 inches square in the pattern stitch you will be using. Pin it down (use a cloth or towel) and block it. Now measure. If you have more stitches to the inch, you are working too tightly, and you should switch to larger size hook or needle. If you get less stitches to the inch use smaller size hook or needle. The size of the implement will not be important after you have obtained the correct stitch gauge. Experiment with different swatches until your gauge is correct.

This gauge measures 2 stitches to 1 inch and 8 rows to 2 inches.

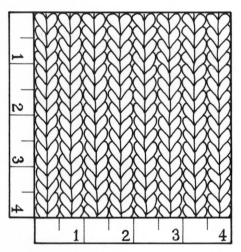

Substituting Yarns. If for some reason you do not have the yarn listed in your instructions or want to change yarns, make a test swatch first and check your gauge. Be sure the gauge is the same for a proper fitting garment. Be sure to buy enough yarn at one time. Dye lots always differ, and you may end up with a sleeve a shade off if you have to buy more yarn.

Dye Lot. A serial number which a manufacturer uses to tell him how much yarn has been dyed at the same time. Always save labels—in case you need to purchase extra quantities of the same yarn.

Choosing Yarns

28 grams	approx. 1 oz.
40 grams	approx. 1½ oz.
50 grams	approx. 1¾ oz.
100 grams	approx. 3½ oz.
113 grams	approx. 4 oz.

Weights

Be sure to use the recommended yarn in any instructions since yarns vary in weight, texture, fiber, and ply. If you substitute yarns it will be difficult, if not impossible, to get the required gauge or even a comparable one. You might end up wearing a tent!

Packaged yarns have bands or wrappers on them. These usually give you specific information: dye lot, weight in ounces, ply. These wrappers also have cleaning or washing instructions, and state the type of fiber such as wool, orlon, cotton, mohair, or acrylic.

If you come across some yarns measured in grams, don't be frightened. The table at left will help you convert the weight from grams into ounces.

The weight of the yarn you use will be determined by the style of the garment you choose to make. Smaller or finer size hooks and needles are usually used with a light weight, soft delicate yarn. Larger hooks and needles are used for a heavier or bulky look. Do not substitute yarns until you have made a test swatch. Yarns are not always interchangeable. Synthetic fibers are most often machine washable—this is especially useful for baby clothes because of the frequent washings.

Putting It Together

Weaving Seams (Duplicate Stitch). Place edges together with right sides up. Thread tapestry needle with matching yarn. Pull needle up through first stitch on your left edge, insert needle through center of first stitch on your right edge, pass under 2 rows, and pull yarn through to right side. Place needle in center of stitch on opposite row of left edge and pass under 2 rows, draw yarn to right side. Continue working in this manner (from side to side) until seam is completed. Always be sure to match rows and/or pattern. Do not pull stitches too tight.

Backstitch Seam. This is the most commonly used method for joining seams. Pin right sides of pieces together. Again be sure your rows and pattern are matching. Use matching yarn in tapestry needle, and take "running" stitches with a backstitch every 1/2 inch—this will keep seams flat.

Crochet Slip Stitch. With right sides facing, insert crochet hook into first stitch at the top, pull yarn through from back. * Insert hook into next stitch, pull this loop through first loop on hook, repeat from * until entire piece is joined.

Sewing in a Sleeve. Pin Pieces together.
1. Place sleeve seam to center underarm.
2. Place center of sleeve cap to shoulder seam. Join with a backstitch seam.

Joining Seams on the Right Side. You might want to use this technique for pillow seams, or handbags.
   Place seams to be joined together, right sides facing. Draw tapestry needle through first stitch at top edge and * draw needle through top stitch of other edge, insert needle into next stitch at top edge, repeat from * until seam is joined. This makes a very neat looking seam. You will not even be able to see it—it magically disappears into the article!

Sewing in a Zipper. Baste the zipper to the knitted or crocheted piece. Sew from the top down. Do not stretch garment or the zipper will bulge.

To Finish a Buttonhole. Work overcast stitch with matching yarn around buttonhole. Ordinary sewing thread matching in color may also be used if the yarn is too bulky.

Center Underarm

Shoulder Seam

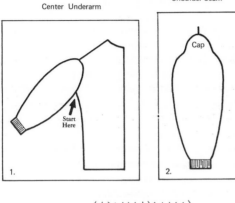

Cap

1.

2.

Start
Here

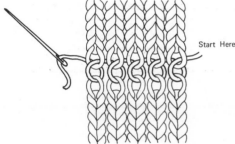

Start Here

The Finished Product

Blocking or Steaming. It is a good idea to block pieces first, then sew them together. Occasionally pieces tend to curl up and therefore have no shape. Blocking them first will hold their shape and make it easier to sew them together.
   Place pieces or garment on ironing board with wrong sides facing, then place a damp cloth on top of garment. Press lightly with a medium hot iron. Never rest iron on articles. You may want to pin pieces or garment to the ironing board. If you do this, leave pins in place until article is dry. Use rust-proof pins, which can be purchased in a five- and ten-cent store.
Caution: Never block or steam ribbing.

How to Line a Garment. Lining can be a very important asset in the making of your garment. A good lining helps to shape the garment and retain the shape.
   Choose a fabric which is appropriate to the weight, style and color of your garment. Bring the garment with you when you shop for lining to be sure of the weight and color.
   After pieces have been blocked, lay them flat on a clean piece of paper and carefully make an outline around each piece. Cut the paper patterns about a half inch wider than the outline (for seam allowance). Place pieces on fabric. Pin in place, cut around the edge of pattern. Make bustline darts on dress or sweater front lining about 2 inches under the armhole, taper to about 3 inches toward center front. Tack a half-inch seam at neck and waistline edges. On the right side of lining stitch all main seams, leave back or side opening in lining. Make allowance for pleats. Baste the seam at neck and waist and sleeves.

Hem garment separately. Collars, pockets, and cuffs should be lined separately. A commercial pattern is also recommended. One can usually be found for any type of garment.

Crocheted Edges. Knitted and crocheted work tends to curl up and have a somewhat unfinished look. The best solution is to crochet the edges: work the single crochet (sc) on the right side of the article; to turn corners, work 2 or 3 single crochet in each corner stitch.

Making Alterations

To Lengthen a Finished Garment. Working from bottom down, attach yarn at seam or center back and work a few rows of pattern; perhaps a different color yarn would be more suitable to give a bordered effect. This will work well on sleeves as well.

To Shorten a Finished Garment. This technique may be used on sleeves or hem. Open the seam, measure amount to be shortened. Cut one thread and draw along row, "Ripping" to length desired. Or turn up hem if the garment is not bulky and sew in place, if you do not wish to "rip" the threads. Steam and block accordingly.

To Narrow a Finished Garment. Mark seams for alteration. Wrong side facing, with sewing machine, sew 2 or 3 rows of elongated stitches along seams edges. Cut away excess.

Washing and Care of Sweaters

By Machine. Synthetics are recommended. Turn garment inside out. The garment is less able to "pill." In the washer use cold water and a mild detergent. Sweaters can be dried at a low or medium temperature.

By Hand. For synthetics and wool trace an outline of the garment on paper. Wash in cold water and gentle detergent. Rinse and place on paper outline. Reshape the garment to fit paper outline. Squeeze water out. Do not twist or rub.

Caring For Sweaters.
1. Never hang a sweater. Fold loosely and keep flat.
2. For storage: clean and place in mothballs.
3. After wearing, air it.
4. "Pills" can be brushed off with a clean dry sponge, brushing lengthwise.

Decorative Effects
and Ornaments

Notions   It's a good idea to investigate a trimming store. You will come up with all sorts of interesting little things to make your knitting and crocheting more fun.

Ribbon: A touch of ribbon woven into a neckline or a sleeve edge brightens the plainest sweater. Make some ribbon bows and sew to childrens' clothing. You can knit and crochet with ribbon too! In fact, that's what "knitting ribbon" is made for.

Appliqués: They can be bought by the yard or one at a time. Use the cotton ones that can be laundered. Appliqués can be quite expensive, so you may want to make them yourself from felt scraps. Just trace a design on the felt and cut it out.

Buttons: Add a touch of ingenuity to your child's favorite sweater or cap by sewing on a button or two. You probably have some in your sewing basket which you don't know what to do with.

Beads, Sequins, Pearls: There are great possibilities with just a handful of beads, sequins or pearls. They can be sewn on or worked right into your piece. Wash finished garment by hand in cold water. Do not use bleach, or dry clean.

Knitting with Beads

Pull out several yards of yarn from skein, cut and thread into tapestry needle, string as many beads as necessary for 1 or 2 rows.

Row 1: Knit.
Row 2: Purl.
Row 3: K 1, * insert right needle into stitch on left needle, draw yarn and bead around right needle, pass left stitch over yarn and bead, pushing bead to front of work, k 3, repeat from * across row.
Row: 4: Purl.
Repeat Rows 1-4 for Pattern Stitch.

Crocheting with Beads

Thread yarn through a tapestry needle and string enough beads for several rows.
Note: work sc in top lp throughout.
Ch 20.
Row 1: Sk first ch, sc in each rem ch, ch 1, turn.
Row 2: Sc in first 3 sc, * push bead against last sc worked, insert hook into top lp, yo hook, push bead and draw yarn through to front of work and complete st, sc in next 3 sc, repeat from * across row, end sc in last 3 sc, ch 1, turn.
Repeat Rows 1 and 2 for Pattern Stitch.

Paillettes: These come 100 per package and provide unusual decorative effects on knits. They are flat and shiny and are available in a wide variety of colors. There is a large eye at the top for a knitting needle to pass through. Use a smaller size needle than the eye of the paillette.

Here are two pattern ideas for incorporating paillettes:

Multiple of 5 stitches plus 2.
Rows 1, 2: Stockinette stitch.
Row 3: * K 3, place paillette on right needle yo and pull paillette over right needle (keep paillette in front of work), repeat from * across row, end k 3.
Row 4: * P 3, p 2 tog, repeat from * across row, end p 2.
Repeat Rows 1-4 for Pattern Stitch

Overlapping Paillette Pattern. Multiple of 4 stitches
Row 1: Knit.
Row 2: Purl.
Row 3: K 1, * place paillette on right needle, insert right needle in next st yo and draw st and paillette over right needle, repeat from * across row, end k 1.
Row 4: Purl.
Repeat Rows 3 and 4 for Pattern Stitch.
Note: Be sure to keep all paillettes in front of work.

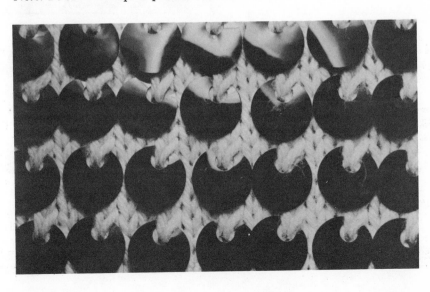

Embroidery Floss: Embroidery floss is very inexpensive and colors are fantastic. It may be purchased in yarn shops. It's great for cross-stitching designs over a stockinette stitch background or other similarly flat knit and crochet pattern stitches.

It's very easy: Use a piece of graph paper to map out your design. Count the squares on the graph sheet, using as many blocks as you have stitches in your article. Use colored pencils for color changes. Begin from the center stitch and work out to the ends; otherwise you might end up with extra stitches at the edges and it will throw the whole design out of order. Work the entire pattern in cross-stitch. See diagrams 1 and 2 for details.

Sample: 25 stitches across row (25 blocks). Use an **X** to designate design and any color changes.

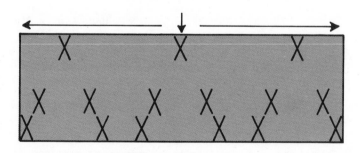

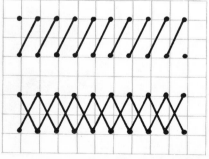

Cross-Stitch: Worked on a stockinette stitch background.
Materials: Tapestry needle, contrasting yarn or embroidery floss

Work from right to left or vice versa.
1. Make a row of diagonal stitches of equal length (usually over 2 rows). Space evenly. Each Dot represents one stitch, each Block represents 1 row.
2. Work back over the same stitches with a diagonal stitch going in the opposite direction. When article is finished, knot ends of thread in back of work.

Cross Stitch Charts

Here are some easy color/design ideas.
Use instructions on preceding page.

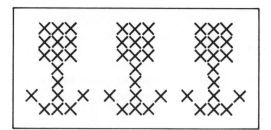

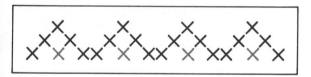

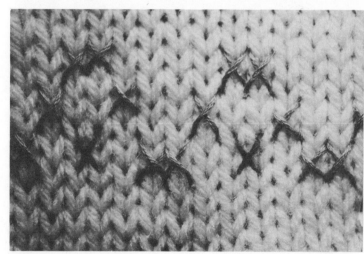

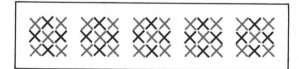

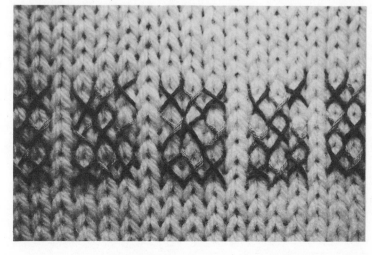

Ornaments

Fringe: Wind yarn around a piece of cardboard. Cut open at one end. Place several strands of yarn together, fold in half. Place crochet hook inside fold and, in desired place for fringe, draw loose ends through fold and tighten. Trim evenly.

Tassels: Wind yarn around a cardboard slightly longer than desired length for each tassel. Tie a loop at one end. Remove from cardboard. Wind a piece of yarn about 1 inch from top. Cut open bottom loop. Trim evenly. Sew in place.

Pom pom: Wind yarn about 25-35 times (depending upon fullness desired) around a cardboard measuring 2 inches in length. Remove from cardboard. Tie a knot in center. Cut open loops at both ends. Trim evenly.

Twisted Cord: Cut a number of strands about 2½ times the desired length for finished cord. Tie one end to stationary point such as a door knob, pull yarn and twist between fingers until yarn begins to buckle, fold the cord in half and twist together. Make a knot at each end, leaving about 3 to 4 inches for fringe. Cut loops open and trim.

Tie: Use double strand of yarn and a crochet hook. Crochet a chain of desired length, end off, weave in ends.

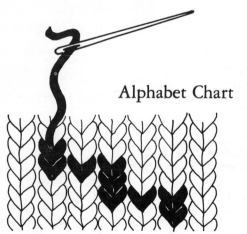

Alphabet Chart

This Alphabet Chart is designed as a guide for making monograms or decorations on your knitted or crocheted work. Work the letters in duplicate stitch.

Duplicate Stitch: * Insert tapestry needle (use a contrasting color) from back to front side of work going through the center of a stitch. Pass needle under the 2 strands of the stitch as shown in the diagram. Pass needle into the center of same stitch, in next stitch repeat from * until you have finished your design.

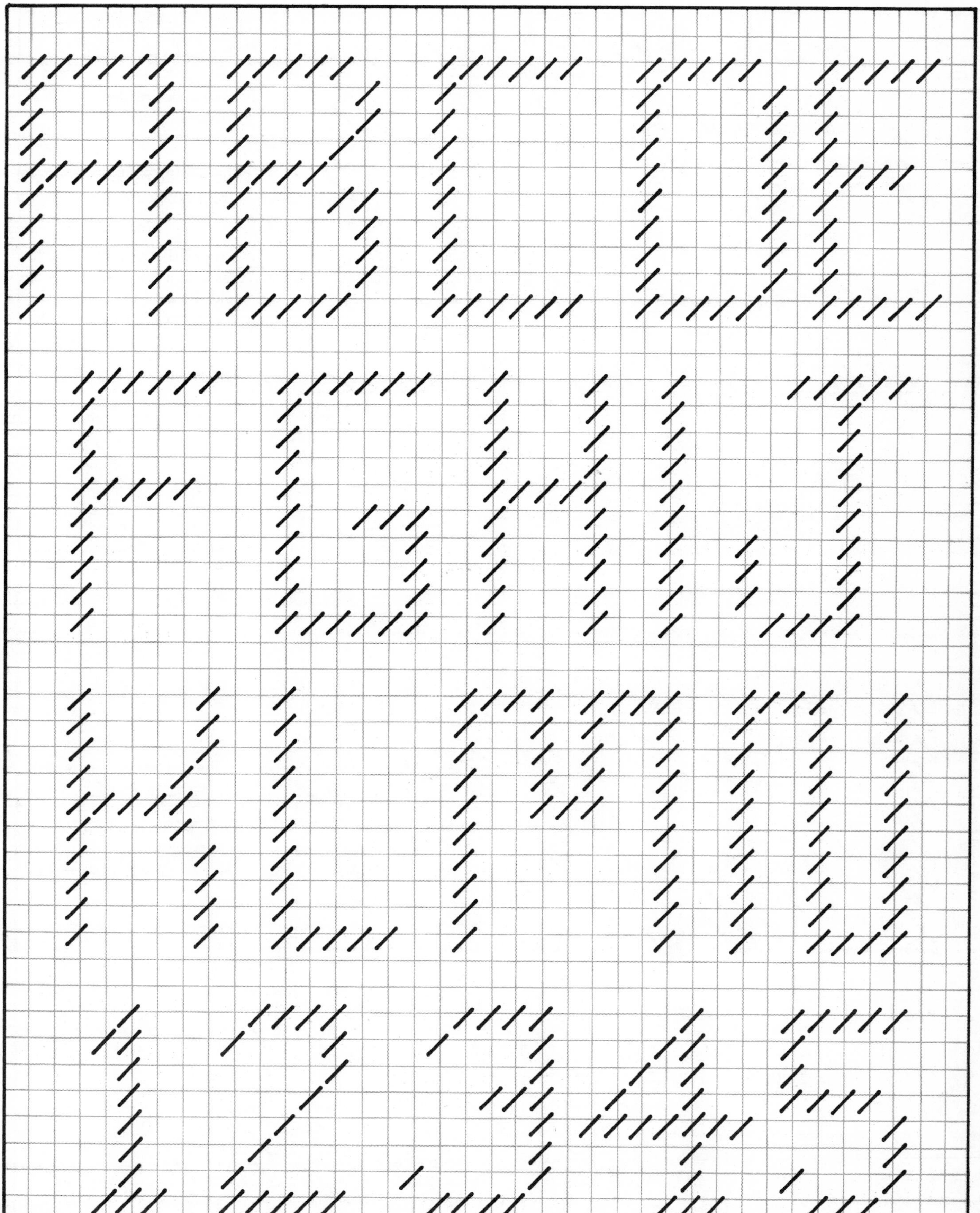

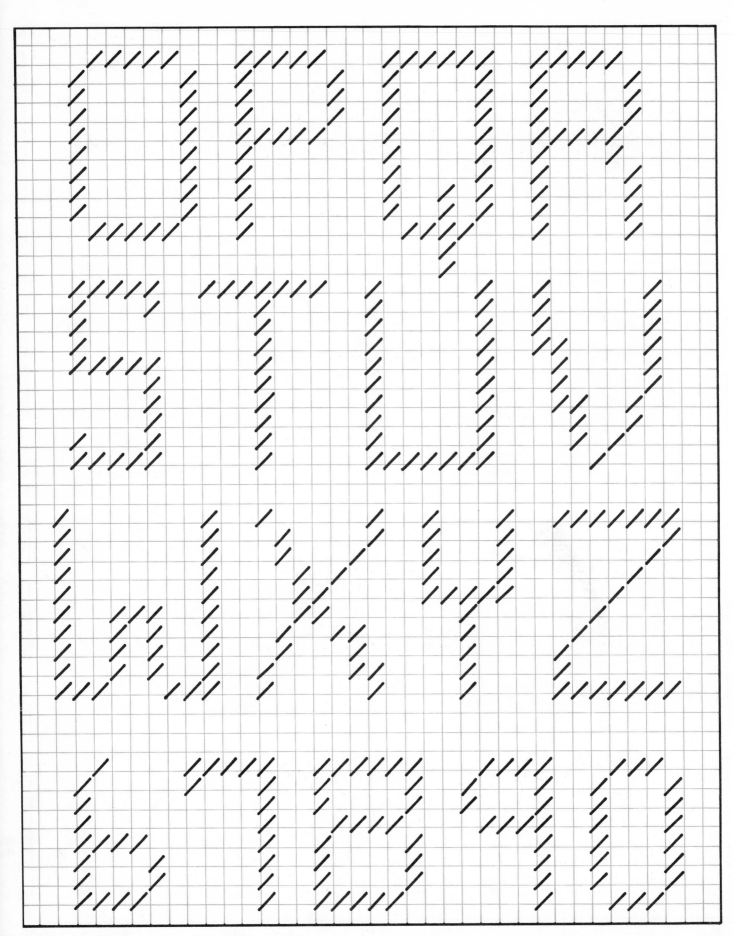

Knitting and Crochet Materials
Their Uses and Effects

Unusual Novelties

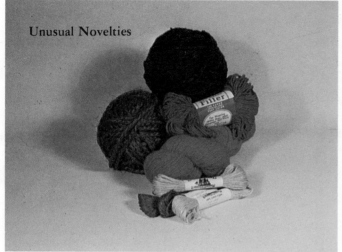

Threads and String

Medium-Weight Yarns

Bulky Yarns

Cord, Twine and Rope

Light-Weight Yarns

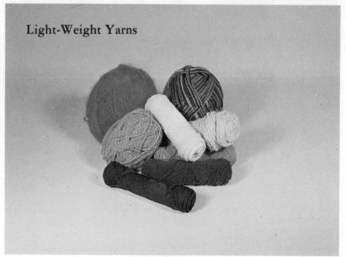

Unusual Novelties—These exotic yarns may not be available in your local store, but you can track them down on page 4. Clockwise from upper left: Mexiskeins' Medium Weight, Lily Cotton's 4-strand Filler, Golden Fleece's Heavyweight Wool, Frederick Fawcett's linen, Golden Fleece's sisal. **Threads and Strings**—A variety of effects can be created with these yarns: combine several strands of cotton and linen for a fabric sturdy enough for a handbag, belt or hat. The shiny rattail makes exciting jewelry, while Crocheted strings make elegant lace table covers. **Medium-Weight Yarns**—These versatile yarns are excellent for warm sweaters, skirts, dresses, pants, afghans, and blankets. **Bulky Yarn**—On large knitting needles or crochet hooks, these yarns are quickly worked into cozy outdoor garments. **Cord, Twine and Rope**—Plant holders, baskets, curtains, casual tablecloths and place mats can be knit or crocheted with these sturdy cotton and nylon fibers, most of which are available at your hardware store. **Light-Weight Yarns**—If you're interested in old-fashioned lacy looks, experiment with these thinner yarns. Lightweight orlon is excellent for baby garments and blankets.

Tools and Implements
Both Common and Exotic

Knitting Needles

Scissors and Shears

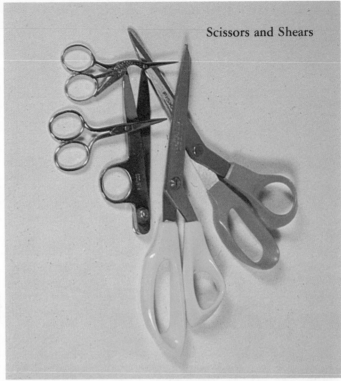

Knitting and Crochet Tools

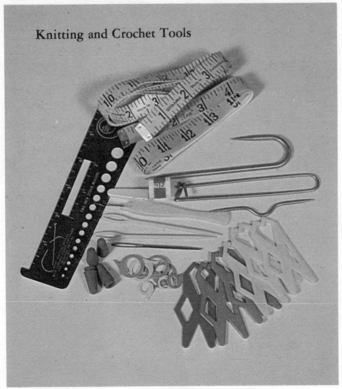

Crochet Hooks

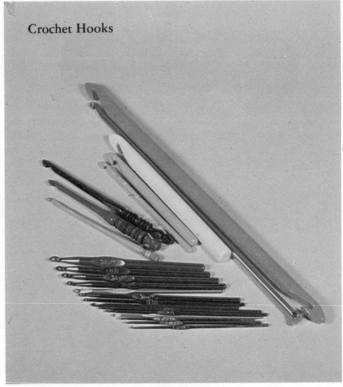

Knitting Needles—Knitting needles range in size from a monster 1½″ in diameter to a needle measured in millimeters. Double pointed and circular needles are used to work on circular or tubular garments. **Scissors and Shears**—These range from tiny, for use on snipping delicate cottons, to hefty models used on heavyweight cords. **Knitting and Crochet Tools**—Reading clockwise from 12 o'clock, tape measure, cable needle, yarn holder, stitch counter, cable needle, yarn

thread ender, tapestry and yarn needles, stitch markers, needle caps and a knitting needle size gauge. **Crochet Hooks**—Whether you work with the finest thread or the heaviest yarn, you can find a crochet hook to fit your needs. Crochet hooks shown here include a knit-cro-hook (with a hook at both ends), afghan hook, and a group of hand-carved rosewood hooks, available at Coulter Studios (see page 4 for address).

Knitting and Crochet Projects

These knitting and crochet projects include detailed instructions charts and illustrations for many useful fashion and home furnishing projects. While showing specific application of stitch patterns, the projects also utilize many unusual materials and decorative techniques to increase design alternatives and expand the art of knitting and crochet.

Flower-in-the-Square Afghan

Afghan measures approximately 64″ x 64″ plus fringe.

Materials
Knitting Worsted (4-oz. skeins), Color A—Winter White, 3 skeins; Color B—Shocking Pink, 4 skeins; Color C—Emerald Green, 4 skeins

Crochet Hook Size I

Blunt End Tapestry needle

Gauge
8 dc to 2″ (diameter of first round); motif is 8″ square.

Motif
Make 64. With Color A ch 7, join with sl st to form ring.

Rnd 1: Ch 3 (counts as 1 dc), work 15 dc in ring—16 dc around. Join with sl st in top of ch-3.

Rnd 2: Ch 9, tr in next dc, * ch 5, tr in next dc, repeat from * around, ch 5, sl st in 4th ch of starting ch; 16 ch-5 spaces around. End off.

Rnd 3: Joining Color B with sl st in any ch-5 sp, ch 3; holding back last lp of each tr, work 3 tr in same sp, yo and then thru all 4 lps on hook, * ch 5; holding back last lp of each tr on hook, work 4 tr in next ch-5 sp, yo and thru all 5 lps on hook. Repeat from * around. End ch 5, sl st in top of starting ch. End off.

Rnd 4: Join Color C with sl st in any ch-5 sp, ch 2, and work 3 dc, ch 1 in same sp, work 4 dc, ch 1 in each of next 2 ch-5 spaces, * in next ch-5 sp work (4 dc, ch 3, 4 dc) for corner, work 4 dc, ch 1 in each of next 3 ch-5 sps, repeat from

* until all 4 corners have been made. Join with sl st in top of ch-2. End off.

Finishing
Sew in all loose ends before sewing together.

Joining
Sew all motifs together with Color C on *wrong side only and sew through back loops only.* Sew 8 squares together to make one strip. Make 8 strips of 8 squares each. Join strips in same manner. Sew in all loose ends.

Note
Do not block or steam squares.

Fringe
Cut 9, 14″ strips of yarn for each fringe and place fringe in each corner of each square and a fringe in center of each square.

Appliquéd Blouse

Directions are written for size 8. Changes for sizes 10 and 12 are in parentheses.

Materials

Knitting Worsted (4 oz. skeins), 3 skeins White

Knitting Needles Size 10½ or size required to obtain the gauge

2 yards cotton appliqués

Sewing needle and cotton thread

Crochet Hook Size I

Gauge

6 sts to 2"; 9 rows to 2"

Front

Cast on 56 (64,72) sts. Knit 2 rows. Work even in stockinette stitch until piece measures 12" (14",15") or desired length to Bodice Pattern.

Bodice Pattern:
Multiple of 8 stitches. Refer to Pattern Number 234. Work even in Diamond Pattern for 8" (10",12"), ending on Row 16 (Row 9, Row 16) of pattern.

Neck:
Work across 16 (21,21) sts, slip these onto a holder. Bind off center 24 (22,30) sts in

pattern. *Shoulder:* Work even on rem 16 (21,21) sts for 4" (5",5"). Bind off in pattern. Work opposite side to correspond.

Back

Cast on 56 (64,72) sts. Work even in stockinette stitch for 12" (14",16"). *Neck:* Work across 16 (21,21) sts, slip these onto a holder. Bind off center 24 (22,30) sts. Bind off in Pattern. Work across rem 16 (19,24) sts. *Shoulder:* Work even for 2" (2",2½"). Bind off. Work opposite side to correspond. Sew shoulder seams together.

Sleeves

On front edge beg 5½" below shoulder, pick up 28 sts, on back edge pick up 28 sts. Work even in stockinette stitch on these 56 sts for 5½". Dec (k 2 tog) every other row until 50 sts remain. Bind off.

Finishing

Sew all remaining seams. Work 1 row sc around neck edge, sleeves, and lower edge of sweater. Steam lightly on wrong side.

Appliqués

Sew 1 flower in each complete diamond and sew a flower in each ½ diamond at neck edge.

Zig Zag Scarf ▶

Measures approximately 8" x 41".

Materials

Knitting Worsted (4 oz. skein), 1 skein of Pale Blue

Knitting Needles Size 10

Gauge

Your gauge will be the width of scarf, 8"

Pattern Stitch

Row 1: Purl.

Row 2: K 1, k 2 tog, k 6, yo, k 1, yo, k 6, k 2 tog, k 2 tog, k 6, yo, k 1, yo, k 6, k 2 tog, k 1.

Row 3: Purl.
Repeat all three rows for Pattern Stitch.

Cast on 36 sts and work even in Pattern for 41" or desired length. Bind off in Pattern Stitch.

Fringe

Wind yarn around a 6" cardboard several times, cut at one end. Place one fringe (8 strands of yarn) in each corner. Place one fringe in center between corners. Trim evenly.

Zig Zag Scarf

Hand Signal Mittens

Directions are written for Child's size 4-5.

Materials

Knitting Worsted, 1 ounce each of Scarlet and Green.
Knitting Needles Size 7
Small amount of White yarn for Embroidery

Gauge

4 sts to 1"; 5 rows to 1"

Mittens

Left Mitten is Scarlet, Right Mitten is Green. Both Mittens are knitted in exactly the same manner. Cast on loosely 20 sts. *Ribbed Cuff:* Work in k 1, p 1 rib for 2".

Palm: Right Side:

Row 1: Knit across row, increasing 6 sts evenly spaced, 26 sts.

Row 2: Purl.

Thumb:

Row 1: K 12, place a marker on needle, inc 1 st in each of the next 2 sts, place a marker on needle, k 12.

Row 2 and even numbered rows: Purl.

Row 3: Knit across to first marker, slip marker, inc 1 st in next st, knit across to within last st, inc 1 st in next st, sl marker, knit across to end of row. Repeat Rows 2 and 3 until there are 8 sts between markers. Purl across next row.

Next Row: K 12 sts and place on a st holder, drop marker, k 8, drop marker, place rem 12 sts on a holder. Work even on the 8 sts in stockinette stitch for 7 rows. End with a purl row.

Next Row: K 2 tog across row. Leaving about 14" of yarn, break off. With tapestry needle, draw yarn through rem sts, remove from needle, pull tightly and sew in place. Sew thumb seam.

Palm:

On right side of work pick up sts from 2nd holder, knit across row, turn, and purl across row, pick up sts from first st holder, purl across row. Work even in stockinette st for 4" from last row of wrist cuff, end with a purl row.

Finger area shaping:

Row 1: * K 2, k 2 tog, repeat from * across row.

Row 2: Purl.

Row 3: * K 1, k 2 tog, repeat from * across row.

Row 4: Purl.

Row 5: K 2 tog across row leaving about 14" of yarn, fasten off. With tapestry needle draw yarn through rem sts, remove from needle, pull up tightly and sew in place.

Embroidery

Follow instructions for making Duplicate stitch; see page 30. The Scarlet Mitten is LEFT. Green Mitten is RIGHT. Embroidery is worked with White Yarn. See charts for stitch guidelines.

Finishing

Sew in all loose ends, sew rem seams.

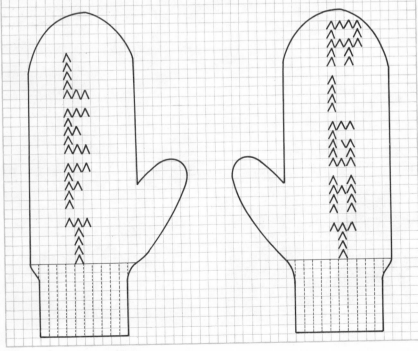

Buttercup Top See Page 76 for instructions

Green and Yellow Basket ▶

Basket is 12″ in diameter across the top, 4″ deep

Materials
Sisal (½ pound hanks); 1 hank Green, 1 hank Yellow
Crochet Hook Size 5

Gauge
1 sc to 1″; 1 row to ¾″

Pattern Stitch
Sc, working in back loop of stitch only.

Basket
With Green ch 4. Join with sl st to form ring.

Rnd 1: Sc 8 into ring.

Rnd 2: Sc 2 in to join each sc (16 sc).

Rnd 3: (Sc 1, sc 2 into next sc) 8 times, (24 sc).

Rnd 4: (Sc in 2 sts, 2 sc into next sc) 8 times, (32 sc).

Rnd 5: (Sc in 3 sts, 2 sc into next sc) 8 times, (40 sc).

Rnd 6: Cut Green. Attach Yellow. With Yellow (sc in 4 sc, 2 sc into next sc) 8 times, (48 sts).

Rnd 7: (First row of side of basket) Ch 1. Sc into first st to left. Work even in back loop of st working around circle to left. Sl st into ch 1.

Rnds 8 and 9: Repeat Round 7

Rnd 10: With Green repeat Rnd 7.

Note: These basic instructions can be used with softer yarns to make smaller baskets. Experiment.

Knit Place Mat

Finished place mat measures approximately 10″ x 16″.

Materials
Frederick J. Fawcett's 10/5 linen (15-yard skeins, ½ pound and pound cones. If not available in your area write to Frederick J. Fawcett. See page 4 for address.) For one place mat, 2 skeins Wild Cherry, 8 skeins White. For 4 place mats, ½ pound Wild Cherry, one pound White.

Knitting Needles Size 6
Tapestry Needle

Gauge
9 sts to 2″; 7 rows to 1″

Place Mat
With Wild Cherry cast on 75 sts.
Rows 1-7: K.
Row 8: K 1, sl 1, k 7, sl 1, attach White.

With White, k 1, p 1 for 55 sts. Attach 2nd ball of Wild Cherry, sl 1, k 7, sl 1, k 1.

Row 9: With Wild Cherry k 10, with White k 1 p 1 for 55 sts, with Wild Cherry k 10.

Repeat Rows 8 and 9 until piece measures 9″. With Wild Cherry, repeat Rows 1 through 7.

Finishing
Block. With tapestry needle, work in loose ends.

Diamond Plaid Afghan ▶

Measures 50″ x 73″

Materials

Knitting Worsted (4-oz. skeins), 10 skeins Winter White, 1 skein Tangerine, 1 skein Orange

Knitting Needles Size 10½

Crochet Hook Size I

Gauge

8 sts to 2″; 10 rows to 2″

Pattern Stitch

Note: *Cross 2L:* Insert right needle behind the first st, knit the second st thru the front lp, leaving st just worked on left needle, knit the first st as usual, remove both sts from left needle. *Cross 2 R:* Knit the second st on left needle, going in front of the first st, knit the first st.

Row 1: Knit.

Row 2 and all even numbered rows: Purl.

Row 3: K 3, * cross 2L, k 6, cross 2 R, k 4, repeat from *, ending last repeat k 3.

Row 5: K 4, * cross 2L, k 4, cross 2 R, k 6, repeat from * across, end last repeat k 4.

Row 7: K 5, * cross 2 L, k 2, cross 2 R, k 8, repeat from * across, end last repeat k 5.

Row 9: K 6, * cross 2 L, cross 2 R, k 10, repeat from * across, end last repeat k 6.

Row 11: K 7, * cross 2 R, k 12, repeat from * across, end last repeat k 7.

Row 13: K 6, * cross 2 R, cross 2 L, k 10, repeat from * across, end last repeat k 6.

Row 15: K 5, * cross 2 R, k 2, cross 2 L, k 8, repeat from * across, end last repeat k 5.

Row 17: K 4, * cross 2 R, k 4, cross 2 L, k 6, repeat from * across, end last repeat k 4.

Row 19: K 3, * cross 2 R, k 6, cross 2 L, k 4, repeat from * across, end last repeat k 3.

Row 21: K 2, * cross 2 R, k 8, cross 2 L, K 2, repeat from * across, end last repeat k 2.

Row 23: K 1, * cross 2 R, k 10, cross 2 L, repeat from * across row, end last repeat k 1.

Repeat Rows 2-23 for Pattern Stitch.

With Winter White cast on 198 sts; work even in Pattern Stitch for 73″. Bind off.

Finishing

Crossing Lines: Do not work tightly. Work evenly to keep work from pulling up. Starting on right side at lower edge at left corner with Tangerine, insert crochet hook in center space between the lowest points of first ½ diamond, draw yarn up thru st. Working on a diagonal to center and crossing of next diamond * insert hook into the next st, draw yarn up thru st and draw thru lp on hook, repeat from * until row is completed. End off. *2nd Crossing Row:* Insert hook into center sp between next ½ diamond and working on a diagonal repeat from * until crossing row is completed. Work in this manner until all diamonds have been crossed.

Contrasting crossing rows (Orange yarn): Begin each row in the same st as for Tangerine crossing lines. Work in the same manner as for Tangerine crossing lines going in the opposite direction. Work 1 row sc around entire afghan, work 3 sc in each corner for a turn.

Fringe

Wind Tangerine yarn around an 8″ cardboard several times. Cut at one end. Place 1 fringe (6 strands of yarn) in each corner and place 1 fringe in st where Tangerine and Orange lines converge. Trim evenly.

41

Diamond Plaid Afghan See Page 41 for instruction

Plain Rattail Choker ▶

Choker is 1″ wide. One size fits all.

Materials
Rattail, 10 yards White, 5 yards Brown
Crochet Hook Size 7
Tapestry Needle

Gauge
4 sc to 1″

Choker
With White ch 45.

Row 1: Sc in second ch from hook, sc in each ch across. Do not turn. Sc twice in last ch, sc once into each st on opposite side of ch, end off.

Row 2: With Brown, ch 31. Sl st into back loop only of each sc. At end of row ch 31. Sl st into bottom of 2nd ch from hook, sl st into bottom of each ch across, sl st into back loop only of each sc and ch; end off.

Finishing
Work loose threads into back of choker. Block.

Rattail Choker with Medallion ▶

Medallion is 3″ in diameter. One size fits all.

Materials
Rattail, 10 yards Peach, 10 yards Lavender
Crochet Hook Size 7

Gauge
4 sc to 1″

Choker
With Peach ch 4, join with sl st to form ring.

Rnd 1: * sc in ring, ch 3, repeat from * 7 times more. Join with a sl st to first sc.

Rnd 2: Sl st in ch-3 sp, * ch 2, in same ch-3 sp (yo draw up a lp, yo and thru 2 lps) 4 times, yo and thru 5 lps on hook, ch 2, draw up a lp in same ch-3 sp, draw up a lp in next ch-3 sp, yo and thru 3 lps on hook, repeat from * around in each ch-3 lp, end sc in last lp worked, sl st in first sc. Cut Peach, join Lavender. With Lavender, sl st through back loop only of sts in 3 clusters. Ch 63, sl st in bottom of 2nd ch from hook, sl st in bottom of next 29 ch, sc in bottom of next 32 ch. Sl st in back loop only of remaining 5 clusters. Ch 63, sl st in bottom of 2nd ch from hook, sl st in bottom of next 29 ch, sc in bottom of next 32 ch, sl st into first sl st of medallion. End off.

Finishing
Work loose threads into back of work. Block.

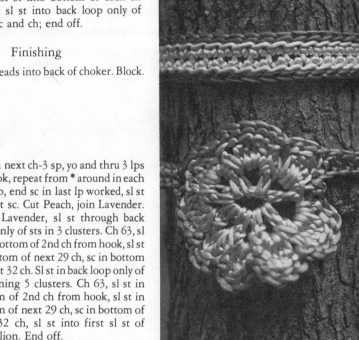

Crocheted Shell Stitch Belt
Simple Crocheted Belt
See Page 65 for instructions

43

Row 1: (Right side) K 4, * k 2 tog, yo, k 1, yo, k 2 tog, k 6, rep from *.
Row 2 and all even rows: P.
Row 3: K 3, * k 2 tog, yo, k 3, yo, k 2 tog, k 4, rep from *, end k 1.
Row 5: K 2, * k 2 tog, yo, k 5, yo, k 2 tog, k 2, rep from *, end k 2.
Row 7: K 1, * k 2 tog, yo, k 7, yo, k 2 tog, rep from *, end k 3.
Row 9: K.
Row 10: P.
Repeat these 10 rows for Pattern.

Back

Note: two strands of yarn are used throughout. Length from hem to waist is planned for 24″ (24″,25″). Make any changes between first 4 decreases. Cast on 114 (125,136) sts. Work in Pattern Stitch for 3″. Then work in stockinette st until otherwise indicated. Simultaneously decrease 1 st each edge every 2½″ (2½″,3¼″), 5 (5,4) times; 104 (115,128) sts. Dec 1 st each edge every ¾″, 15 (16,16) times; 74 (83,96) sts. Mark for waistline.

Bodice:
Inc 1 st each end every ¾″, 12 (14,13) times; 98 (111,122) sts. Work even until bodice measures 10″ (10½″,11″) from waist or desired length to underarm.

Armholes:
Bind off 3 (6,8) sts at beg of next 2 rows; dec 1 st each edge every other row 3 (5,7) times; 86 (89,92) sts. *Next row:* K 3 (4,0), place marker, work in Pattern Stitch to within last 2 (4,0) sts, k to end. Working Pattern St between markers, work even until armholes measure 7″ (7½″,8″) above sts.

Shoulders:
Bind off 7 sts at beg of next 6 rows; bind off 6 sts at beg of next 2 rows; bind off rem 32 (35,38) sts.

Front

Work same as for back until armholes measure 2½″ (3″,3½″). Work first 35 (36,36) sts. Attach another double strand of yarn. Bind off center 16 (17,20) sts. Work to end of row. Working on both sides at once, dec one st each side of center bind-off every other row 8 (9,9) times. Work even until armholes measure same as for back.

Shoulders:
Bind off 7 sts at each arm edge 3 times; bind off 6 sts at each arm edge once.

Finishing

Block pieces. Sew side seams. With right side facing, work one row picot sts around neckline, armholes, and bottom.

Picot Stitch

Attach yarn, * ch 3, sl st in base of ch-3, sc in next 2 sts. Repeat from * around.

Lacy Skimmer Dress

Instructions are for Misses size small (8-10). Changes for Size medium (12-14) and large (16-18) are in parentheses.

Materials

Cum's Cot/Lin (5¼ oz. skeins. If not available in your area contact School Products, Inc. See credit page for address.) 4 (5,6) skeins Green (9081)

Knitting Needles Size 1
Steel Crochet Hook Size 1
Tapestry Needle

Gauge

6 sts to 1″; 8 rows to 1″ with yarn worked double

Pattern Stitch

(Multiple of 11 sts plus 4)

Textured Pullover

Instructions are for size small (8-10). Changes for sizes medium (12-14) and large (16-18) are in parentheses.

Materials

Knitting Worsted, Rust (4-oz. skeins): 4 (4,5) skeins

Knitting Needles Size 5 and 7

Crochet Hook Size H

Tapestry needle

Gauge

Pattern st is 5½ sts to 1"; 6 rows to 1"

Cable is ¾" wide

Pattern Stitch

Row 1: (Right side) P 1, k 1 in back of st.
Row 2: K.

Cable Pattern

Row 1: (Right side) P 2, sl 3 to cable needle and hold in front of work, k 3, k 3 from cable needle, p 2, sl 3 to cable needle and hold in back of work, k 3, k 3 from cable needle, p 2.
Row 2: K 2, (p 6, k 2) twice.
Row 3: P 2, (k 6, p 2) twice.
Row 4: Rep Row 2.
Row 5: P 2, sl 3 to cable needle and hold in back of work, k 3, k 3 from cable needle, p 2, sl 3 to cable needle and hold in front of work, k 3, k 3 from cable needle, p 2.
Row 6: Repeat Row 2.
Row 7: Repeat Row 3.
Row 8: Repeat Row 2.
Repeat these 8 rows for Cable Pattern.

Sweater Back

Beg at lower edge, with size 5 needles cast on 68 (76,88) sts.

Ribbing

Row 1: K 1, p 1 across row. Repeat this row for ribbing for 2". Change to size 7 needles and work in Pattern St, inc'g 1 st each end every ¾", 12 (13,12) times; 92 (102,112) sts. Work even until back measures 12½" (13",13½") or desired length to underarm.

Underarm

Bind off 3 (5,6) sts at beg of next 2 rows. Dec 1 st each end every other row 3 (4,6) times; 80 (84,88) sts. Work even until armhole measures 7½" (8",8½") above bound-off sts.

Shape shoulders

Bind off 5 sts at beg of next 10 rows. Bind off rem 30 (34,38) sts.

Front

Work same as for back to end of ribbing. Change to size 7 needles. To establish placement of Cable Pattern: Work in Pattern St for next 7 (11,17) sts. Work Row 1 of Cable Pattern. Work in Pattern St for next 18 sts. Work Row 1 of Cable Pattern. Work in Pattern St for last 7 (11,17) sts. Continue working Pattern st and Cable pattern as established, increasing as for back, until armhole bind-off, ending with a wrong side row. *Next row:* With right side facing, work in Pattern st and first Cable Pattern as established. Rep Cable pattern across next 18 sts. Finish row with Cable Pattern and Pattern St as established. Continuing to work 3 repeats of Cable Pattern across front, simultaneously shape armholes as for back.

Shape neck

When armholes measure 3", with right side facing, work first 32 (33,34) sts. Attach second ball of yarn. Bind off next 16 (18,20) sts. Work to end of row. Working on both sides at once, dec one st each side every other row 7 (8,9) times. Work even until armholes measure same as for back.

Shape shoulders

Bind off 5 sts at beg of each arm edge 5 times.

Sleeves

With #5 needles, cast on 42 (46,48) sts. Work 2" in k 1, p 1 ribbing. Change to #7 needles. To establish placement of Cable Pattern: Work 12 (14,15) sts in Pattern St. Work next 18 sts in Cable Pattern. Work rem 12 (14,15) sts. Continuing to work in Pattern St and Cable Pattern as established, inc 1 st each end every 1½", 9 (9,10) times; 60 (64,68) sts. Work even until piece measures 17" or desired length to underarm.

Shape cap

Bind off 4 (5,6) sts at beg of next 2 rows. Dec 1 st each end every other row 18 (19,20) times. Bind off rem 16 sts.

Finishing

Sew shoulder, side, and sleeve. With center of cap bind-off at shoulders and sleeve seam at underarm, sew in sleeves. With right side facing, work one row sc around neck.

Child's Yo-Yo Party Dress

◄Child's Yo-Yo Party Dress

Directions are written for size 6. Changes for size 8 are in parentheses.

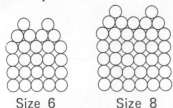

Size 6   Size 8

Materials

Knitting Worsted, 4 ounces Raspberry

Knitting Needles Size 8

Crochet Hook Size H

Small pieces of cotton fabric, assorted patterns

Two 20″ pieces Forest Green satin ribbon 5/16″ wide.

Gauge

9 sts to 2″; 11 rows to 2″

Front

Cast on 66 (75) sts and work even in stockinette stitch for 9″ (11″), ending on a purl row. *Next Row:* * K 1, k 2 tog, repeat from * across row. Bind off on next row, leaving about 15″ of yarn, thread through tapestry needle and weave yarn using small running stitches across last row, gather slightly until waist measures 8″ (10″), knot and fasten off.

Back

Work same as for front ending with k 1, k 2 tog across row. *Next Row:* * K 1, p 1, repeat from * across row. *Row 2:* * P 1, k 1, repeat from * across row. Work even in ribbing for 2¼″ (3½″). Bind off in Pattern Stitch.

Bodice

Yo Yo's: Make 26 (37). Cut a circle with a 4″ diameter out of cardboard. Steam fabric. Trace circle on fabric and cut out. On wrong side of fabric turn under a 1/8″ hem. With sewing needle and thread work small running stitches around entire circle and pull tightly until circle is puckered, knot and fasten off.

Joining

Join Yo Yo's on wrong side in straight rows. 5 (6) Yo Yo's across and 4 (5) Yo Yo's vertically. See diagrams above. *Next row:* Place 1 Yo Yo between 2 Yo Yo's of previous row—4 (5) across row. *Next row:* Place 1 Yo Yo between the first 2 Yo Yo's at each arm edge. Sew ribbon in back of last 2 Yo Yo's for straps.

Finishing

Sew skirt seams. Sew first row of Yo Yo's to front of skirt using needle and thread. Sew ribbed edges of back to sides of halter top—about 1½ (2½) Yo Yo's on each side. *Skirt hem:* Starting on right side and center back, join yarn with a sl st, ch 3, sl st in top of first sl st, * sc in next 3 sts, ch 3, sl st in base of ch-3, repeat from * around, ending with a sl st. Fasten off.

Child's Sundress

See Page 75 for instructions

Kangaroo Dress

See Page 67 for instructions

Indian Afghan See Page 72 for instructions

Pink Bumpy Stitch Sweater
See Page 69 for instructions

Fiesta Sweater
See Page 76 for instructions

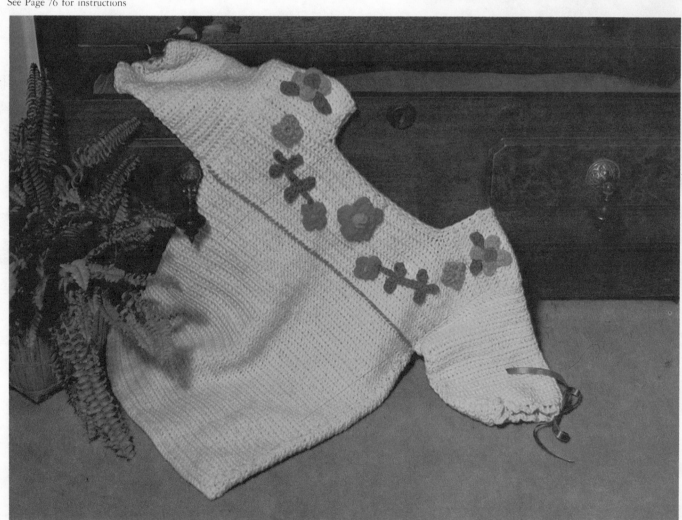

49

September Plaid Afghan

◄ September Plaid Afghan

Measures approximately 45½" x 62½".

Materials

Knitting Worsted (4 oz skeins), 6 skeins Winter White, 3 skeins Tangerine, 3 skeins Dark Brown

Crochet Hook Size I

Blunt End Tapestry Needle

Gauge

4 mesh to 2"; 4 mesh rows to 2"

Filet Mesh Pattern Stitch

Row 1: 1 dc in 6th ch from hook, * ch 1, sk 1 ch, 1 dc in next ch, repeat from * across row, ch 4, turn.

Row 2: Turning ch counts as first dc, 1 dc in next dc, * ch 1, 1 dc in next dc, repeat from * across row, working last dc in turning ch, ch 4, turn.

Repeat Row 2 for Pattern Stitch.

Note

When changing colors, always work off last 2 loops of last dc with next color. Color Code: A—Winter White, B—Tangerine, C—Dark Brown.

Afghan

With Color A ch 184 and work in Pattern Stitch for 2 rows, * with Color B work in Pattern Stitch for 2 rows, with Color C work in Pattern Stitch for 2 rows, with Color A work in Pattern Stitch for 4 rows, repeat from * working for 62½", ending with Color A—4 rows, Color B—2 rows, Color C—2 rows, Color A—2 rows.

Weaving

Run a basting thread from bottom to top through center mesh. Thread 3 strands of Color A into a tapestry needle, each strand approximately 110" long. Starting in first mesh to the left of basting thread, bring needle through to right side and draw strands through leaving 9" ends hanging at lower edge. Weave strands over first bar, under 2nd bar, over 3rd bar and continue in this manner to top.

Note: Be sure to alternate the unders and overs at the beg of each stripe. With Color A weave center mesh and 2 stripes to right of center. Working towards right side weave * 2 stripes with Color C, 2 stripes with Color B, 4 stripes with Color A, repeat from * to side edge. Working towards left side, repeat from * to side edge.

Fringe

Draw the 3 strands of yarn remaining at end of each stripe over or under the first bar and through the first mesh (loop made), hold loop with forefinger and twist to the right, bring ends through this loop and tighten. Trim evenly.

Blue on Blue Afghan See Page 67 for instructions

Toddler's Alphabet Blanket See Page 77 for instruction

Baby Booties and Snuggle Cap ▶

Directions are written for infants to 8 months old.

Materials

Orlon (4 oz. skein) 1 skein Peach

Needles Size 7

Crochet Hook Size G

Gauge

4 sts to 1"; 17 rows to 2"

Booties

Make 2. Cast on 48 sts. Work in garter stitch for 24 rows. Bind off 10 sts at beg of next 2 rows. Knit even for 13 rows. Bind off.

Sewing

Fold booties in half. Sew front seam. Sew back seam.

Ties

Make 2. Crochet a chain 15"-16" long. Bind off. Weave through ankle of each bootie.

Cap

Cast on 64 sts and work in garter stitch until piece measures 6". Bind off loosely. Fold in half. Sew back seam.

Tie

Crochet a chain 39"-40" long, end off. Weave through base of cap.

Pom pom

Wind yarn 35-40 times around a 2" cardboard. Cut at one end, tie a knot at top. Sew on cap where desired or as shown in picture.

Rick Rack Baby Afghan ▶

Afghan measures 28" x 36".

Materials

Orlon Baby Yarn (1 oz skeins), 4 skeins each Light Green, Light Yellow and White

Crochet Hook Size E

Gauge

1 "V" equals 3½"

Pattern Stitch

Row 1: Sk first st from hook; working in back lp of ch, work 1 sc in each of next 2 chs, sk 1 st, * 1 sc in each of next 11 sts, 3 sc in next st, 1 sc in each of next 11 sts, sk 2 sts. Repeat from *, end sk 1 st, 1 sc in each of last 2 sts, ch 1, turn.

Row 2: 1 sc in each of first 2 sts, sk 1 st, * 1 sc in back lp of each of next 11 sts, 3 sc in back lp of next st, 1 sc in back lp of each of the next 11 sts, sk 2 sts. Repeat from *, end sk 1 st at end of point, 1 sc in each of last 2 sts working in both lps of st below. (The first and last 2 stitches are worked in both lps to prevent edge from curling.)

Repeat Row 2 for Pattern Stitch.

Afghan

With Green ch 205 sts. Work in Pattern Stitch as follows: ** 4 rows Green, 4 rows Yellow, 2 rows White. Repeat from ** until afghan measures 36", ending with 2 rows White. End off.

Angora Cardigan

Instructions are for Girl's size small (4-6). Changes for medium (8-10) and large (12-14) are in parentheses.

Materials

100% angora (10 gram balls), 16 (19,22) balls Mimosa, 1 (2,2) balls White

Knitting Needles Size 3 and Size 5

Crochet Hook Size 7

7 buttons

1½ yards 1¼" wide grosgrain ribbon

Gauge

4 sts to 1"; 5 rows to 1"

Back

Beg at lower edge, with Mimosa and #3 needles, cast on 46 (52,54) sts. Work in k 1, p 1 ribbing for 1½". Switch to #5 needles. Work in stockinette st. Increase one st each end every 2½" (2", 1½"), 2 (3,4) times; 50 (58,62) sts. Work even until back measures 8" (9½",11") or desired length to underarm, end with purl row.

Armholes:
Bind off 2 (3,3) sts at beginning of next 2 rows. Dec one st each side every other row 1 (2,2) times; 44 (48,52) sts. Work even until armhole measures 4½" (5",6½") above bound-off sts.

Shoulders:
Bind off 6 sts at beg of next 4 rows. Bind off remaining 20 (24,28) sts.

Left Front

Beg at lower edge, with Mimosa and #3 needles cast on 26 (28,30) sts. Work in k 1, p 1 ribbing to last 6 sts. K these last 6 sts on this row and each row for buttonhole placket. Continue working in k 1, p 1 ribbing for 1½". Switch to #5 needles. Work in stockinette st until front measures same as back to underarm, ending with a p row.

Armholes and Neck:
With right side facing, bind off 2 (3,3) sts at beg of row (arm edge). Dec one st at arm edge every other row 1 (2,2) times. Work even until armholes measure 0" (1",2½"). For small size only, begin neckline shaping at first row of armhole shaping. With right side facing, work to 2 sts before buttonhole placket. Dec one st. K rem 6 sts. Dec one st in this manner every other row 5 more times, ending with a k row; 17 (17,19) sts. Bind off 4 sts at beg of next row. Dec 1 st at neck edge every other row 1 (1,3) times. Work even until armhole measures same as back.

Shoulders:
Bind off 6 sts at beg of arm edge twice.

Right Front

Work same as for left front, reversing shaping

and making 6 buttonholes, evenly spaced on placket, with first buttonhole ½" above bottom of sweater and last buttonhole 2 rows below neckline. Bind-off.

Buttonholes

Row 1: With right side facing, work until 1 st of buttonhole placket has been completed. Bind off 3 sts. K final 2 sts.

Row 2: K 2, cast on 3 sts above bound-off sts of previous row, k 1, p to end of row.

Sleeves

Beg at lower edge, with Mimosa and #3 needles, cast on 24 (26,28) sts. Work in k 1, p 1 ribbing for 1½". Change to #5 needles and stockinette st. Work in stockinette st, increasing 1 st each end every 5th row 10 (11,12) times; 44 (48,52) sts. Work even until piece measures 12" (15",16½") from start or desired length to underarm, ending with p row.

Shape Cap:

Bind off 2 (3,3) sts at beg of next 2 rows. Dec 1 st each side every other row 10 (11,19) times. *For small and med. sizes only:* Bind off 2 sts at beg of next 6 rows. *For large size only:* Work even 7 rows after last decrease. Bind off remaining 8 (6,8) sts.

Collar

With White and #5 needles, cast on 48 (48,62) sts. Working in stockinette st, increase one st each side every other row until collar measures 1½". Bind off loosely in stockinette st.

Finishing

Block pieces lightly. Do not block ribbing. With backstitch, sew shoulder seams; sew sleeve seams. With center of cap bind-off at shoulder seam and sleeve seam at underarm, sew in sleeves. Sew grosgrain ribbon to wrong side of button placket. Slash for buttonholes and work overcast st around buttonholes. Sew on collar. Starting at lower edge of left front, with right side facing, sc one row of white along center edge, around collar, down other center edge. Beginning at neckline, work one row sc with white along inner edge of right front placket. Sew on buttons.

Granny Square Baby Afghan

Blanket measures approximately 25½" x 25½".

Materials

Made of odd skeins Knitting Worsted or Orlon.

Crochet Hook Size G

Tapestry Needle

Squares

Make 49 Squares. Follow Geometric Pattern Number 612. Work through Rnd 4.

Joining

Sew all loose ends in on wrong side. Sew together 7 squares—this makes one panel.

Make 6 more panels of 7 squares each. Join each panel—one to the other.

Border

Work 6 rows of single crochet around entire blanket, increasing 3 sc in each corner for turn on each row.

Sunrise Afghan See Page 72 for instructions

▲ Crocheted Bath Mat

Finished mat measures 20″ x 27″.

Materials

Lily cotton—The Sugar and Cream Yarn (125-yard skeins) (See pg. 4 for address) 4 skeins White, 1 skein Blue, 1 skein Peach

Crochet Hook Size I

Tapestry Needle.

Gauge

3 clusters = 2″

Pattern Stitch

Chain loosely.

Row 1: Sk 2 chs * sc, hdc, sc in next ch, sk 1 (one cluster), repeat from * across row, end ch 1, turn.

Row 2: (Sc, hdc, sc) in each hdc across row, end ch 1, turn.

Repeat Row 2 for pattern.

Mat

Chain loosely 61 sts with White. In Pattern St, work 4 clusters White, 2 Peach, 9 White, 4 Peach, 10 White (color pattern A). Work with these colors for 3″. *Next row:* Substitute Blue for White, continuing with Peach as established (color pattern B). Work with these colors for 2″. *Next row:* Return to color Pattern A and work in that for 12″. Return to color pattern B for 4″. Return to color pattern A for 5″.

Finishing

Work in all loose ends. Block.

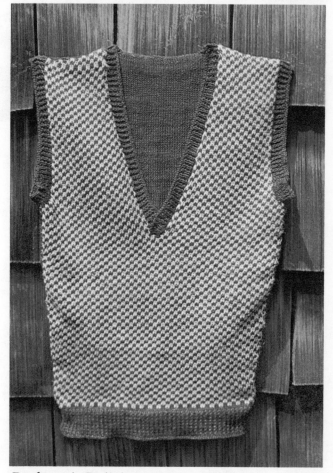

Professor's Delight See Page 75 for instructions

57

Little Kid's Silly Jumper

Directions are written for Girl's size 4. Directions for sizes 6 and 8 are in parentheses.

Materials

Knitting Worsted or Orlon Knitting Yarn (4 oz skeins), 2 skeins Turquoise.

Knitting Needles Size 8 or size required for gauge.

Crochet Hook Size H

Plastic Beads: assorted colors, diameter ¼", approximately 200-250.

Gauge

8 sts to 2"; 12 rows to 2".

Thread beads onto yarn, push back on skein until sts have been cast on.

Front

Cast on 66 sts (70, 82). Knit one row, purl next row (stockinette stitch).

Beading

Each beaded row will be different. Place a bead where you think it will look nice. * Knit a couple of sts and then insert right needle into next st on left needle, draw yarn and one bead around right needle, pass left st over both yarn and bead, pushing bead to front of work, repeat from * across row. Left-handed knitters will work in reverse. Purl across next row. *Do not work beads* on the Purl side of work. Work even in stockinette stitch, dec 1 st each end of every row every 1½" until 61 (65, 72) sts remain, then work even for 11" (12", 13") or desired length to underarm.

Armholes

Bind off 5 (6, 7) sts, work across next 20 (20, 22) sts and place on a holder, bind off center 11 (13, 14) sts, work across remaining 20 (20, 22) sts.

Shoulders

Next row at neck edge dec 1 st every other row 4 times and at the same time dec 1 st at armhole every row until 10 (11,12) sts remain. Work even for 5½" (6",6½"). Bind off. Work opposite shoulder to correspond.

Back

Work exactly the same as for front. Omit beading.

Finishing

Sew shoulder seams together. Work 1 row sc around neck edge. Work 1 row sc around armholes. Sew side seams.

Lower Edge: On right side at center back, work 1 row sc, join with sl st in first sc, * ch 3, sl st in top of ch-3, sc in next 3 sc, repeat from * around. Join with sl st. Fasten off.

Washing Instructions

Wash by hand in mild soap powder; never place in an automatic clothes dryer—temperature may affect bead work.

Fleur-de-Lis Afghan

Measures approximately 57″ x 76″.

Materials

Knitting Worsted (4 oz. skeins), 6 skeins Winter White, 1 skein each of Beige, Gold, Tangerine, Turquoise, and 2 ounces each of Dark Brown, Avocado, Orange

Knitting Needles Size 10½

Crochet Hook Size I

Gauge

8 sts to 2″; 8 rows to 2″

Afghan

Work in stockinette stitch throughout. With Gold yarn cast on 209 sts.

Striped Pattern:
Rows 1-4: * With Gold work for 4 rows.
Rows 5-8: With Tangerine work for 4 rows.
Rows 9-12: Join Winter White and work for 4 rows.
Rows 13-16: Join Beige and work for 4 rows.

Rows 17-18: Join Winter White and work for 2 rows. See chart and work Fleur-de-Lis-Pattern until completed.

Repeat from * for Striped Pattern Alternate Fleur de-Lis and Striped Pattern until afghan measures 73½″, ending with complete Striped Pattern. Bind off on next row. Fasten off.

Borders

On right side of afghan with crochet hook and Turquoise work 1 sc in each st along each longer side of afghan (approximately 226 sts), work sc for 4 rows. Fasten off.

Key for Chart

1. Make Fleur-de-Lis on a background of Winter White for entire Pattern Stitch.
2. Each square represents *1 st* horizontally and *1 row* vertically.
3. Each X represents 1 st made with a particular color; the same color is worked across entire row of pattern for 3 rows. Color Code: B—Dark Brown, O—Orange, T—Turquoise, A—Avocado.

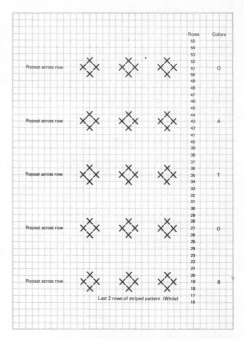

Child's Camisole See Page 70 for instructions

Pink Cloud Ribbon Dress

Directions are written for Child's size 4. Sizes 6 and 8 are in parentheses.

Materials

Knitting Worsted (4 oz. skeins), 2 skeins Dusty Pink

Mint Green Satin Ribbon 5/16″ wide approximately 23 (24,25) feet long

Knitting Needles Size 7

Crochet Hook Size F.

Gauge

9 sts to 2″; 12½ rows to 2″

Eyelet Pattern

Row 1: K 1,* yo, k 2 tog, repeat from * across row, end k 2 tog, k 1.
Row 2: Purl.
Repeat Rows 1 and 2 for Eyelet Pattern.

Front

Cast on 70 (76,80) sts. Work in stockinette stitch for 12″ (12½″, 13″) or 1½″ below desired length to underarm. Change to Eyelet Pattern and work for 1½″.

Armholes:
Bind off 6 sts, work across row in Eyelet Pattern. On next row bind off 6 sts. Continue working in Eyelet Pattern for 5″ (5½″,6″).

Neck:
Change to st st and work across 17 (19,21) sts, place center 24 (26,26) sts and last 17 (19,21) sts on a holder.

Shoulders:
Work even in st st for 5 rows; bind off. Work other shoulder to correspond.

Back

Cast on 70 (76,80) sts and work even in st st for 14″ (14½″, 15″).

Armholes:
Bind off 6 sts beg of next 2 rows, then work even in st st for 5″ (5½″,6″). Work across next 17 (19,21) sts, place center 24 (26,26) sts and last 17 (19,21) sts on a holder.

Shoulders:
Work even in st st for 5 rows more; bind off. Work other shoulder to correspond.

Weaving

Cut a piece of ribbon approximately 48″ (50″,52″) and save for sleeve trim. Place a safety pin in beginning of rem ribbon and starting in first eyelet row work under, then over each eyelet across row; turn and work across next row in same manner being careful to alternate unders and overs. Continue in this manner until all eyelet rows are woven with ribbon. With sewing needle and matching colors sew in all loose ends on wrong side.

Sleeves

Sew shoulder seams together. Starting at armhole on front side and working around to back armhole pick up and knit 50 (54,58) sts. Work in st st for 4½″ (5″,5½″). Change to Eyelet Pattern and work through Row 2. Bind off.

Finishing

Sew side seams and sleeve seams. *Sleeve Ribbon:* With the remaining ribbon cut 2 pieces approximately 24″ (25″,26″) each. Find center of sleeve by counting eyelets from seam to seam. Place a safety pin at beginning of ribbon and starting in center eyelet weave around sleeve going under and over each eyelet to center eyelet, pull ribbon slightly and tie a bow.

Picot Edging

Neck: At the center back with crochet hook attach Pink yarn, sl st,*ch 2, sl st in same st, sl st in next 2 sts, repeat from * around to beg, end with a sl st. End off. *Hemline:* Work same as for neck edge.

Caterpillar Afghan

Measures 63″ x 44″

Materials

Knitting Worsted, 2 ounces each of the following colors: Black, Scarlet, Purple, Dark Green, Brown, Lt. Orange, Tangerine, Turquoise, Pink, Lt. Green, Bright Pink

Knitting Needles Size 10

Crochet Hook Size H

Gauge

7 sts to 2″; 10 rows to 2″

Afghan

With Black cast on 216 sts. Knit 4 rows, * join Scarlet and work in stockinette stitch for 5 rows, join Purple and knit 4 rows, repeat from * for Pattern Stitch. Alternate colors as desired or work as follows. Reminder: All knit rows are worked for 4 rows, and all stockinette rows are worked for 5 rows.

Finishing

Sew in all loose ends on wrong side only. Steam lightly. With Black crochet 1 row sc around entire afghan.

Color sequence from start of afghan

#	Stitch	Color	#	Stitch	Color
1.	Knit	Black	25.	Knit	Dk. Green
2.	St st	Scarlet	26.	St st	Black
3.	Knit	Purple	27.	Knit	Purple
4.	St st	Lt. Orange	28.	St st	Tangerine
5.	Knit	Bright Pink	29.	Knit	Scarlet
6.	St st	Black	30.	St st	Dk. Green
7.	Knit	Brown	31.	Knit	Black
8.	St st	Turquoise	32.	St st	Lt. Green
9.	Knit	Dk. Green	33.	Knit	Purple
10.	St st	Br. Pink	34.	St st	Scarlet
11.	Knit	Tangerine	35.	Knit	Dk. Green
12.	St st	Scarlet	36.	St st	Pink
13.	Knit	Turquoise	37.	Knit	Tangerine
14.	St st	Purple	38.	St st	Lt. Green
15.	Knit	Lt. Green	39.	Knit	Turquoise
16.	St st	Pink	40.	St st	Black
17.	Knit	Brown	41.	Knit	Lt. Green
18.	St st	Tangerine	42.	St st	Pink
19.	Knit	Purple	43.	Knit	Brown
20.	St st	Scarlet	44.	St st	Scarlet
21.	Knit	Dk. Green	45.	Knit	Dk. Green
22.	St st	Pink	46.	St st	Purple
23.	Knit	Lt. Orange	47.	Knit	Pink
24.	St st	Turquoise	48.	St st	Black

Girl's Peasant Dress

Directions are written for Girl's size 4. Directions for sizes 6 and 8 are in parentheses.

Materials

Knitting Worsted (4 oz. skeins), 3 skeins White

Knitting Needles Size 10½

Crochet Hook Size I

Satin Ribbon ½" wide, 2 yards each of Pale Pink, Mint Green, Gold, Scarlet and 3 yards Turquoise

Sewing Needle

Cotton Thread

Tapestry Needle

Gauge

6 sts to 2"; 9 rows to 2"

Eyelet Pattern:

Row 1: Knit.
Row 2: Purl.
Row 3: K 1, k 2 tog across row.
Row 4: * K 1, knit horizontal bar before next st, k next st, repeat from * across row.

Front

Cast on 54 (65,75) sts, knit 2 rows (this will keep the edges from curling up). Then work even in stockinette stitch until piece measures 10" (11",14") or desired length to yoke.

Yoke:

Knit 2 rows, purl next row and work in Eyelet Pattern for 3" (4",5") ending on a purl row.

Neck Edge:

Work across Row 3 of Pattern and at the same time slip first 14 (16,19) sts onto a holder. Bind off center 26 (34,37) sts, work in pattern across rem 14 (16,19) sts.

Shoulders:

Work in established pattern for 2½". Bind off on a knit row. Work opposite shoulder to correspond. Bind off.

Back

Work same as for front to Yoke. Purl 2 rows and continue in st st for 3" (4",5").

Neck Edge:

Work across 14 (16,19) sts and slip to a holder, bind off center 26 (34,37) sts and work across rem 14 (16,19) sts.

Shoulders:

Work in st st on the 14 (16,19) sts until shoulder measures 2½". Bind off. Work opposite shoulder to correspond.

Sleeves

Sew shoulder seams. Starting at armhole on right side and working around to back armhole pick up and knit 36 (40,46) sts, work even in st st for 4" (4½",5"). Work rows 3 and 4 of Eyelet Pattern, then work 2 rows st st. Bind off.

Finishing

Neck Edge: Start at center back on right side and work 1 sc in each st around. *Next Row:* Work 1 sc in first sc of previous row, * skip 1, sc in next sc, repeat from * around. End off. *Lower Edge and Sleeves:* Work 1 row sc around these edges.

Ribbon

For Bodice: Cut 2 ribbons of each color except Turquoise approximately 15" (15",16") long. *For Shoulder:* Cut 2 ribbons of each color except Turquoise approximately 5" (5",6") long.

Weaving Ribbon

Beg with first row of Eyelet Pattern, weave Pale Pink Ribbon through back of stitches across row. Ribbon is drawn *under each eyelet.* Do not alternate unders and overs as for regular weaving. Alternate colors as follows, * Mint Green, Scarlet, Gold, Pale Pink, repeat from * until entire yoke and shoulders are woven. On wrong side sew one end of ribbon to inside sleeve edge, pull ribbon slightly to gather eyelets, be sure to keep ribbons flat. Sew all ribbons to opposite sleeve edge, cut away any excess ribbon.

Neck Edge:

Cut a piece of Turquoise 60" long. Beg at center front, weave in and out of first row of sc. Pull through st first entered at center, pull ribbon to tighten and tie a bow.

Sleeves:

Cut rem Turquoise ribbon in half and begin at center top of sleeve and weave around to beg, pull slightly, and tie a bow.

Rainbow Hat and Scarf

Rainbow Hat and Scarf

Materials

Knitting Worsted (4-oz. skeins), 1 skein each of Red, Orange, Yellow, Green, Blue, Violet.

Knitting Needles Size 8

Tapestry Needle

Scarf

Scarf measures 13" x 42".

Gauge

11 sts to 2"; 8 rows to 1"

Pattern Stitch

Row 1: K 1, k 2 tog * k 10, (k 2 tog) twice. Repeat from *, end k 10, k 2 tog, k 1.
Row 2: K 1, (k 1, p 1) in next st * k 10, (k 1, p 1 into same st) twice. Repeat from *, end k 10, (k 1, p 1) into next st, k 1.
Repeat these 2 rows for pattern.

With Red, cast on 72 sts. Working in pattern, work colors as follows: 14 rows each of Red, Orange, Yellow, Green, Blue, Violet: (2 rows each of Red, Orange, Yellow, Green, Blue, Violet) 4 times; 2 rows Red, 4 rows Orange, 6 rows Yellow, 8 rows Green, 10 rows Blue, 12 rows Violet. Work colors in reverse order, beginning with 10 rows Blue. Bind off.

Finishing

Work in loose ends with tapestry needle. No blocking is necessary.

Hat

Instructions are for size small. Changes for sizes medium and large are in parentheses.

Gauge

4 sts to 1"

Pattern Stitch

Violet
Row 1: K 2, p 2.
Row 2: Repeat Row 1.
Row 3: P 2, k 2.
Row 4: Repeat Row 3.
Repeat these 4 rows for pattern.

Blue
Rows 1 and 3 (wrong side): K.
Row 2: K 1, p 1.
Row 4: P 1, k 1.
Repeat these 4 rows for pattern.

Green
Row 1: K 2, p 2.
Row 2: P 1, k 2 * p 2, k 2, repeat from *, end p 1. Repeat these 2 rows for pattern.

Yellow
Rows 1 and 2: P 1, k 1.
Rows 3 and 4: K 1, p 1.

Repeat these 4 rows for pattern.

Orange
Row 1: K 2, p 2.
Row 2: K 1 * p 2, k 2, repeat from *, end k 1.
Row 3: P 2, k 2.
Row 4: P 1, * k 2, p 2, repeat from *, end p 1.
Repeat these 4 rows for pattern.

Red
Row 1: K 1, p 1.
Row 2: P 1, k 1.
Repeat these 2 rows for pattern.

With Violet cast on 76 (80,84) sts. Work in pattern for Violet for 4". Break off Violet. Attach Blue. Work in Blue pattern for 1¼". Continue working 1¼" of each color, using the pattern for that color, in the following order: Green, Yellow, Orange. Work even in Red for ¾". *Next row:* Decrease 25 (26,28) sts evenly spaced; 51 (54,56) sts. *Next row:* Dec 25 (27,28) sts evenly spaced; 25 (27,28) sts. Cut off Red, leaving a 6" tail. Thread tapestry needle with yarn and bring it through sts on needle, slip sts from needle and bring yarn through again, pulling tight into a circle. Knot and break off yarn.

Finishing

Sew side seam. Weave ends back in. No blocking is necessary.

Crocheted Shell Stitch Belt
See Page 43 for color illustration

Belt is 1½" wide.

Materials

Guimpe (sold only in pound skeins, which are enough for many belts.) Tan and Red
Steel Crochet Hook Size 0

Gauge

With guimpe worked double, one tr shell is 1"; one dc shell is ½"

Belt

With 2 strands Red, ch a multiple of 10 plus 5 long enough to go around your waist. Belt is stretchy so don't make ch too long. Work 5 more chs with 2 strands Tan. Continuing with Tan, work 2 tr in 6th ch from hook, ch 1, 3 tr in same ch * ch 1, sk 4 ch, (3 dc) in next ch (dc shell). Ch 1, sk 4 ch, (3 tr, 1 ch, 3 tr) in next ch (tr shell). Repeat from * to last ch. *Make buttonhole:* In last ch work one tr shell. Do not turn. Ch 1. In same ch, work 3 tr, ch 1, work 1 tr shell. Work from * along bottom of ch. In last ch work one tr shell. Do not turn. Ch 1. In same ch, work 3 tr, sl st to top ch of first shell. With one strand Red and one strand Tan worked tog, sc in each st all around belt. End off.

Make Button

With 2 strands Red ch 3. Join with sl st to form ring. Work 6 sc into ring.
Rnd 1: (Sc 1 into next sc, sc two into next sc) 3 times.
Rnd 2: Sc into every other sc. Stuff cup with guimpe. Sl st cup closed. Sew button to beginning of belt, at opposite end from buttonhole.

Finishing

With crochet hook, work in loose ends. No blocking is necessary.

Simple Crocheted Belt
See Page 43 for color illustration

Belt is 1½" wide.

Materials

Guimpe (sold only in pound skeins, which are enough for many belts.) Green and Yellow.

Steel Crochet Hook Size 0

Gauge

With guimpe worked double, 5½ sc to 1"; 2 rows to ⅜"

To Make

With 2 strands Yellow, ch enough to go around your waist plus 1" overlap. Belt is stretchy, so don't make ch too long.

Rnd 1: Sc in second ch from hook, sc in each ch across. At last ch, do not turn. Sc 2 more into this ch, then sc into bottom of each ch across. Work to end of ch, working 3 sc into last ch to turn. Sl st to first sc.
Rnd 2: With 1 strand Green and 1 strand Yellow, work same as Rnd 1 until 1" before end of Rnd 1.

Buttonhole:
Ch 4, skip 4 sc. Continue to sc to end of row as in Rnd 1.

Rnds 3 and 4: With 2 strands Green, work same as Rnd 1, inc 1 st at either side of center st at end.
Rnd 5: Sl st into each sc.

Button:
With 2 strands Green, follow instructions for button of shell belt. Sew button to end of belt opposite buttonhole.

Finishing

With crochet hook, work in loose ends. No blocking is necessary.

Boy's Fisherman Sweater

Instructions are for Boys' size small (6-8). Changes for Size medium (10-12) and large (14-16) are in parentheses.

Materials

Lightweight unscoured fisherman yarn (2 oz. skeins) 5 (7,11) skeins

Knitting Needles Size 3 and 5

Tapestry Needle

Gauge

4 sts to 1"; 5 rows to 1"

Pattern Stitch

Side Cables:
Rows 1 and 3: P 4, k 4.
Row 2: (Sl 1 yib, k 1, yo, pass sl st over k st and yo) 4 times.
Repeat these 3 rows for Pattern.

Center Cable:
Row 1: (Right side) Sl 3 to cable needle and hold in front of work, k 3, k 3 from cable needle.
Row 2: P 6.
Row 3: K 6.
Row 4: P 6.
Row 5: K 6.
Row 6: P 6.
Row 7: Sl 3 to cable needle and hold in back of work, k 3, k 3 from cable needle.

Rows 8-12: Rep Rows 2 through 6. Repeat these 12 rows for Pattern.

Note: Reverse stockinette st is worked at sides and between all cables.

Back

With #3 needles cast on 54 (58,72) sts. Work even in k 1, p 1 ribbing for 2". Change to #5 needles. *Next row: (Right Side)* To establish pattern, p 4 (6,13) (row 1, reverse stockinette st), work Row 1 side cable for next 8 sts, p 8. Work Row 1 center cable, p 2, work Row 1 center cable, P 8. Work Row 1 side cable, p to end of row. Continue working in pattern as established for 10" (11",13") or desired length to underarm.

Armholes:
Bind off 3 (3,4) sts at beg of next 2 rows. Dec 1 st each end every other row 3 (2,3) times; 42 (48,58) sts. Work even until armholes measure 3½" (5",6½") above bound-off sts.

Neck:
Work first 12 (14,17) sts; place center 18 (20,24) sts on holder; work to end of row. Dec one st each side of holder every other row 2 (2,7) times. Work even until armholes measure 4½" (6",7½").

Shoulders:
Bind off 5 (6,7) sts at beg of next 4 rows.

Front

Work same as back.

Sleeves:
With #3 needles cast on 24 (28,32) sts. Work even in k 1, p 1 ribbing for 2". Change to #5 needles. *Next row:* (Right side) To establish pattern, P 5 (7,9) sts, work row 1 center cable, p 2, work row 1 of center cable, p remaining sts. Working in pattern as established, inc 1 st each end every 1½", 4 (6,8) times; 32 (40,48) sts. Work even until piece measures 11" (14",17") or desired length to underarm.

Shape cap

Bind off 3 (3,4) sts at beg of next 2 rows. Dec 1 st each end every other row 4 (8,11) times. Bind off 2 sts at beg of next 4 rows. Bind off remaining 10 sts.

Finishing

Sew shoulder seams. With right side facing, pick up 26 (28,32) sts around front neck shaping, including sts on holders. Work in k 1, p 1 ribbing for 5" (5½",6"). Bind off loosely. Repeat with sts at back of neck. Sew side, sleeve, neck seams. With center of cap bind-off at shoulder seams and sleeve seam at underarm, sew in sleeves.

Blue on Blue Afghan

See Page 51 for color illustration

Afghan measures 44" x 68" plus fringe.

Materials

Knitting Worsted (4-oz. skeins), 2 skeins each of Pale, Light, Medium and Dark Turquoise

Crochet Hook Size 8

Gauge

One shell to 1¼"; 2 rows to ¾"

Pattern Stitch

Row 1: 1 sc into next 2 sts, * ch 3, 1 sc into each of 3 center dc of group, rep from *, end ch-3, sc into last 2 sts, 1 ch turn.

Row 2: 1 sc into first st, * 5 dc into ch-3 sp, sk 1 sc, 1 sc into next st, rep from *, turn.

Row 3: * ch 3, 1 sc into each of 3 center dc of group, rep from *, end ch 2, 1 sc into last st, ch 3, turn (counts as first dc of next row).

Row 4: 2 dc into ch-2 sp, * 1 sc into center st of 3 sc of previous row, 5 dc into ch-3 sp, rep from *, 1 sc into center st of 3 sc of previous row, 3 dc in last sp, ch-1, turn. Rep these 4 rows for Pattern.

Afghan

With Dark Turquoise, ch 213 sts.

Row 1: Sk 8 chs, sc into next ch, * ch 6, sk 5 chs, sc in next ch, rep from * across row, end ch 6, sk 5 sts, sc in last ch.

Row 2: Ch 6, turn, * 1 sc under next ch-6 lp, ch 6, rep from * across row, ending 1 sc in ch-8 sp, ch 3, 1 dc in 4th ch of ch-8 lp, ch 1, turn. Change to Medium Turquoise and Pattern St, working Row 1 of first repeat of Pattern St as follows: 2 sc into ch-3 sp, * ch 3, 3 sc into next ch-6 sp, rep from *, end ch 3, 4 sc into next ch-6 sp, 1 ch turn.

Work 3 more rows in Pattern St in Med Turquoise. Change to Light Turquoise. Work 4 rows in Light, change to Pale Turquoise, work 4 rows in Pale. Change to Dark Turquoise and work 8 rows. Continue to work 8 rows in each color until 168 rows have been worked, ending with 8 rows of dark. Change to Pale Turquoise and work 4 rows each of Pale, Light, and Medium Turquoise. Change to Dark Turquoise. Ch 6, * 1 sc into 3rd dc of 5-dc group, ch 6, rep from *, ending 1 sc into top of ch-3.

Next row: Ch 6, turn, * 1 sc under next ch-6 sp, ch 6, rep from * across row, ending 1 sc under last ch 6 sp.

Make Fringe

Cut 70, 13" lengths of each shade. Knot 4 strands, one of each color, into center of each ch-6 sp at each end.

Kangaroo Dress

See Page 47 for color illustration

Directions are written for size 6.
Directions for size 8 are in parentheses.

Materials

Knitting Worsted (4 oz. skeins), 1 skein Winter White, 2 skeins Royal Blue and a small amount of Scarlet
Knitting Needles Size 7
Crochet Hook Size F

Gauge

9½ sts to 2"; 12 rows to 2"

The Pattern for the Front and the Back are exactly the same. However, the Front is knitted with Winter White, and the Back is knitted with Royal Blue.

Front and Back

Cast on 69 (78) sts and knit 2 rows. Work in st st for 16½" (17") or desired length to underarm. *Armholes:* Dec 1 st at arm edge every other row until 53 (62) sts remain. Work even for 3" (4"). *Neck and shoulder:* Work across 17 (20) sts place next 21 (22) sts on a holder, work across next 17 (20) sts and place on a holder. *Left Shoulder:* Work on the 17 (21) sts decreasing 1 st at neck edge every row. Work for 1½" (2"). Fasten off. Work opposite shoulder to correspond.

Sleeves:
Cast on 32 (36) sts. Knit 2 rows. Work even in st st for 2". Increase 1 st at beg and end of row every inch until sleeve is 11" (12") long. Work even in st st until sleeve measures 12" (13"). *Shape Cap:* Bind off 4 sts at beg of next 2 rows. Dec 1 st each end of every row until 6 sts remain. Bind off.

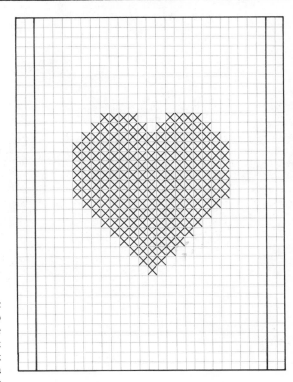

Kangaroo Pouch:

On Front of dress (Winter White Side) and on first row at the bottom, count across 22 (26) sts and mark with a pin. Hold a tape measure in a vertical position on pin and place another pin 3¼" (4") up from first pin. With knitting needle and working *across* row pick up 25 (29) sts. With Royal Blue work in st st for 10 rows. Heart will be knitted into pouch with Scarlet yarn, please see chart for instructions. When pouch is completed steam with a light iron and sew side seams with Royal Blue.

Kangaroo Pouch

1. Each horizontal square represents 1 stitch.

2. Each vertical square represents 1 row.

3. Each X represents 1 stitch worked with scarlet yarn.

4. The inside lines of this rectangle are directions for Size 6.

5. The outside lines of this rectangle are directions for Size 8.

Finishing

Sew shoulder seams. Sew sleeves in place. Sew dress seams and sleeve seams. *Neck Ribbing: Front:* With Royal Blue start at left shoulder seam with right side facing pick up 38 (42) sts (this includes sts from holder) and work in k 1, p 1, ribbing along neck edge. Work in rib st for 1". Bind off in pattern. *Back Neck:* Work same as for Front ribbing. Sew seams. *Lower edge of Dress:* With crochet hook and Royal Blue starting in center back, join yarn with a slip st and work 1 row single crochet around edge. Join with sl st. Fasten off.

Crochet Pocketbook

Finished pocketbook is 11″ in diameter.

Materials

Frederick J. Fawcett's 10/5 linen (15-yard skeins. If not available in your area, contact Frederick J. Fawcett; see page 4 for address.), 8 skeins Yellow, 4 skeins Orange, 4 skeins Peach, 4 skeins Pink, 2 skeins White

Crochet Hook Size 8

Tapestry Needle

Gauge

4 sts to 1″; 4 rows to 1″

Pocketbook Back

With Yellow ch 6. Join with slip st to make a ring.

Rnd 1: Work 12 sc into ring, join.

Rnd 2: Work 2 sc into each stitch.

Rnd 3: (sc into 1 sc, 2 sc in next st) 6 times; join.

Rnd 4: (sc into 2 sc; 2 sc into next sc) 6 times, join.

Rnd 5: (sc into 3 sc; 2 sc into next sc) 6 times, join.

Rnd 6: (sc into 4 sc; 2 sc into next sc) 6 times, join.

Rnd 7: (sc into 5 sc; 2 sc into next sc) 6 times, join.

Continuing in same manner, increasing 6 sts evenly spaced in each rnd, work colors as follows: *Rnd 8:* Orange; *Rnds 9-11:* Peach; *Rnds 12-16:* Yellow; *Rnds 17-18:* White; *Rnds 19-22:* Pink; *Rnd 23:* White; *Rnd 24:* Peach; *Rnd 25:* Slip st with Orange. End off.

Front

Make same as back.

Strap

With Orange ch 10 sts.

Row 1: Sk first ch; holding all lps on hook, pull up lp in each ch across, end yo and pull through 1 lp, * yo and pull through 2 lps, repeat from * across to last lp on hook.

Row 2: Insert hook under 1 vertical bar and next horizontal bar and pull up lp. Work same in each st across. Work off lps as before.

Rep Row 2 for Pattern. Work in pattern until strap measures 22″, or desired length, allowing 29″ to sew bag sides. Break off Orange. Attach Yellow. Work in Yellow for another 25″.

Finishing

Block pieces. Sew one edge of strap to front of pocketbook; sew other edge of strap to back of pocketbook; sew ends of strap together. With Orange work one row of slip st along outer edges of strap.

Pink Bumpy Stitch Sweater

See Page 49 for color illustration

Instructions are for size small (8-10). Changes for Sizes medium (12-14) and large (16-18) are in parentheses.

Materials

Fingering yarn (1 oz. skein) Pale Pink, 10 (12,14) skeins

Knitting Needles Size 2 and 4

Steel Crochet Hook Size 0

Tapestry Needle

Gauge

7 sts to 1″; 8 rows to 1″ with yarn worked double

Pattern Stitch

Row 1: (Right side) * P 5, k 1; repeat from *.
Row 2: P 1, k 5.
Row 3: * P 5, (k 1, p 1, k 1) in next st, p 5, k 1; repeat from *.
Row 4: * P 1, k 13; repeat from *.
Row 5: * P 5, k 3, p 5, k 1; repeat from *
Row 6: Rep Row 4.
Row 7: Rep Row 5.
Row 8: * P 1, k 5, p 3 tog, k 5; repeat from *.
Row 9: Rep Row 1.
Row 10: Rep Row 2.
Row 11: Rep Row 1.
Row 12: Rep Row 2.
Row 13: P 5, k 1, * P 5, (k 1, p 1, k 1) in next st, p 5, k 1, rep from *, end p 5, k 1.
Row 14: P 1, k 5, * p 1, k 13, rep from *; end p; k 5.
Row 15: P 5, k 1, * p 5, k 3, p 5, k 1, rep from *; end p 5, k 1.
Row 16: Rep Row 14.
Row 17: Rep Row 15.
Row 18: P 1, k 5; * p 1, k 5, p 3 tog, k 5. Rep from *, end p 1, k 5.
Row 19: Repeat Row 1.
Row 20: Repeat Row 2.
Repeat these 20 rows for Pattern.

Back

With #2 needles cast on 84 (96,108) sts.

Ribbing

K 1, p 1. Repeat this row for ribbing for 2″. Change to #4 needles and Pattern St. Increase 1 st each end every ½″, 17 times; 118 (130,142) sts. Work even until piece measures 12½″ (13″,13½″) or desired length to underarm.

Underarms:
Bind off 4 (6,9) sts at beg of next 2 rows. Dec 1 st each end every other row 4 (6,8) times; 102 (106,108) sts. Work even until armhole measures 6¾″ (7¼″,7¾″).

Shape Neck: Work first 32 sts; attach second ball of yarn; bind off center 38 (42,44) sts; work to end of row. Working on both sides at the same time, continue working even until armholes measure 7½″ (8″,8½″). Bind off 8 sts at each arm edge 4 times.

Front

Work same as for back until armholes measure 5½″ (6″,6½″).

Neck:
Work first 36 sts; attach second ball of yarn; bind off center 30 (34,36) sts; work to end of row. Working on both sides of center at same time, dec one st each side of center every other row 4 times. Work even until armholes measure same as for back.

Shoulders:
Bind off 8 sts at each arm edge 4 times.

Sleeves:
With # 2 needles cast on 78 (84,90) sts. Work even in k 1, p 1 ribbing for 2″. Change to #4 needles and pattern st. Work even for 3″.

Shape Cap

Bind off 4 (6,8) sts at beg of next 2 rows. Dec 1 st each end every other row 17 (19,20) times. Bind off 4 (3,3) sts at beg of next 4 rows. Bind off rem. 20 (22,22) sts.

Finishing

Sew shoulder, side, and arm seams. With center of cap bind-off at shoulder and sleeve seam at underarm, sew in sleeves. With right side facing, work one row sc around neck.

Fleur-de-Lis Pillow

See Page 62 for color illustration

Pillow measures 14″ square.

Materials

Knitting Worsted (4 oz. skeins) 1 skein each of Hot Pink and Aqua

Knitting Needles Size 8

Tapestry Needle

Pillow 14″ square

Gauge

9 sts to 2″

Pattern Stitch
See Pattern Number 86.

Front

With Hot Pink cast on 59 sts. Work 6 rows in stockinette stitch. Join Aqua and work from chart for Fleur-de-Lis design (stockinette stitch). Work in pattern until 6 rows of Fleur-de-Lis have been worked or piece measures 14″. Bind off loosely.

Back

With Hot Pink cast on 54 sts and work in stockinette stitch until piece measures same as for front. Bind off loosely.

Finishing

Steam both pieces lightly on wrong sides. Wrong sides facing, sew around 3 seams, leave one end open to insert pillow. Sew final seam on front side.

Fringe

For each fringe wind yarn 14 times around 8½″ cardboard. Cut at one end. Place fringe in each of the four corners. Trim evenly.

Dotted Swiss Pillow

See Page 62 for color illustration

Pillow measures 14″ square.

Materials

Orlon (4 oz. skeins), 1 skein each of Royal Blue and Scarlet

Knitting Needles Size 8

Tapestry Needle

Pillow 14″ square

Gauge

8 sts to 2″

Pattern Stitch

Rows 1, 3: With Scarlet, knit.
Rows 2, 4: Purl.
Rows 5, 6: With Royal Blue, * k 2, sl 1, repeat from * across row, end k 2.

Front

With Scarlet cast on 55 sts and work even in Pattern Stitch until piece measures 14″. Bind off.

Back

Cast on 50 sts and work even in stockinette stitch until piece measures same as for front. Bind off.

Finishing

Steam each piece lightly. Sew together around three sides. Insert pillow and sew remaining side closed.

Plant Holder

Fits a 3½-inch pot.

Materials

Lightweight Cotton Twine (used by bakeries), 1 ball.

Crochet Hook Size I

15 Beads with a ¼" diameter

Note:
Plant holder is worked with 2 strands of cotton throughout. Make a bobbin several yards long. String beads onto double strand.

Ch 5, join with a sl st to form a ring.
Rnd 1: Ch 2, work 15 dc in center. Join with a sl st to top of ch-2, * ch 5, sk 1 dc, sc in next dc, repeat from * around.
Rnd 2: Sc in first lp, ** ch 5, sc in next lp, repeat from ** around. Repeat Rnd 2, 3 times more.
Rnd 6: Repeat Rnd 2 slipping one bead between 2nd and 3rd chs of each ch-5—7 beads.
Rnd 7: Repeat Rnd 2 working sc in top of lp surrounding each bead.
Rnd 8: Sc in first lp. * ch 3, sc in next lp, repeat from * around. Fasten off. Weave in loose ends.

Tassels
Cut 25 strands of cotton 8" long. Fold in half. Tie a knot at top and sew to base of holder.

Ties
Cut 8 strands of cotton 15" long, place 2 strands together for each tie and attach in every other sc of last rnd. Place a bead at base of each tie. Make a knot approx 4" from first bead and string another bead. Join all ties 6" from last beads and make a knot.

Child's Camisole
See Page 60 for color illustration

Directions are written for Toddlers size 2. Directions for size 3 are in parentheses.

Materials
Knitting Worsted (4 oz. skeins), 1 (2) skeins Pale Gray, few yds each White, Yellow and Violet

Knitting Needles Size 8

Crochet Hook Size F

Gauge
9 sts to 2"; 14 rows to 2"

Pattern Stitch
Multiple of 2 sts plus 1.
Row 1: * K 1, yarn in front sl 1, yarn in back repeat from * across row, end k 1 (sl 1).
Row 2: Purl.
Row 3: * Yarn in front sl 1, yarn in back k 1, repeat from * across row, end sl 1 (k 1).
Row 4: Purl.
Repeat Rows 1-4 for Pattern Stitch.

Front and Back
Front and back are exactly the same. Cast on 45 (50) sts. Work even in Pattern Stitch for 9½" (10").
Armholes:
Bind off 4 sts at beg of next 2 rows. Dec 1 st each end of next row. Work even in Pattern Stitch for 3" (3½").

Shoulders:
Work across 10 (12) sts and place on a st holder, bind off center 15 (16) sts, work across rem 10 (12) sts. Work even for 1½" (2"). Bind off. Work opposite side to correspond.

Flowers:
Make 2. *Note:* Leave about 16" of yarn on each flower for sewing. With White ch 4; join with a sl st to form a ring.
Rnd 1: In ring (sc, ch 2, dc, ch 2) 4 times. Join with a sl st.
Stem: Ch 16, sk first ch, sl st in next 4 chs, * ch 4 for leaf, sk 1, sc in next ch of leaf, dc in next ch, sl st in next ch, carry yarn in back of stem and make a sl st in stem, repeat from * once more, sl st in center of 2 leaves just made, sl st in rem'g sts of stem; end off.

Embroidery
Sew shoulder seams. Pin flowers to bodice as seen in photograph and sew in place. *Bodice Border:* With Yellow starting at armhole about 2 rows above beginning of armhole, insert hook into first st, * draw yarn up through st and draw through lp on hook, insert hook into next st and repeat from * across row. End off. *Center Stripes:* Place a pin in center of Bodice Border. Place 2 more pins 1/16" to either side of center pin. Join Yellow with a sl st on right side of center pin. Working to lower edge, work in same manner as for Bodice Border. Repeat on left side of center. *Cross Stitch (Bodice):* With Violet beg at top right shoulder and work cross sts randomly across entire Bodice.

Finishing
Sew side seams. With Yellow work 1 row sl st around armholes, neckline, and lower edge. End off; sew in all loose ends.

Autumn Afghan

Afghan measures approximately 47″ x 52″.

Materials

Knitting Worsted (4-oz. skeins), 4 skeins each of Scarlet, Beige, and Gold

Knitting Needles Size 10

Gauge

The gauge for this afghan is the width of each panel. Each panel measures approximately 8″ x 52″. No row gauge is needed.

Pattern Stitch

Row 1: Purl.
Row 2: K 1, k 2 tog, k 6, yo, k 1, yo, k 6, k 2 tog, k 2 tog, k 6, yo, k 1, yo, k 6, k 2 tog, k 1.
Row 3: Purl.
Repeat all *three* rows for Pattern Stitch.

Panels

Make 2 panels of each color yarn. Cast on 36 sts and work in Pattern Stitch until panel measures about 52″ long. Bind off in pattern stitch.

Follow diagram for joining panels.

Fringe

Wind Scarlet and Gold around a 6″ cardboard several times, cut at one end. Place one Scarlet fringe (8 strands of yarn) in each corner; alternating colors, place other fringes in space where panels have been joined.

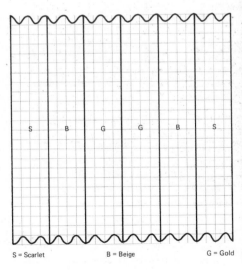

S = Scarlet   B = Beige   G = Gold

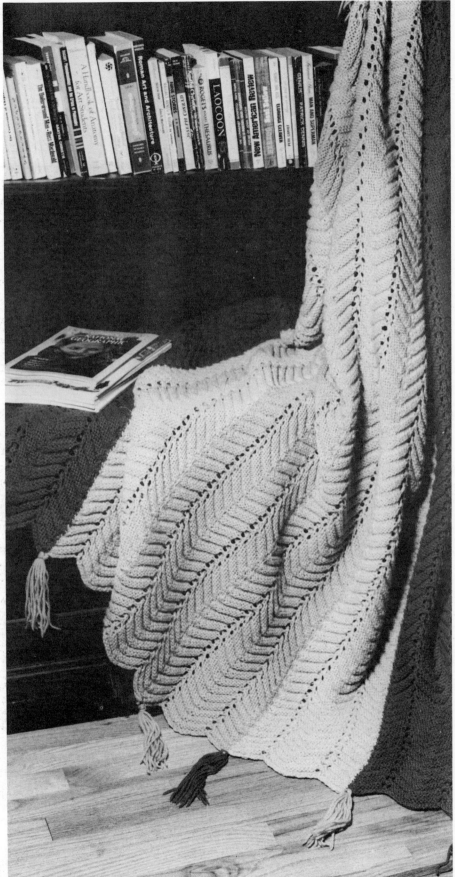

Indian Afghan

See Page 48 for color illustration

Afghan measures approximately 42" x 68".

Materials
Knitting Worsted (4 oz. skeins) 2 skeins each of Red, Yellow, Green, 1 skein White, 3 skeins Blue

Crochet Hook Size J

Blunt End Tapestry Needle

Gauge
7 hdc to 2"; 15 rows to 6"

Each Panel measures approximately 6" x 66"

Pattern
Make 7 panels. See Diagram for color sequence and length of each color space.

Chain 21.
Row 1: Sk 1 ch, hdc in each remaining ch, ch 1, turn. 20 hdc across row.
Row 2: Hdc in each hdc across row, ch 1, turn.
Repeat Row 2 for Pattern Stitch.

Note:
To change colors work last 2 loops of last hdc on now off with next color, ch 1, turn.

Finishing
Pin panels in place—see diagram. Sew panels together on wrong side only. Back stitch panels when sewing. Use matching colors for sewing. Sew in all loose ends. Steam lightly. With Blue work 1 row hdc on short ends of Afghan, working on wrong side only.

Fringe
Cut 15, 9" strands of Green yarn for each fringe. Place a fringe on each corner of Afghan.

Follow Chart as indicated for measurements and colors. All Squares not numbered are approximately 6" x 6". Work rectangle length stated in each space.

Blue	Green	9½" Yellow	13"	9½" Yellow	Green	Blue
	Blue				Blue	
		Blue		Blue		
25" Red	13" Green	13" Yellow	13" Blue	13" Yellow	13" Green	25" Red
		Blue		Blue		
	Blue				Blue	
Blue	Green	13" Yellow	16"	13" Yellow	Green	Blue
	Blue				Blue	
		Blue		Blue		
25" Red	13" Green	Yellow	13" Blue	Yellow	13" Green	25" Red
		Blue		Blue		
	Blue				Blue	
Blue	Green	9½" Yellow	13"	9½" Yellow	Green	Blue

Sunrise Afghan

See Page 56 for color illustration

Measures approximately 54" x 57½".

Materials
Knitting Worsted (4 oz. skeins), 3 skeins Gold, 2 skeins each of Orange, Winter White, 1 skein each of Pink, Cerise, Beige, Tangerine, and Grey

Knitting Needles Size 10½

Crochet Hook Size I

Gauge
8 sts to 2"; 9 rows to 2"

Note:
When changing colors always twist the yarns around each other to prevent holes forming.

Pattern Stitch
Row 1: With Grey k 2, join White, * k 1, with Grey k 6, repeat from * across row, ending with White k 1, with Grey k 2.
Row 2: With Grey p 1, * with White p 3, with Grey p 4, repeat fom * across row, ending with White p 3, with Grey p 1.
Row 3: With White k 5, * with Grey k 2, with White k 5, repeat from * across row, ending with Grey k 2, with White k 5.
Row 4: With White purl.
Row 5: With White knit.
Rows 6-21: Continuing in stockinette st, alternate colors as follows: 2 rows Orange, 2 rows Pink, 2 rows Beige, 2 rows Tangerine, 8 rows Gold.
Row 22: With Orange purl across row.
Row 23: * With Cerise k 2, sl 1, repeat from * across row ending, sl 1, k 2.
Row 24: With Orange purl across row.
Repeat Rows 1-24 for Pattern Stitch.

Afghan
Entire Afghan is worked in stockinette stitch. With Grey cast on 215 sts and work for 2 rows. Work in Pattern Stitch until Afghan measures approximately 56" (ending with Row 24 of Pattern Stitch. Repeat Rows 1-5 once more. Bind off on next row.

Finishing
Borders: With crochet hook and Orange work 1 sc in each st along each side of afghan. Work sc for 1 more row. Fasten off.

Warm-Up Sweater

Instructions are to fit sizes 2T. Directions for (3T) and (4T) are in parentheses.

Materials

Variegated Orlon Knitting Yarn (4-oz. skeins), 3 skeins.

Crochet Hook Size G

Gauge

8 hdc to 2″; 6 rows to 2″

Back

Ch 41 (43,45).

Row 1: Hdc in 2nd ch from hook and in each ch across row, ch 1, turn.

Row 2: 1 hdc in each hdc across row, ch 1, turn. Repeat Row 2 for Pattern Stitch.

Work even for 10″ (11″,11″).

Raglan Armholes:
Sl st across first 2 sts, ch 1, work to last 2 sts, ch 1, turn.

Decrease: Draw up a loop in each of first two sts, yo and through all 3 lps for a dec, work to last 2 hdc, dec 1 st same as before, ch 1, turn. Dec on every other row 2 (2,3) times more. Dec on every row until 14 (14,16) hdc rem. End off.

Front

Work same as for back to underarm.

Raglan Armhole and Neck Opening:
Sl st across first 2 sts, ch 1, work next 18 (19,20) sts, ch 1, turn.

Following Row: Work to last 2 sts, dec 1 st for armhole, ch 1, turn. Repeat Raglan Dec every other row 2 (2,3) times, then every row until 13 (14,14) sts rem. End at raglan edge.

Next Row: Dec 1 st at raglan, work to last 5 (5,6) sts, ch 1, turn. Dec 1 st at neck edge on next row and dec at raglan every row until 2 sts rem. End off. Work other side to correspond.

Sleeves:
Ch 26 (26,27).

Row 1: Hdc in 2nd ch from hook and in each ch across row ch 1, turn.

Row 2: Hdc in each hdc, ch 1, turn.

Inc: Work 2 hdc in 1 hdc. Inc 1 hdc on each side of next row then every 4th row 3 times more. Work on the 34 (34,35) sts for 10″ (10½″,11″).

Sleeve Cap:
Sl st across 2 sts, ch 1, work to last 2 sts, ch 1, turn. Dec 1 st each side of next row, then every other row 3 times, then every row until 6 sts rem. End off.

Hood:
Ch 61 (63,65) work in pattern for 7″. End off.

Sewing

Sew in sleeves. Sew side seams

Hood: Fold hood in half lengthwise, sew seam on one edge, matching seam to center back of sweater, sew from this point around to left front and around to right front.

Cord

Crochet a 35-37″ ch. Work 1 sc in each ch. End off. Thread cord from right side through left front neck edge and from wrong side through right neck edge.

Adobe Tapestry/Afghan

Afghan measures approximately 53" x 57".

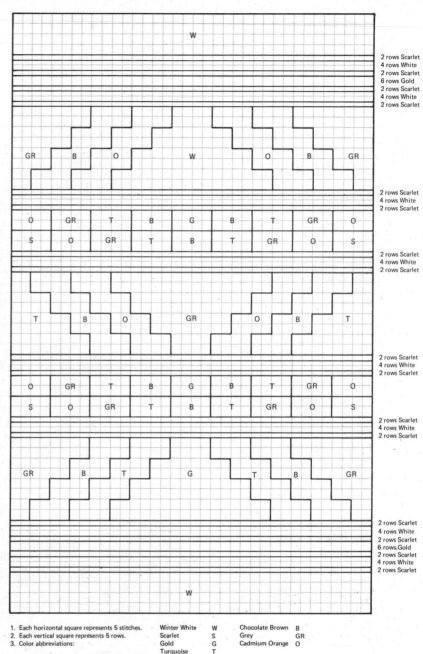

2 rows Scarlet
4 rows White
2 rows Scarlet
6 rows Gold
2 rows Scarlet
4 rows White
2 rows Scarlet

2 rows Scarlet
4 rows White
2 rows Scarlet

2 rows Scarlet
4 rows White
2 rows Scarlet

2 rows Scarlet
4 rows White
2 rows Scarlet

2 rows Scarlet
4 rows White
2 rows Scarlet

2 rows Scarlet
4 rows White
2 rows Scarlet
6 rows Gold
2 rows Scarlet
4 rows White
2 rows Scarlet

1. Each horizontal square represents 5 stitches.
2. Each vertical square represents 5 rows.
3. Color abbreviations:

Winter White	W	
Scarlet	S	
Gold	G	
Turquoise	T	
Chocolate Brown	B	
Grey	GR	
Cadmium Orange	O	

Materials

Knitting Worsted (4 oz. skein), 2 skeins Winter White, 1 skein each Scarlet, Gray, Cadmium Orange, Chocolate Brown, Gold and Turquoise

Knitting Needles Size 10½

Crochet Hook Size I

Wooden dowel for hanging Tapestry, 59" long, ¾" wide

Gauge

7 sts to 2"; 10 rows to 2"

Afghan

Note: When changing colors twist yarn in back to prevent holes from forming in work.

Entire afghan is worked in stockinette stitch. With Winter White cast on 180 sts and follow the chart.

Bobbins: Make 2 Bobbins each of the following colors, Turquoise, Brown, Grey, Orange. See general instructions for making bobbins.

Finishing

With crochet hook and Winter White work 1 row single crochet across top and bottom of afghan. Work 1 row single crochet with Scarlet along sides of afghan.

To Hang as Tapestry

Casing: Fold approximately 3" at top of afghan to the wrong side and hem using matching yarn, put dowel through casing.

74

Child's Sun Dress
See Page 47 for color illustration

Directions are written for size 6. Directions for size 8 are in parentheses.

Materials

Knitting Worsted (4 oz. skeins), 1 skein each of Winter White, Yellow, Avocado

Crochet Hook Size H

Knitting Needles Size 7

Satin Ribbon 5/16" wide, 12 (15) yards each of White, Green, Yellow

Gauge

4 mesh to 2"; 4 mesh rows to 2"

Knitting Gauge

11 sts to 2"; 11 rows to 2"

Filet Mesh Pattern Stitch

Row 1: 1 dc in 6th ch from hook, * ch 1, sk 1 ch, dc in next ch, repeat from * across row, ch 4, turn.

Row 2: Turning ch counts as first dc, dc in next dc, * ch 1, 1 dc in next dc, repeat from * across row, working last dc in turning ch, ch 4, turn. Repeat Row 2 for Pattern Stitch.

Note

When changing colors, always work off last 2 lps of last dc with next color.

Skirt

With Winter White chain 168 (172) = 82 mesh (100 mesh). Join with sl st in first ch. Be careful not to twist chain; ch 4. Work from * of Row 1 of Pattern Stitch, ending with sl st in 4th ch of ch-4 at beg of Rnd 1, do not turn work. Work Row 2 of Pattern Stitch, ending with sl st in 3rd ch of ch-4 of beg of Rnd 2. Working in this manner work next 2 rows with Avocado, 2 rows Yellow, 4 rows Winter White, * 2 rows Avocado, 2 rows Yellow, ending with 4 rows Winter White. For size 8, repeat from * once more. End off all yarn.

Shirred Waist and Bodice:
Front and back are exactly the same; however, they are worked separately. *Back:* Place a marker in center back of skirt (where all rnds are joined). Count across 20 (25) mesh on each side of center back and place markers. Starting at first marker (right side) with knitting needle pick up first st, * sk 1 st, pick up next st (top of dc), repeat from * until 42 (58) sts are on knitting needle. With Avocado work in Rib Pattern:

Row 1: * K 1, p 1, repeat from * across row, ending with p 1.

Row 2: * K 1, p 1, repeat from * across row, ending with p 1.

Note: Do not break yarn at end of rows; carry yarn at back of work. Work even Rib Pattern alternating colors as follows; * 2 rows Yellow, 4 rows Winter White, 2 rows Avocado, repeat from * for 5½" (7½"), end

with 2 rows Winter White. Bind off on next row. Work front to correspond.

Weaving

Cut 10 (11) strands of White ribbon each 36" (52") long. Cut 10 (11) strands each of Green ribbon and Yellow ribbon approximately 19" (27") long. Place a safety pin in end of white ribbon. Starting at lower edge in 2nd mesh to the left of center back, bring safety pin through to right side and draw ribbon through leaving 2" end. Weave ribbon over 1st bar, under 2nd bar, over 3rd bar, continue in this manner to end of row. Work 3 more rows White. *Note:* Be sure to alternate the unders and overs at the beg of each mesh row. Continue working around skirt to right. Work next * 2 rows with Yellow, next 2 rows with Green, 4 rows White, repeat from *.

Finishing

Sew ends of ribbon on wrong side of work as you would sew a dress hem. Seam binding may be added to ribbon and then sewed in place. Sew ribbed seams on right side. Weave in all loose ends.

Bodice Trim:

With crochet hook and Yellow yarn, on right side, make a sl st at center back, * ch 3, sk 1 st, sc in next st, repeat from * around. Join with sl st. Fasten off.

Straps

Cut 4 strips of Green ribbon approximately 14" or desired length. Sew each ribbon approximately 2" from side seams.

Professor's Delight
See Page 57 for color illustration

Instructions are for Men's small size (34-36). Changes for medium (38-40) and large (42-44) are in parentheses.

Materials

Frederick J. Fawcett's 10/2 linen (½ pound and pound cones. If not available in your area write to Frederick J. Fawcett. For address see page 4 .), ½ (1,1) pound Dark Blue, ½ (½,1) pound Natural

Knitting Needles Size 1

Tapestry Needle

Gauge

6 sts to 1"; 9 rows to 1"

Color Pattern

Row 1: K 2 with Natural, k 2 with Blue. (Note: carry color not in use loosely behind.)

Row 2: P 2 with Blue, p 2 with Natural.

Row 3: K 2 with Blue, k 2 with Natural.

Row 4: P 2 with Natural, p 2 with Blue.

Repeat these 4 rows for pattern.

Back

Beg at lower edge, cast on 96 (108,120) sts in Blue. Work even in k 1, p 1 ribbing for 2". Tie on Natural. Work in Color Pattern, increasing 1 st each side every 2¼", 6 times; 108 (120,132) sts. Work even until piece measures 15" (16",16½") or desired length to underarm, ending with a p row.

Underarms:
Bind off 5 (6,7) sts at beg of next 2 rows. Dec 1 st each side every other row 4 (6,7) times; (90 (96,104) sts. Work even until armholes measure 8½" (9½",10½"), ending with a p row.

Shoulders:
Bind off 6 (7,7) sts at beg of next 4 rows, 5 (5,6) sts at beg of next 6 rows. Place remaining 36 (38,40) sts on holder.

Front

Work same as for back until vest measures 2" below underarm, ending with a p row.

V-neck:
Work 54 (60,66) sts. Attach second ball of each

color. Work to end of row. Working on both sides at once, with separate strands of each color for each side of V, dec 1 st at each neck edge of next row, then 1 st each side of center every ½", 16 (18,19) times more. Simultaneously, when piece measures same as back to underarm, repeat underarm shaping as for back. When armholes measure same as back, bind off for shoulder shaping same as for back.

Finishing

Block pieces. With backstitch sew left shoulder seam. From right side, with Blue, pick up 36 (38,40) sts from back holder. Work in k 1, p 1 ribbing for 1". Bind off. With right side facing, pick up 90 sts along left side of neck. Work in k 1, p 1 ribbing for 1". Repeat along right side of neck. Sew side seams. From right side pick up 80 (90,100) sts around one armhole, work in k 1, p 1 ribbing for 1". Repeat with other armhole. Sew ribbing from back of neck to neckline ribbing. Sew loose edge of ribbing from right side of neck to left edge of V. Sew loose edge of ribbing from left side of neck to right edge of V. (Left side ribbing should cross over right side ribbing.)

75

Fiesta Sweater
See Page 49 for color illustration

Directions are written for size small; directions for sizes medium and large are in parentheses.

Materials

Knitting Worsted (4 oz. skeins), Winter White 3(4,4) skeins. Small amounts Scarlet, Orange, Kelly Green, Turquoise, Gold, Brown. Kelly Green Satin Ribbon 5/16 inches wide, 2 yards long

Crochet Hook Size H

Gauge
9 sts to 2"; 8 rows to 2"

Pattern Stitch
Row 1: Sk first ch, sc in each ch across to end, ch 1, turn.
Row 2: Sc in front lp of each sc across row, ch 1, turn.
Repeat Row 2 for Pattern Stitch.
Front and back are exactly the same: Sweater measures across chest 15" (17", 19"). Chain 67 (75,83) sts and work even in Pattern Stitch for 17" (18",19") or desired length to neck edge. *Shoulders:* Work across 16 (18,20) sts, ch 1, turn. Work even on the 16 (18,20) sts for 3"(4",5"). Fasten off. Work opposite shoulder to correspond. End off.

Crocheted Flowers

Small Scarlet Flowers and stem with leaves. Make 2. *Note:* Leave several inches of yarn on each flower for sewing. With Scarlet ch 4, join with sl st to form a ring. In ring (sc, ch 2, dc, ch 2) 4 times. Join with a sl st. End off. *Stem:* Join Kelly Green in any sc, ch 16, sk first ch, sl st in next 4 chs, * ch 4 for leaf, sk 1, sc in next ch of leaf, dc in next ch, sl st in next ch, carry yarn in back of stem and make a sl st in stem, repeat from * once more, sl st in center of 2 leaves just made, sl st in next 6 chs of stem, repeat from * ch 4 until 2 more leaves are made. End off.

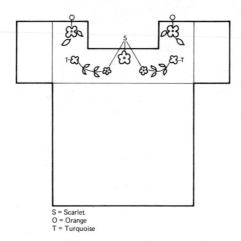

S = Scarlet
O = Orange
T = Turquoise

Orange Flowers and 2 leaves:
Make 2. Ch 5, join with sl st to form a ring.
Rnd 1: Work 8 sc in ring, join with a sl st in top of first sc.
Rnd 2: * Ch 2, hold back last lp of each dc, work 3 dc in same sp, yo and thru all 4 lps on hook, sl st in next 2 sc in ring, repeat from * around until 4 petals are made.
Leaves: Join Kelly Green in any sc between 2 petals, ch 4, sk 1 ch, sc in next ch, dc in next sc in next ch, sl st in first ch, ch 4, carry the ch-4 in back of petal, sl st in next sc, repeat from * once more. Fasten off.

Turquoise Flowers:
Make 2. Work same as for small Scarlet flowers omitting stem and leaves.

Large Scarlet Flower:
Ch 6, join to first ch with sl st to form a ring.
Rnd 1: Work 15 sc in ring, join with a sl st to first sc.

Rnd 2: Sc in next sc, * 2 dc, tr, 2 dc in next sc, sc in next 2 sc, repeat from * around, join with sl st to first sc. End off.

See Diagram for application. Pin all flowers in place and sew to front. *Embroidery* (centers of large Scarlet and Orange Flowers): Thread tapestry needle with Orange yarn for Scarlet flower and Brown yarn for Orange flower. Bring needle up through center of flower, wind yarn 4 times around index finger (holding finger close to center of flower) hold yarn in place and remove finger, set down in center and sew down. Embroidery for centers of small flowers: Use Orange yarn and work same as for larger flowers, winding yarn around finger just once.

Border
Thread tapestry needle with Scarlet, bring needle up through first st at side edge approximately 2 rows below last flower. Work 1 row overcast st across row.

Sleeves:
Sew shoulder seams. On right side starting at border st and working around to back of sweater work sc in 56 (60,64) sts. Work even in Pattern Stitch for 9"(9½",10").

Finishing
Sew sleeve and side seams on wrong side. With white yarn start at center back neck and work * sc, sk 1 st, repeat from * around neck. Join with sl st and fasten off. At lower edge and starting at back on right side and with Winter White yarn work 1 row sc, join with sl st and fasten off. Sleeves: Cut 2 pieces of ribbon each about 28" long and starting at top of each sleeve edge weave around to beg of ribbon, gather and tie a bow.

Buttercup Top
See Page 39 for color illustration

Directions are written for Girl's size 6. Directions for size 8 are in parentheses.

Materials

Knitting Worsted (4 oz. skein), 1 (2) skein(s) Yellow

Knitting Needles Size 8
Crochet Hook Size I

6 Glass mirrors from Pakistan. Ordered from Jean Simpson's Mini Mirrors, Box 5042, Glendale, California 91201. 1 package of 20 mirrors and instructions costs $1.50 plus 50 cents for postage.

Small amount of Royal Blue Knitting Worsted for Embroidery.

Gauge
9 sts to 2"; 14 rows to 2"

Pattern Stitch
Multiple of 2 plus 1.
Row 1: * K 1, yarn in front sl 1, yarn in back repeat from * across row, end k 1 (sl 1).
Row 2: Purl.
Row 3: * Yarn in front sl 1, yarn in back k 1, repeat from * across row, end sl 1.
Row 4: Purl.
Repeat Rows 1-4 for Pattern Stitch.
Front and Back are exactly the same: Cast on 45 (50) sts. Work even in Pattern Stitch for 9½" (11½").

Armholes: Bind off 6 sts at beg of next 2 rows. Dec 1 st each end of next 2 rows. *Size 8 only:* Dec 1 st beg and end of next 2 row . Size 6: 31 sts remain. Size 8: 34 sts remain. Work even on remaining number of sts for 2" (3") from beg of armhole. *Shoulders:* Work across 7 sts (and place on a holder). Bind off center 17 (20) sts, work across remaining 7 sts. Work even on these 7 sts for 4" (6"). Bind off. Work opposite shoulder to correspond.

Finishing

Fastening mirrors to top. Fasten mirrors according to instructions included with mirrors. Sew shoulder seams. Sew side seams. Work 1 row sc around neck and armholes.

Delft Tile Afghan

Measures approximately 56" x 70".

Materials

Knitting Worsted (4 oz. skeins), 6 skeins Aqua and 4 skeins Eggshell

Crochet Hook Size I

Gauge

Each square measures approximately 11" x 11"

Squares

Make 30. With Aqua ch 5, join with sl st to form ring.

Rnd 1: Ch 7, (dc in ring, ch 4) 5 times, sl st in 3rd st of ch-7—6 sps.

Rnd 2: Sc, hdc, dc, tr, dc, hdc, and sc in each sp around. Join with sl st in first sc.

Rnd 3: * Ch 4, keeping ch in back of petal, sl st between next 2 petals; repeat from *, ending sl st in first st of starting ch.

Rnd 4: In each ch-4 make 1 sc, 1 hdc, 2 dc, 1 tr, 2 dc, 1 hdc and 1 sc. Join with sl st in first sc.

Rnd 5: Join Eggshell, * ch 6, sc in top of next tr, ch 6, sc between next 2 petals; repeat from *, ending ch 6, sc in tr of last petal, ch 3, dc in joining of last rnd.—12 lps.

Rnd 6: * Ch 6, sc in 3rd ch of next ch-6, ch 10, sc in same st for corner, (ch 6, sc in next lp) twice; repeat from * 3 times, ending last repeat after 4th corner lp, ch 6, sc in next lp, ch 3, dc in dc of Rnd 5.

Rnd 7: Ch 6, sc in next lp, ch 6, * make a shell of 1 sc, 1 hdc, 3 dc, 1 tr, 3 dc, 1 hdc and 1 sc in corner ch-10 lp, (ch 6, sc in next lp) 3 times; repeat from *, ending ch 6, sc in next lp after 4th corner ch-3, dc in dc.

Rnd 8: (Ch 6, sc in next lp) twice, * ch 6, sc in tr of corner shell, join Aqua and ch 10, sc in same st, (ch 6, sc in next lp) 4 times; repeat from * ending after 4th corner ch-6, sc in next lp, ch 3, dc in dc.

Rnd 9: (Ch 6, sc in next lp) 3 times, * ch 6, join Eggshell and work a shell as on Rnd 7 in corner lp, (ch 6, sc in next lp) 5 times; repeat from * ending after 4th corner ch-6, sc in next lp, ch 3, dc in dc.

Rnd 10: (Ch 6, sc in next lp) 4 times, * ch 6, sc in next tr, join Aqua and ch 10, sc in same st, (ch 6, sc in next lp) 6 times; repeat from * ending after 4th corner ch-6, sc in next lp, ch 6, join in top of dc. Fasten off.

Finishing

With Aqua sew squares together on wrong side in strips of 5 squares each. Sew all strips together.

Fringe

Wind yarn (Eggshell) around an 8" cardboard, cut at one end. Make a few with Aqua also. Place 7 strands of Eggshell and 1 strand of Aqua (1 fringe) in each corner of Afghan and 1 fringe where each square is joined together.

Toddler's Alphabet Blanket

See Page 52 for color illustration

Afghan measures approximately 43" x 48".

Materials

Knitting Worsted (4 oz skeins), 5 skeins Mandarin Blue, 1 skein Yellow, 1 oz each Purple, Turquoise, Tangerine and Kelly Green (enough for 1 square), small amounts Violet, Scarlet, Pink, White and Chartreuse

Afghan Crochet Hook Size J

Crochet Hook Size I

Gauge

4 sts to 1"; 3 rows to 1"

Afghan Stitch

Row 1: Draw up a lp in each ch, leaving all lps on hook; to take off lps, yo hook and through 1 lp, * yo hook and through 2 lps, repeat from * across row, end with 1 lp on hook.

Row 2: Count lp on hook as first st, draw up a lp in each upright st across row, insert hook in center of last st (to keep from going on a diagonal). Take off lps as before.

Repeat Row 2 for Pattern Stitch.

Squares

Each measures about 7½" x 6½". Make 30—20 Blue, 1 Violet, 1 Purple, 2 Tangerine, 1 Turquoise, 1 Green, 4 Yellow. With afghan hook, ch 30 and work in Afghan Stitch for 20 rows. *Last Row:* Sl st (going into each upright st) across row. End off.

To Embroider

Block squares first. Each square has 1 letter of the alphabet or a number embroidered on it. Work design in Cross Stitch, 1 Cross Stitch over 1 Afghan Stitch. Make a diagonal stitch and work back over the same stitch with a diagonal stitch going in the opposite direction. When each letter has been made, knot end of yarn in back of work. Embroider letters following Alphabet Chart on page 31 in following colors—

A	Scarlet letter on Blue square
B	Pink letter on Blue square
C	Yellow letter on Blue square
D	Turquoise letter on Violet square
E	Chartreuse letter on Blue square
F	Pink letter on Tangerine square
G	Yellow letter on Blue square
H	Violet letter on Yellow square
I	Pink letter on Purple square
J	Red letter on Blue square
K	Red letter on Blue square
L	Tangerine letter on Blue square
M	Scarlet letter on Blue square
N	Yellow letter on Blue square
O	White letter on Blue square
P	Pink letter on Tangerine square
Q	Pink letter on Turquoise square
R	Scarlet letter on Blue square
S	Violet letter on Yellow square
T	Pink letter on Blue square
U	White letter on Green square
V	Turquoise letter on Blue square
W	White letter on Yellow square
X	Scarlet letter on Blue square
Y	Pink letter on Blue square
Z	Chartreuse letter on Blue square
1	Yellow number on Blue Square
2	Scarlet number on Blue square
3	White number on Blue square
4	Purple number on Yellow square

To Join Squares

Afghan is made of 6 horizontal panels consisting of 5 squares each. The letters are arranged alphabetically from left to right with the last 4 blocks on the last panel containing numbers. Join the squares to form panels as follows: With I hook join Blue on right side of work at upper right hand corner, ch 4, sc in first st of next square (upper left hand corner), * ch 3, sk 2 sts of first square, sc in next st, ch 3, sk 2 sts of 2nd square, sc in next st, repeat from * until 2 squares are joined. Work in this manner until there are 5 squares in each panel. Join the 6 panels in the same manner.

Border

With Blue on right side work across top and bottom edges in half double crochet for 5 rows each. Work along side edges in half double crochet for 2 rows each side.

Heavy Crochet Jacket

Pattern Stitch

Row 1: 1 sc into 2nd st from hook, 1 sc into each st, turn.

Row 2: Ch 2, work one hdc into back loop of each st to make ridge.

Note: Jacket is worked in vertical ribs.

Back

With Tangerine, ch 43 (46,49) or desired length to underarm. Work in Orange in pattern st for 3 rows. Attach Eiderdown; cut Tangerine. At end of first row of Eiderdown, ch 24 (26,28) sts; 63 (72,77) sts. Continue in Pattern St with Eiderdown until piece has total of 31 (34,38) rows. Attach Tangerine, cut Eiderdown. With Tangerine, work 43 (46,49) sts, turn. Work on this number of sts for a total of 3 rows. End off.

Right Front

Work same as for back until piece measures 13 (14,15) rows.

Neck:
At end of next row leave 9 (10,11) sts; 54 (62,66) sts. Work even for 4 (4,5) rows. End off.

Left Front

Work as for right front, reversing shaping, until end of neck shaping. Work even for 5 (5,6) rows. End off.

Sleeves:
(Worked horizontally) With Tangerine ch 37 (41,43) sts. Work even in pattern st for 17" or desired length to underarm. Leave 5 sts at end of next 2 rows. Dec 1 st each end 5 (4,5) times; leave 3 sts at end of next 2 (4,4) rows. End off.

Make Pocket

With Tangerine, ch 19 (20,21) sts. Work even in pattern st for 10 (11,12) rows.

Finishing

Sew seams; sew in sleeves. Right side facing, starting at right side seam on lower edge with Tangerine and working 3 sc in corners, sc along lower right front edge, sc up right front, making 6 ch-5 loops evenly spaced; sc around neck, down left front, and along lower edge to right side seam. Join; end off. Sew on buttons. Sew pocket along bottom edge of right front.

Instructions are for Misses size small (8-10). Changes for size medium (12-14) and large (16-18) are in parentheses.

Materials

Mexiskeins Lightweight (½ lb. skeins, available from Mexiskeins; see page 4 for address), 2½ (3,3½) skeins derdown (#2), 1 skein Tangerine (#24)

Crochet Hook Size K
Tapestry Needle
6 buttons

Gauge

3 sts to 1"; 2 rows to 1"

Stitch Patterns

This collection of stitch patterns is intended to be an invaluable reference source in your craft library for many years to come. Browse through the sections, choosing just that stitch you see in your mind's eye which will create the perfect skirt, shawl or afghan. Once you have mastered the rudiments of knitting and crochet, you will realize that achieving the effect you want depends on judicious stitch selection.

It is very important that you do some preliminary stitching before actually beginning to work your article. Always knit or crochet a swatch of the pattern you have chosen as a sort of "trial run" before actually starting a project. This will give you an idea of how long it will take to make, how much yarn you will need—and above all, you will know for sure if this particular stitch pattern will produce the desired effect and whether you enjoy working it.

Preliminary stitch preparation is fun. Think of the article you are about to start as a composition, and as you work a stitch pattern, experiment with color and thread variations as if you were a painter with a palette. Let your ideas run free. Once you have achieved the textural and visual effect you want, begin your project.

Selecting from a sea of stitch patterns isn't as overwhelming as you might first think. Knitting and crochet patterns have been divided into categories which will help you narrow stitch selection according to visual effect and practical needs. Before choosing a stitch make sure its characteristics conform to what you plan to make. Each stitch pattern division is preceded by a brief description of what you may expect from it along with helpful design ideas to spark your imagination.

Knitting

Simple to Make
Stitch Patterns

These quick and easy patterns are mostly 2 or 4 row designs. They are practically instant knits. Work them on jumbo knitting needles, and zip along! The faster you memorize them, the faster you can work.

Most of the patterns are knit and purl combinations, so if you're a newcomer to knitting, try these first. Before you know it, you'll be whipping up sweaters, coats, dresses and caps.

1. Multiple of 3 stitches plus 2.
   Note: For Rows 2 and 4 slip the yo.
   Row 1: K 1, * yo, sl 1, k 2 tog, repeat from * across row, end k 1.
   Row 2: K 3, * sl 1, k 2, repeat from * across row, end sl 1, k 1.
   Row 3: K 1, * k 2 tog, yo, sl 1, repeat from * across row, end k 1.
   Row 4: K 2, * sl 1, k 2, repeat from * across row.
   Repeat Rows 1-4 for Pattern Stitch.

2. Multiple of 2 stitches plus 1.
   Row 1: Knit.
   Row 2: Purl.
   Row 3: Knit.
   Row 4: Purl.
   Rows 5, 6, 7: Knit.
   Row 8: K 1, * p 1, k 1, repeat from * across row.
   Row 9: Knit.
   Row 10: Knit.
   Row 11: Knit.
   Row 12: Repeat Row 8.
   Rows 13, 14: Knit.
   Repeat Rows 1-14 for Pattern Stitch.

3. Even number of stitches.
Row 1: Knit.
Row 2: * P 2 tog (hold on needle), k same 2 tog and sl from needle tog,
    repeat from * across row.
Row 3: Knit
Row 4: P 1, repeat from * of Row 2, end p 1.
Repeat Rows 1-4 for Pattern Stitch.

4. Multiple of 2 stitches.
Row 1: Knit.
Row 2: Purl.
Row 3: K 2 tog across row.
Row 4: * K 1, k the horizontal bar before next st, repeat from * across row.
Repeat Rows 1-4 for Pattern Stitch.

5. Any number of stitches.
Row 1: Knit.
Row 2: Purl.
Rows 3, 4: Knit.
Row 5: Purl.
Row 6: Knit.
Repeat Rows 1-6 for Pattern Stitch.

6. Multiple of 7 stitches plus 1.
Row 1: * K 7, yo, k 2 tog, repeat from * across row, end k 6.
Row 2: Knit.
Row 3: K 6, * k 2 tog, yo, k 7, repeat from * across row.
Row 4: Knit.
Repeat Rows 1-4 for Pattern Stitch.

7. Multiple of 3 stitches.
Row 1: Purl.
Row 2: K 2, * k 2 tog, yo, k 1, repeat from * across row, end k 1.
Row 3: Purl.
Row 4: K 2, * yo, k 1, k 2 tog, repeat from * across row, end k 2 tog.
Repeat Rows 1-4 for Pattern Stitch.

8. Even number of stitches.
Rows 1, 3: Knit.
Rows 2, 4: Purl.
Row 5: * K 1, p 1, repeat from * across row.
Row 6: * P 1, k 1, repeat from * across row.
Repeat Rows 1-6 for Pattern Stitch.

9. Multiple of 6 stitches.
Rows 1, 5: * K 1, p 1, k 4, repeat from * across row.
Row 2 and even-numbered rows: K the p's and p the k's.
Row 3: * P 1, k 1, p 1, k 3, repeat from * across row.
Rows 7, 11: * K 4, p 1, k 1, repeat from * across row.
Row 9: * K 3, p 1, k 1, p 1, repeat from * across row.
Row 12: Repeat Row 2.
Repeat Rows 1-12 for Pattern Stitch.

10. Multiple of 2 stitches.
Row 1: Knit.
Row 2: Purl.
Row 3: * K 1, p 1, repeat from * across row.
Row 4: Purl.
Repeat Rows 1-4 for Pattern Stitch.

11. R.P.
Multiple of 2 stitches plus 1.
Row 1: K 1, yo, k 2 tog, repeat from * across row, end k 1.
Rows 2, 3, 4: Purl.
Repeat Rows 1-4 for Pattern Stitch.

12. Multiple of 2 stitches.
Row 1: Knit.
Row 2: K 2 tog across row.
Row 3: K into the front and back of each st across row.
Row 4: Purl.
Repeat Rows 1-4 for Pattern Stitch.

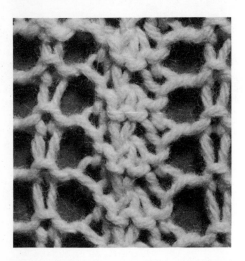

13. Multiple of 6 stitches plus 1.
Row 1: K 1, * yo, k 1, k 3 tog, k 1, yo, k 1, repeat from * across row.
Row 2: Knit.
Repeat Rows 1 and 2 for Pattern Stitch.

14. Odd number of stitches.
Row 1, 2: Knit.
Row 3: K 1, * yo, k 2 tog, repeat from * across row.
Rows 4, 5, 6: Knit.
Repeat Rows 3-6 for Pattern Stitch.

15. Multiple of 4 stitches.
Row 1: * K 2, sl 1, k 1 in row below, repeat from * across row.
Row 2: Knit.
Repeat Rows 1 and 2 for Pattern Stitch.

16. Multiple of 4 stitches.
Row 1: K 1, * sl 2, yif k 2, repeat from * across row, end k 1.
Row 2: K 1, p 2, * sl 2, yib p 2, repeat from * across row, end k 1.
Repeat Rows 1 and 2 for Pattern Stitch.

17. Multiple of 4 stitches.
Row 1: * K 2, p 2, repeat from * across row.
Row 2 and even-numbered rows: K the p's and p the k's.
Row 3: * K 1, p 2, k 1, repeat from * across row.
Row 5: * P 2, k 2, repeat from * across row.
Row 7: * P 1, k 2, p 1, repeat from * across row.
Repeat Rows 1-7 for Pattern Stitch.

18. R.P.
Multiple of 2 stitches.
Row 1: Knit.
Row 2: * K 1, k 1 (in back of st), repeat from * across row, end k 1.
Repeat Row 2 for Pattern Stitch.

19. Multiple of 6 stitches.
Row 1: * K 3, p 3, repeat from * across row.
Row 2 and even-numbered rows: Purl.
Row 3: P 1, * k 3, p 3, repeat from * across row, end k 3, p 2.
Row 5: P 2, * k 3, p 3, repeat from * across row, end k 3, p 1.
Row 7: * P 3, k 3, repeat from * across row.
Row 9: Repeat Row 5.
Row 11: Repeat Row 3.
Row 12: Purl.
Repeat Rows 1-12 for Pattern Stitch.

20. Multiple of 7 stitches plus 1.
Row 1: Purl.
Row 2: * K 2 tog, k 2, inc 1 st (knit the st below next st, k st just above it), k 2, repeat from * across row, end k 3.
Row 3: Purl.
Row 4: K 3, * inc 1, k 2, k 2 tog, k 2, repeat from * across row, end k 2 tog.
Repeat Rows 1-4 for Pattern Stitch.

21. Multiple of 2 stitches.
Row 1: * P 1, sl 1 yib, repeat from * across row.
Rows 2, 4: Purl.
Row 3: * Sl 1 yib, p 1, repeat from * across row.
Repeat Rows 1-4 for Pattern Stitch.

22. Even number of stitches.
Rows 1, 2, 3: Purl.
Row 4: * Yo, sl 1, k 1, psso, repeat from * across row, end psso.
Repeat Rows 1-4 for Pattern Stitch.

23. Even number of stitches.
Row 1: * Sl 1, k 1, yo, psso (k st over), repeat from * across row, end psso.
Row 2: Purl.
Repeat Rows 1 and 2 for Pattern Stitch.

24. Multiple of 3 stitches.
Rows 1, 3: * K 2, p 1, repeat from * across row.
Row 2: * K 1, p 2, repeat from * across row.
Row 4: Knit.
Repeat Rows 1-4 for Pattern Stitch.

25. Even number of stitches.
Row 1: K 1 under first lp of k st, * k same st, k 1 under next bar, repeat from * across row.
Row 2: P 2 tog across row.
Row 3: Knit.
Row 4: Knit.
Repeat Rows 1-4 for Pattern Stitch.

26. Multiple of 6 stitches plus 3.
Row 1: * K 3, p 1, k 1, p 1, repeat from * across row, end k 3.
Row 2: P 4, * k 1, p 5, repeat from * across row, end p 4.
Repeat Rows 1 and 2 for Pattern Stitch.

27. Odd number of stitches.
Row 1: * K 1, yo needle 2 times, repeat from * across row, end k 1.
Row 2: * K 1, drop yo's from needle and repeat from * across row, end k 1.
Row 3: Knit.
Row 4: Knit.
Repeat Rows 1-4 for Pattern Stitch.

28. Multiple of 2 stitches.
Row 1: * K 1, yif sl 1, yib, repeat from * across row, end sl 1.
Row 2: Purl.
Repeat Rows 1 and 2 for Pattern Stitch.

29. Multiple of 2 stitches.
Row 1: * K 1, sl 1, repeat from * across row, end sl 1.
Repeat Row 1 for Pattern Stitch.

30. Even number of stitches.
Row 1: * K 2, p 2, repeat from * across row, end k 2.
Row 2: * P 2, k 2, repeat from * across row, end p 2.
Row 3: * P 2, k 2, repeat from * across row, end p 2.
Row 4: * K 2, p 2, repeat from * across row, end k 2.
Repeat Rows 1-4 for Pattern Stitch.

31. Odd number of stitches.
Row 1: * K 1, p 1, repeat from * across row, end p 1.
Row 2: * P 1, k 1, repeat from * across row, end k 1.
Repeat Rows 1 and 2 for Pattern Stitch.

32. Even number of stitches.
Row 1: * K 1, sl 1, repeat from * across row.
Rows 2, 4: Purl.
Row 3: * Sl 1, k 1, repeat from * across row.
Repeat Rows 1-4 for Pattern Stitch.

33. Even number of stitches.
Row 1: Knit.
Row 2: K 2 tog across row.
Row 3: K first st, * k into bottom 2 loops of same st, k 1, repeat from *
    across row, end k in bottom 2 lps of last st.
Row 4: Knit.
Row 5: Purl.
Repeat Rows 2-5 for Pattern Stitch.

34. Even number of stitches.
Row 1: Knit.
Row 2: * K 1, k 1 under loop of next st, repeat from * across row.
Repeat Rows 1 and 2 for Pattern Stitch.

35. Even number of stitches.
Row 1: * Yo, k 2, psso (1 k st over), repeat from * across row.
Row 2: Purl.
Repeat Rows 1 and 2 for Pattern Stitch.

36. Even number of stitches.
Rows 1, 2: Knit.
Row 3: * Yo, k 2 tog, repeat from * across row.
Row 4: * Yo, p 2 tog, repeat from * across row.
Repeat Rows 1-4 for Pattern Stitch.

37. Multiple of 4 stitches plus 2.
Row 1: K 2, * p 2, k 2, repeat from * across row.
Row 2: Purl.
Row 3: P 2, * k 2, p 2, repeat from * across row.
Row 4: Purl.
Repeat Rows 1-4 for Pattern Stitch.

38. Multiple of 10 stitches.
Row 1: * K 3, p 7, repeat from * across row, end k 3.
Row 2: * P 3, k 7, repeat from * across row.
Row 3: Repeat Row 1.
Row 4: Purl.
Row 5: P 5, * k 3, p 7, repeat from * across row, end p 5.
Row 6: K 5, * p 3, k 7, repeat from * across row, end k 5.
Row 7: Repeat Row 5.
Row 8: Purl.
Repeat Rows 1-8 for Pattern Stitch.

39. R.P.
Odd number of stitches.
Row 1: * K 1, yo, sl 1, repeat from * across row, end k 1.
Row 2: K across row, * knit yo and sl 1 tog, repeat from * across row, end k 1.
When binding off—knit yo and sl 1 tog.
Repeat Rows 1 and 2 for Pattern Stitch.

40. Multiple of 7 stitches.
Row 1: * P 1, p 2 tog, yo, k 1, yo, p 2 tog, p 1, repeat from * across row.
Rows 2, 4: Purl.
Row 3: Knit.
Repeat Rows 1-4 for Pattern Stitch.

41. Any number of stitches.
Row 1: Knit.
Repeat Row 1 for Pattern Stitch.

42. Any number of stitches.
Row 1: Knit.
Row 2: Purl.
Repeat Rows 1 and 2 for Pattern Stitch.

43. Any number of stitches.
Row 1: Knit in the back of each stitch.
Row 2: Purl.
Repeat Rows 1 and 2 for Pattern Stitch.

44. Multiple of 5 stitches plus 2.
Row 1: * K 2, p 3, repeat from * across row, end k 2.
Row 2: * P 2, k 3, repeat from * across row, end p 2.
Row 3: Repeat Row 1.
Row 4: * P 2, yo, sl 1, k 2 tog, psso, yo, repeat from * across row, end yo, p 2.
Repeat Rows 1-4 for Pattern Stitch.

45. Any number of stitches.
Row 1: Purl.
Row 2: K 1, * k under bar before next st, k 1, psso, repeat from * across row.
Repeat Rows 1 and 2 for Pattern Stitch.

46. Multiple of 4 stitches.
Row 1: Yo, sl 1, k 2 tog, psso, * yo, k 1, yo, sl 1, k 2 tog, repeat from * across row, end yo, k 1, yo.
Row 2: Purl.
Row 3: Yo, k 2 tog, * yo, sl 1, k 2 tog, psso, yo, k 1, repeat from * across row.
Row 4: Purl.
Repeat Rows 1-4 for Pattern Stitch.

47. Multiple of 6 stitches plus 3.
Row 1: K 3, * p 3, k 3, repeat from * across row.
Repeat Row 1 for Pattern Stitch.

48. Multiple of 8 stitches plus 2.
Row 1: * K 2, p 8, repeat from * across row.
Row 2: Knit.
Repeat Rows 1 and 2 for Pattern Stitch.

49. Multiple of 10 stitches.
Row 1: * P 3, k 1, p 3, k 3, repeat from * across row.
Row 2: * P 3, k 3, p 1, k 3, repeat from * across row.
Row 3: Repeat Row 1.
Row 4: Knit.
Repeat Rows 1-4 for Pattern Stitch.

50. Multiple of 2 stitches.
Row 1: Knit.
Row 2: Knit.
Row 3: * K 1, p 1, repeat from * across row, end p 1.
Row 4: * K 1, p 1, repeat from * across row, end p 1.
Repeat Rows 1-4 for Pattern Stitch.

51. R.P.
Multiple of 2 stitches plus 1.
Row 1: * K 1, yif sl 1, yib repeat from * across row, end k 1.
Row 2: Purl.
Row 3: * Yif sl 1, yib k 1, repeat from * across row, end sl 1.
Row 4: Purl.
Repeat Rows 1-4 for Pattern Stitch.

52. Multiple of 3 stitches plus 1.
Row 1: * K 1, sl 1, k in front loop of next st, psso, repeat from *, end k.
Row 2: Purl.
Repeat Rows 1 and 2 for Pattern Stitch.

53. Multiple of 4 stitches plus 1.
Rows 1, 3, 5, 7: Purl.
Row 2: K 1, * sl 3, k 1, repeat from *
Row 4: K 2, * insert needle under strand into next st and k as 1 st, k 3, repeat from *, end k 2.
Row 6: K 3, * sl 3, k 1, repeat from *, end k 3.
Row 8: K 4, repeat from * of row 4, end k 4.
Repeat Rows 1-8 for Pattern Stitch.

54. Multiple of 4 stitches plus 3.
Row 1: K 1, * sl 1, k 3, repeat from *, end sl 1, k 1.
Row 2: P 1, * sl 1, p 3, repeat from *, end sl 1, p 1.
Row 3: Repeat Row 1.
Row 4: Knit.
Repeat Rows 1-4 for Pattern Stitch.

55. Multiple of 4 stitches plus 3.
Row 1: * K 3, p 1, repeat from * across, end k 3.
Row 2: Purl.
Row 3: Knit.
Row 4: Purl.
Repeat Rows 1-4 for Pattern Stitch.

56. Multiple of 2 stitches.
Row 1: Knit.
Row 2: * K 1, k 1 in back of st, repeat from *, end k 1 in back of st. Repeat
Row 2 for Pattern stitch.

Color
Stitch Patterns

These patterns provide an endless amount of fun and experimentation, and are an excellent way to develop color sense too. Choose two contrasting colors (or more if you wish) to create arresting visual effects. Try straight-up or off-beat stripings and checkerboards. Advanced colorists paint pictures on sweaters with needles and yarns.

Interesting tweed effects may be created by combining several yarn colors into stitches.

Work in color groupings of related soft pastels, bold scarlets or bright blues. Treat color as icing on a cake—use it for borders and trimmings. Make an afghan using all the colors of the rainbow.

Patterns 67 and 70 can be used to knit giant patch pockets on a coat or jacket.

57. Multiple of 4 stitches.
Row 1: With Color B, * k 3, p 1, repeat from * across row.
Row 2 and even-numbered rows: With B-Purl.
Rows 3, 7: With B-Knit.
Row 5: With A-K 1, * p 1, k 3, repeat from * across row, end p 1, k 2.
Row 6: With A-Purl.
Repeat Rows 1-6 for Pattern Stitch.

58. Multiple of 4 stitches plus 3.
Cast on with White and knit a row.
Row 1: K 2 White, * k 2 Green, k 2 White, repeat from * across row, end k 1 Green.
Row 2: P 2 Green, * p 2 White, p 2 Green, repeat from * across row, end p 1 White.
Row 3: K 2 Green, * k 2 White, k 2 Green, repeat from * across row, end k 1 White.
Row 4: P 2 White, p 2 Green, p 2 White, repeat from * across row, end p 1 Green.
Repeat Rows 1-4 for Pattern Stitch.

59. Multiple of 16 stitches plus 1.
Rows 1, 2: Color A-Knit.
Row 3: Color B-K 1, * yo, k 6, sl 2, k 1, psso (2 over), k 6, yo, k 1, repeat from * across row.
Row 4: Color B-Purl.
Row 5: Color B-Repeat Row 3.
Row 6: Color B-Purl.
Rows 7, 8: Color A-Knit.
Repeat Rows 1-8 for Pattern Stitch.

60. Odd number of stitches.
Row 1: With Main Color, Knit.
Row 2: Purl.
Row 3: Knit.
Row 4: Purl.
Row 5: With 2nd color, K 1, k 2 tog across row.
Row 6: * K 1, k horizontal bar before next st, repeat from * across row.
Row 7: Knit.
Row 8: Purl.
Row 9: K 1, k 2 tog across row.
Row 10: Repeat Row 6.
Repeat Rows 1-10 for Pattern Stitch.

61. Use Color Pattern 60 for background. Thread tapestry needle with contrasting color for surface design. Follow diagram for design. Circles indicate eyelets in knitted background. Dotted lines indicate yarn on wrong side only.

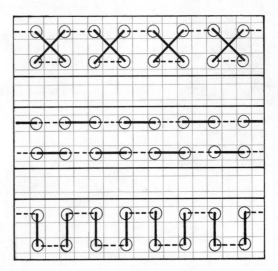

62. Multiple of 4 stitches plus 3.
Use Colors A, B, C.
Row 1: C-* K 3, sl 1, repeat from * across row, end k 3.
Row 2: C-Purl.
Row 3: A-K 1,* sl 1, k 3, repeat from * across row, end sl 1, k 1.
Row 4: A-Purl.
Rows 5, 6: B-Repeat Rows 1 and 2.
Rows 7, 8: A-Repeat Rows 3 and 4.
Repeat Rows 1-8 for Pattern Stitch.

63. Multiple of 3 stitches plus 2.
Row 1: K 1, * yo, sl 1, k 2 tog, repeat from * across row, end k 1.
Repeat Row 1 for Pattern Stitch.
Weaving: Thread tapestry needle with double strand of yarn several feet
long (use a contrasting color). Work from right to left: Weave
over and under the stitches in first ridge, * go under and over the
stitches in next ridge, repeat from * until the piece is finished. Sew
all loose ends on wrong side.

64. Even number of stitches.
Row 1: K 1, * yo, k 2 tog, repeat from * across row, end k 1.
Row 2: Purl.
Repeat Rows 1 and 2 for Pattern Stitch.
Weaving: Use triple strand of yarn. Work over and then under each ridge
of each row. Weave each row twice. Alternating colors: * with A-4
rows, with B-6 rows, repeat from * until piece is finished. Sew all
loose ends on wrong side.

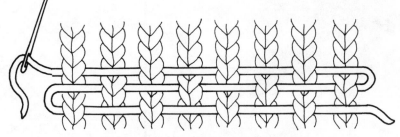

Stitch has been exaggerated to show weaving technique.

For Pattern Number 63, vertical weave, turn diagram once to the
left. Proceed in the same manner.

65. Multiple of 4 stitches plus 2.
Rows 1, 3: With Color A-Knit.
Rows 2, 4: With A-Purl.
Row 5: With B-K3, * sl 2 yif, k 2, repeat from * across row, end sl 2, k 1.
Row 6: With B-K 1, * sl 2 yif, k 2, repeat from * across row, end sl 2, k 3.
Rows 7, 8, 9, 10: With A-Repeat Rows 1, 2, 3, 4.
Row 11: With B-Repeat Row 6.
Row 12: With B-Repeat Row 5.
Repeat Rows 1-12 for Pattern Stitch.

66. R.P.
Multiple of 2 stitches plus 1.
Row 1: Color A-Knit.
Row 2: Color A-Purl.
Row 3: Color B-K 1, * yif, sl 1, k 1, repeat from * across row.
Row 4: Repeat Row 3.
Repeat Rows 1-4 for Pattern Stitch.

67. Star Motif: Entire pattern is made in stockinette stitch. Star is worked with a contrasting color. Work each X as one stitch, and each block as one stitch.

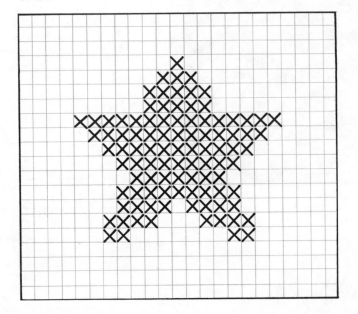

68. Stripe pattern is all stockinette stitch (knit one row, purl one row). Alternate colors as follows:
6 Rows with Color A.
2 Rows with Color B.

69. R.P.
Multiple of 2 stitches plus 1.
Rows 1, 3: Color A-Knit.
Rows 2, 4: Color A-Purl.
Row 5: Color B, * K 2, sl 1, repeat from * across row, end k 2.
Row 6: * K 2, sl 1 yib, repeat from * across row, end k 2.
Repeat Rows 1-6 for Pattern Stitch.

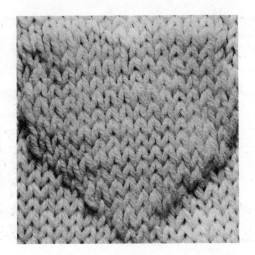

70. Heart Motif: Use 2 colors. See Chart: Work in stockinette stitch. Each block counts as one stitch.

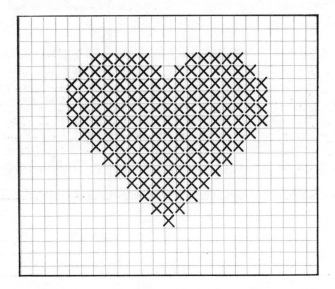

71. Multiple of 6 stitches plus 5.
Row 1: With Color A-Knit.
Row 2: With B, * K 5, sl 1, repeat from * across row, end k 5.
Row 3: B, * K 5, yif sl 1, repeat from * across row, end k 5.
Row 4: A, * K 2, sl 1, repeat from * across row, end k 2.
Row 5: A, * K 2, yif sl 1, repeat from * across row, end k 2.
Row 6: A-K 2, * sl 1, k 2, repeat from * across row, end k 2.
Repeat Rows 1-6 for Pattern Stitch.

72. Multiple of 2 stitches plus 2.
Purl one row.
Row 1: K 1, * p 1, k 1, repeat from * across row.
Row 2: Purl.
Row 3: P 1, * k 1, p 1, repeat from * across row.
Row 4: Purl.
Repeat Rows 1-4 for Pattern Stitch.
Weaving: Use double strand of yarn (use a contrasting color). Begin at upper right-hand corner and working on a diagonal draw yarn through each purl st of each row (diagonal). Work evenly.

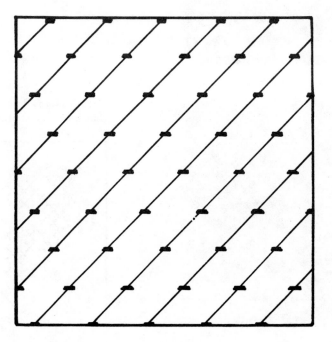

73. Even number of stitches.
With Color A, Purl a row.
Row 1: With Color B-K 1, * sl 1, k 1 in back of next st, repeat from * across row, end k 1.
Row 2: With B-Purl.
Row 3: A-K 1, * k 1 in back of next st, sl 1, repeat from * across row, end sl 1.
Row 4: A-Purl.
Repeat Rows 1-4 for Pattern Stitch.

74. Odd number of stitches.
Row 1: With Color A, * K 1, sl 1, repeat from * across row, end k 1.
Row 2: A-Purl.
Row 3: With B-K 2, * sl 1, k 1, repeat from * across row, end k 1.
Row 4: B-Purl.
Row 5: A-Repeat Row 1.
Row 6: A-Purl.
Row 7: With B-Knit.
Row 8: B-Purl.
Repeat Rows 1-8 for Pattern Stitch.

75. Multiple of 4 stitches plus 3.
Row 1: With Color B-K 1, * sl 1, k 3, repeat from * across row, end sl 1, k 1.
Row 2: With B-Purl.
Row 3: With A-K 1, * sl 1, k 3, repeat from * across row, end sl 1, k 1.
Row 4: With A-P 1, * yif sl 1, p 3, repeat from * across row, end p 1.
Row 5: B-K 3, * sl 1, k 3, repeat from * across row.
Row 6: B-Purl.
Row 7: A-K 3, * sl 1, k 3, repeat from * across row.
Row 8: A-P 3, * yif sl 1, p 3, repeat from * across row.
Repeat Rows 1-8 for Pattern Stitch.

76. Multiple of 6 stitches.
With Color A, knit a row, purl a row.
Row 1: With A-K 3, B-k 3, * A-k 3, B-k 3, repeat from * across row.
Row 2: Purl across row, matching colors.
Row 3: * B-K 3, A-k 3, repeat from * across row.
Row 4: Purl across row, matching colors.
Rows 5, 6: With A, knit a row, purl a row.
Row 7: A-K 6, * C-k 2, A-k 6, repeat from * across row, end A-k 3.
Rows 8, 10: Purl across row, matching colors.
Row 9: C-K 2, * A-k 2, C-k 2, repeat from * across row, end A-k 1.
Row 11: A-K 2, C-k 2, * A-k 6, C-k 2, repeat from * across row, end A-k 2.
Row 12: Purl across row, matching colors.
Row 13: With A-Knit.
Row 14: With A-Purl.
Repeat Rows 1-14 for Pattern Stitch.

77. R.P.
Multiple of 4 stitches plus 2.
With Color A, purl one row.
Row 1: With B-K 1, * sl 2 yif, k 2, repeat from * across row, end sl 2, k 3.
Row 2: With B-K 1, * p 2, sl 2 yif, repeat from * across row, end k 1.
Row 3: With A-K 3, * sl 2 yif, k 2, repeat from * across row, end sl 2 yif, k 1.
Row 4: With A-K 1, * sl 2 yif, p 2, repeat from * across row, end k 1.
Repeat Rows 1-4 for Pattern Stitch.

78. R.P. Reversible Pattern.
Multiple of 2 stitches plus 1.
Row 1: With Color B-K 1, * yib, sl 1, k 1, repeat from * across row.
Rows 2,4,6: With B-Purl.
Rows 3, 5: B-Knit.
Row 7: A-Sl 1, * k 1, sl 1, repeat from * across row.
Row 8: With A-Purl.
Row 9: With Color C-Repeat Row 1.
Row 10: C-Purl.
Row 11: C-Knit.
Row 12: C-Purl.
Row 13: With A-Repeat Row 7.
Row 14: With A-Repeat Row 8.
Repeat Rows 1-14 for Pattern Stitch.

79. Any number of stitches. Entire stripe pattern is worked in stockinette stitch (knit one row, purl one row).
* 4 rows with Color A, 4 rows with Color B, repeat from * for color pattern. Carry yarn on side edge; do not break off yarn.

80. Multiple of 12 stitches plus 5.
Rows 1-5: With Color B-Knit.
Row 6: With A-Purl.
Row 7: With A-K 3, * yo, k 4, sl 1, k 2 tog, psso, k 4, yo, k 1, repeat from * across row, end k 3.
Row 8: With A-K 2, purl across row, end k 2.
Repeat Rows 7 and 8 alternately for 4 rows, then repeat Row 7 once more.
Row 14: With B, Purl.
Repeat Rows 1-14 for Pattern Stitch.

81. Multiple of 4 stitches plus 3.
With Color A, purl a row.
Row 1: With B, * K 1, p 1, k 1, sl 1, repeat from * across row, end k 1, p 1, k 1.
Row 2: B, * K 1, p 1, k 1, yif sl 1, repeat from * across row, end k 1, p 1, k 1.
Row 3: A-K 1, p 1, * k 3, p 1, repeat from * across row, end k 1.
Row 4: A, * K 1, p 1, repeat from * across row, end k 1.
Row 5: A, * K 1, p 1, k 1, sl 1, repeat from * across row, end k 1, p 1.
Row 6: A, * K 1, p 1, repeat from * across row, end k 1.
Repeat Rows 1-6 for Pattern Stitch.

82. Multiple of 3 stitches plus 2.
Row 1: With Color A-K 2, * sl 1, k 2, repeat from * across row.
Row 2: A-K 2, * yif sl 1, k 2, repeat from * across row.
Row 3: A-K 1, * sl 1, k 2, repeat from * across row, end k 3.
Row 4: A-K 3, * yif sl 1, k 2, repeat from * across row, end sl 1, k 1.
Row 5: With B, Yib sl 1, * k 2, sl 1, repeat from * across row, end k 1.
Row 6: B-K 1, * yif sl 1, k 2, repeat from * across row, end sl 1.
Repeat Rows 1-6 for Pattern Stitch.

83. R.P.
Odd number of stitches.
Row 1: With Color A-Knit.
Row 2: A-Knit.
Row 3: With B-K 1, * sl 1, k 1, repeat from * across row.
Row 4: B-K 1, * yif sl 1, k 1, repeat from * across row.
Repeat Rows 1-4 for Pattern Stitch.

84. R.P.
Multiple of 12 stitches plus 3.
With Color A-Knit 1 row.
Row 1: With B-K 1, sl 1, k 1, psso, * k 9, sl 2, k 1, pass 2 over, repeat from * across row, end k 9, k 2 tog, k 1.
Row 2: With B-K 1, * p 1, k 4, (k 1, yo, k 1) in next st, k 4, repeat from * across row, end p 1, k 1.
Rows 3, 4: With A-Repeat Rows 1 and 2.
Repeat Rows 1-4 for Pattern Stitch.

85. Multiple of 4 stitches plus 4.
Rows 1, 3: * Color A-K 4, Color B-k 4, repeat from * across row, end A-k 4.
Rows 2, 4: * Color A-P 4, B-p 4, repeat from * across row, end A-p 4.
Rows 5, 7: * Color B-K 4, C-k 4, repeat from * across row, end B-k 4.
Rows 6, 8: * B-P 4, C-p 4, repeat from * across row, end B-p 4.
Repeat Rows 1-8 for Pattern Stitch.

86. Multiple of 6 stitches plus 3.
Rows 1, 3: Color A-K 3, * Color B-k 1, A-k 5, repeat from * across row.
Row 2: B-P 1, * A-p 3, B-p 3, repeat from * across row, end B-p 1.
Rows 4, 6: A-P 2, * B-p 1, A-p 5, repeat from * across row, end B-p 1.
Row 5: B-K 2, * A-k 3, B-k 3, repeat from * across row, end A-k 1.
Repeat Rows 1-5 for Pattern Stitch.

87. Motif: Use a contrasting color for motif. Background and design are worked at the same time. See Chart: Work in stockinette stitch throughout. Work each x as one stitch and each block as one stitch.

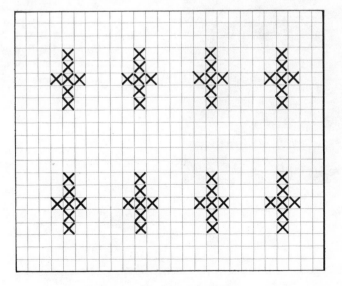

88. Multiple of 4 stitches.
Row 1: Color A-K 1, * Color B-k 1, A-k 3, repeat from * across row, end B-k 1, A-k 2.
Row 2: * B-P 3, A-p 1, repeat from * across row.
Row 3: * B-K 3, A-k 1, repeat from * across row.
Row 4: A-P 1, * B-p 1, A-p 3, repeat from * across row, end B-p 1, A-p 2.
Repeat Rows 1-4 for Pattern Stitch.

89. R.P.
Any number of stitches.
Row 1: With Color A-Purl.
Row 2: With Color A-Knit.
Row 3: With Color B-Purl.
Row 4: With Color B-Knit.
Repeat Rows 1-4 for Pattern Stitch.

90. Multiple of 4 stitches plus 4.
Row 1: With Color A-Knit one row.
Row 2: * A-K 4, B-k 4, repeat from * across row, end A-k 4.
Row 3: * A-P 4, B-p 4, repeat from * across row, end A-p 4.
Rows 4, 5: Repeat Rows 2 and 3 once more.
Row 6: * B-K 4, A-k 4, repeat from * across row, end B-k 4.
Row 7: * B-P 4, A-p 4, repeat from * across row, end B-p 4.
Rows 8, 9: Repeat Rows 6 and 7 once more.
Repeat Rows 2-9 for Pattern Stitch.

91. Multiple of 4 stitches plus 3.
Row 1: With Color B-Knit one row.
Row 2: A, * K 3, sl 1, repeat from * across row.
Row 3: A, * K 3, sl 1 yif, repeat from * across row.
Row 4: B-K 1, * sl 1, k 3, repeat from * across row, end sl 1, k 1.
Row 5: B-K 1, * sl 1 yif, k 3, repeat from * across row, end sl 1, k 1.
Repeat Rows 2-5 for Pattern Stitch.

92. R.P.
Multiple of 4 stitches plus 3.
Cast on with Color A and purl a row.
Rows 1, 3: B-K 3, * sl 1, k 3, repeat from * across row.
Rows 2, 4: B-K 3, * sl 1 yif, k 3, repeat from * across row.
Row 5: With A-Knit.
Row 6: With A-Purl.
Repeat Rows 1-6 for Pattern Stitch.

93. R.P.
Odd number of stitches.
Row 1: With Color A-Knit.
Row 2: A-K 1, * k st in row below, k 1, repeat from * across row.
Row 3: With B-Knit.
Row 4: B-K 2, * k st in row below, k 1, repeat from * across row, end k 1.
Repeat Rows 1-4 for Pattern Stitch.

94. Multiple of 3 stitches plus 1.
Cast on with Color A and knit a row.
Row 1: B-K 3, * sl 1, k 2, repeat from * across row, end k 3.
Row 2: B-K 3, * yif sl 1, k 2, repeat from * across row, end k 3.
Row 3: C, * K 2, sl 1, repeat from * across row, end k 1.
Row 4: C-K 1, * yif sl 1, k 2, repeat from * across row.
Row 5: A-K 1, * sl 1, k 2, repeat from * across row.
Row 6: A, * K 2, yif sl 1, repeat from * across row, end k 1.
Repeat Rows 1-6 for Pattern Stitch.

95. Multiple 6 stitches.
Row 1: Color A, * K 1, yo, k 2 tog, Color B-k 1, yo, k 2 tog, repeat from * across row, end A-k 1, yo, k 2 tog.
Row 2: With A-Purl.
Row 3: With B, * K 1, yo, k 2 tog, repeat from * across row.
Row 4: With A-Purl.
Row 5: With A, * k 1, yo, k 2 tog, repeat from * across row.
Row 6: With B-Purl.
Repeat Rows 3-6 for Pattern Stitch.

96. R.P.
Multiple of 2 stitches plus 1.
Row 1: With A-Knit.
Row 2: With A-Purl.
Row 3: B-K 1, * sl 1, k 1, repeat from * across row.
Row 4: B, * K 1, yif sl 1, yib k 1, repeat from * across row.
Repeat Rows 1-4 for Pattern Stitch.

97. R.P.
Multiple of 2 stitches.
Row 1: A, * yif sl 1, yib k 1, repeat from * across row.
Row 2: A, * yif sl 1, yib p 1, repeat from * across row.
Row 3: B-Repeat Row 1.
Row 4: B-Repeat Row 2.
Repeat Rows 1-4 for Pattern Stitch.

98. Multiple of 3 stitches.
Row 1: With Color A-Purl.
Row 2: A-K 2, * yo, k 3, pass first st of the 3 k sts over the 2nd and 3rd sts, repeat from * across row, end k 1.
Row 3: With B-Purl.
Row 4: B-K 1, * k 3, pass first st of the 3 k sts over the 2nd and 3rd sts, yo, repeat from * across row, end k 2.
Repeat Rows 1-4 for Pattern Stitch.

99. Multiple of 2 stitches plus 2.
Row 1: * K 1, k 1 in next st in row below, repeat from * across row, end k 2.
Row 2: Knit.
Row 3: K 2, * k 1 in next st in row below, k 1, repeat from * across row.
Row 4: Knit.
Repeat Rows 1-4 for Pattern Stitch. For color sequence: Work 4 rows with Color A, 2 rows with Color B, and 6 rows with Color C. Repeat these 12 rows for color pattern.

100. Multiple of 2 stitches plus 1.
Row 1: Color A-Knit.
Row 2: Color A-Purl.
Row 3: Color B-Knit.
Row 4: Color C-P 1, * sl 1, p 1, repeat from * across row.
Row 5: C-K 1, * sl 1, k 1, repeat from * across row.
Row 6: B-Purl.
Repeat Rows 1-6 for Pattern Stitch.

101. R.P.
Multiple of 4 stitches plus 3.
Cast on with Color D.
Row 1: A-K 1, * sl 1, k 3, repeat from * across row, end sl 1, k 1.
Row 2: A-P 1, * yif sl 1, p 3, repeat from * across row, end sl 1, p 1.
Row 3: B, * K 3, sl 1, repeat from * across row, end k 3.
Row 4: B, * P 3, yif sl 1, repeat from * across row, end p 3.
Rows 5, 6: With C-Repeat Rows 1 and 2.
Rows 7, 8: With D-Repeat Rows 3 and 4.
Repeat Rows 1-8 for Pattern Stitch.

102. Odd number of stitches.
Row 1: With A-K 1, * sl 1, k 1, repeat from * across row.
Row 2: A-Purl.
Row 3: B-Sl 1, * k 1, sl 1, repeat from * across row, end sl 1.
Row 4: B-Purl.
Repeat Rows 1-4 for Pattern Stitch.

103. Multiple of 4 stitches plus 3.
Row 1: A-P 1, * k 1, p 1, repeat from * across row.
Row 2: With A, Repeat Row 1.
Row 3: B-P 1, k 1, p 1, * sl 1 yib, p 1, k 1, p 1, repeat from * across row.
Row 4: B-P 1, k 1, p 1, * sl 1 yif, p 1, k 1, p 1, repeat from * across row.
Repeat Rows 1-4 for Pattern Stitch.

104. R.P.
Multiple of 4 stitches plus 1.
Row 1: With Color A-Purl.
Row 2: B-K 1, * yif sl 1, k 3, repeat from * across row, end yif sl 1, k 1.
Row 3: B-K 1, yib sl 1, * p 3, sl 1, repeat from * across row, end k 1.
Row 4: A-K 1, * k 2, yif sl 1, k 1, repeat from * across row, end k 2.
Repeat Rows 2-5 for Pattern Stitch.

105. Multiple of 4 stitches plus 2.
Row 1: With A-Knit.
Row 2: With A-Purl.
Row 3: B-K 2, * sl 2, k 2, repeat from * across row.
Row 4: B-K 2, * sl 2, k 2, repeat from * across row.
Rows 5, 6: With A-k 1 row, with B-purl 1 row.
Row 7: B-Sl 2, * k 2, sl 2, repeat from * across row.
Row 8: B-Sl 2, * k 2, sl 2, repeat from * across row.
Repeat Rows 1-8 for Pattern Stitch.

106. Multiple of 2 stitches.
Row 1: A, * Sl 1, k 1, repeat from * across row.
Row 2: With A-Purl.
Row 3: B, * K 1, sl 1, repeat from * across row.
Row 4: With B-Purl.
Repeat Rows 1-4 for Pattern Stitch.

107. Multiple of 4 stitches plus 2.
Row 1: Knit.
Row 2: * P 3 tog-hold on needle, yo, p the same 3 sts tog, slip off left needle, k 1, repeat from * across row, end k 1, p 1.
Row 3: Knit.
Row 4: P 1, * k 1, p 3 tog-hold on needle, p the same 3 sts tog, slip off left needle, repeat from * across row.
Repeat Rows 1-4 for Pattern Stitch. Alternate colors every 2 rows.

108. Multiple of 8 stitches plus 3.
Note: On right side of work sl sts are slipped with yib; on wrong side of work sl sts are slipped with yif.
Rows 1, 2: With A-Knit.
Row 3: B-K 3, * (sl 1, k 1) twice, sl 1, k 3, repeat from * across row.
Row 4: B-P 3, * (sl 1, k 1) twice, sl 1, p 3, repeat from * across row.
Rows 5, 6: A-K 1, sl 2, * k 5, sl 3, repeat from * across row, end sl 2, k 1.
Rows 7, 8: With B-Repeat Rows 3 and 4.
Rows 9, 10: With A-Knit.
Row 11: B, (K 1, sl 1) twice, * k 3, (sl 1, k 1) twice, sl 1, repeat from * across row, end (sl 1, k 1) twice.
Row 12: B, (K 1, sl 1) twice, * p 3, (sl 1, k 1) twice, sl 1, repeat from * across row, end (sl 1, k 1) twice.
Rows 13, 14: A-K 4, * sl 3, k 5, repeat from * across row, end k 4.
Rows 15, 16: With B-Repeat Rows 11 and 12.
Repeat Rows 1-16 for Pattern Stitch.

109. Multiple of 4 stitches.
Row 1: B-K 1, * sl 2 yib, k 2, repeat from * across row, end sl 2, k 1.
Row 2: B-K 1, * sl 1 yib, sl 1 yif, p 2, repeat from * across row, end sl 1 yib, sl 1 yif, k 1.
Row 3: A-K 3, * sl 2 yib, k 2, repeat from * across row, end sl 2, k 3.
Row 4: A-K 1, * p 2, sl 1 yib, sl 1 yif, repeat from * across row, end p 2, k 1.
Repeat Rows 1-4 for Pattern Stitch.

110. R.P.
Even number of stitches.
With Color A-Knit one row.
Row 1: A-K 1, * p 1, k 1 in row below, repeat from * across row, end k 1.
Row 2: With A-Knit.
Row 3: B-K 1, * k 1 in row below, p 1, repeat from * across row, end k 1.
Row 4: With B-Knit.
Repeat Rows 1-4 for Pattern Stitch.

111. R.P.
Even number of stitches.
Row 1: B, * K 1, sl 1 yib, repeat from * across row, end sl 1.
Row 2: B, * K 1, sl 1 yif, repeat from * across row, end sl 1.
Rows 3, 4: With A-Repeat Rows 1 and 2.
Repeat Rows 1-4 for Pattern Stitch.

112. Multiple of 4 stitches plus 2.

Row 1: With Color A-Purl.

Row 2: B-K 1, sl 1 yib, * k 2, sl 2 yib, repeat from * across row, end k 2, sl 1, k 1.

Row 3: B-P 1, sl 1 yif, * p 2, sl 2 yif, repeat from * across row, end p 2, sl 1, p 1.

Row 4: With A-Knit.

Row 5: A-P 2, * sl 2 yif, p 2, repeat from * across row.

Row 6: A-K 2, * sl 2 yib, k 2, repeat from * across row.

Repeat Rows 1-6 for Pattern Stitch.

Cable and Twist
Stitch Patterns

Cable and Twist Patterns are terrific for big bulky sweaters—make one for your next ski trip. Work miniature cables on a carriage cover to keep baby warm in winter. A single band of cables down the center of a dress or sweater is an elegant effect. Side-routed twists or cables twining around sleeves add impact and drama to simple designs.

Cables are good combination makers. Mix a Cable and Twist Pattern with lacy openwork. Or incorporate a couple of different cables in one sweater, each a contrasting color. Fun and uncomplicated. Just be sure to keep a pencil handy to mark off completed pattern rows to avoid a muddle.

And since Cable and Twist Patterns tend to pull in or squeeze up a bit, it's often wise to add an extra inch to your measurements.

113. Multiple of 6 stitches plus 2.
Row 1: Knit (loosely).
Row 2: K 1, * (sk 3 sts, purl the 4th st off needle and pull over the 3 skipped sts), purl the 3 skipped sts, repeat from * across row, end k 1.
Repeat Rows 1 and 2 for Pattern Stitch.

114. Multiple of 13 stitches.
Row 1: P 2, * k 9, p 2, repeat from * across row.
Row 2: K 2, * p 9, k 2, repeat from * across row.
Row 3: * P 2, sl 3 sts to dpn in front, k 3, k 3 from dpn, k 3, repeat from * across row, end k 3, p 2.
Rows 4, 6: Repeat Row 2.
Row 5: Repeat Row 1.
Row 7: * P 2, k 3, sl 3 sts to dpn in back, k 3, k 3 sts from dpn, repeat from * across row, end p 2.
Row 8: Repeat Row 2.
Repeat Rows 1-8 for Pattern Stitch.

115. Multiple of 3 stitches plus 2.
Row 1: P 2, * yo, k 1, yo, p 2, repeat from * across row.
Row 2: K 2, * p 3, k 2, repeat from * across row.
Row 3: P 2, * k 3, p 2, repeat from * across row.
Row 4: K 2, * p 3 tog, k 2, repeat from * across row.
Repeat Rows 1-4 for Pattern Stitch.

116. Multiple of 10 stitches plus 6.
Row 1: * P 2, yo, sl 1, k 1, psso, p 2, k 4, repeat from * across row, end p 2, yo, sl 1, k 1, psso, p 2.
Row 2: * K 2, p 2, k 2, p 4, repeat from * across row, end k 2, p 2, k 2.
Row 3: * P 2, k 2 tog, yo, p 2, sl next 2 sts to dpn, hold in front of work, knit next 2 sts, k 2 from dpn, repeat from * across row, end p 2, k 2 tog, yo, p 2.
Row 4: Repeat Row 2.
Repeat Rows 1-4 for Pattern Stitch.

117. Multiple of 5 stitches.
Row 1: * K 3, sl 1, k 1, yo, psso, repeat from * across row.
Row 2: Purl.
Repeat Rows 1 and 2 for Pattern Stitch.

118. Multiple of 5 stitches.
Row 1: * P 3, sl 1, yib k 1, yo, psso, repeat from * across row.
Row 2: Knit.
Repeat Rows 1 and 2 for Pattern Stitch.

119. Multiple of 3 stitches plus 1.
Row 1: * K 1, sl 1, k 1, psso-place on left needle and knit it, repeat from *
across row.
Row 2: Purl.
Repeat Rows 1 and 2 for Pattern Stitch.

120. Multiple of 7 stitches plus 3.
Row 1: * P 3, k 4, repeat from * across row, end p 3.
Row 2: * K 3, p 4, repeat from * across row, end k 3.
Row 3: Repeat Row 1.
Row 4: Repeat Row 2.
Row 5: * P 3, sl 2 sts on a cable needle at back of work, k 2, k 2 sts from
cable needle, repeat from * across row, end p 3.
Rows 6, 8, 10: Repeat Row 2.
Rows 7, 9: Repeat Row 1.
Row 11: * P 3, sl 2 sts to cable needle and leave at front of work, k 2, k 2 sts
from cable needle, repeat from * across row, end p 3.
Row 12: Repeat Row 2.
Repeat Rows 1-12 for Pattern Stitch.

121. Multiple of 8 stitches plus 1.
Row 1: K 1, * k 3 tog (p 2 tog, k 2 tog), k 1, repeat from * across row.
Rows 2, 4: Purl.
Row 3: Knit.
Repeat Rows 1-4 for Pattern Stitch.

122. Multiple of 5 stitches.
Row 1: K 1, * insert needle between 2nd and 3rd sts, pull thru a lp, k 3, repeat from * across row.
Row 2: P 1, * p 2, p 2 tog, repeat from * across row.
Repeat Rows 1 and 2 for Pattern Stitch.

123. R.P.
Multiple of 3 stitches plus 2.
Row 1: P 2, * yo, k 1, yo, p 2, repeat from * across row.
Row 2: K 2, * p 3, k 2, repeat from * across row.
Row 3: P 2, * k 3, p 2, repeat from * across row.
Row 4: K 2, * p 3 tog, K 2, repeat from * across row.
Repeat Rows 1-4 for Pattern Stitch.

124. Multiple of 4 stitches.

Row 1: K 1, * sk 1, and knit the 2nd st thru back lp, keep on needle, then k the skipped st thru front and sl both sts from needle together, k 2, repeat from * across row, end k 1.

Row 2: K 1, * yif sk 1, purl 2nd st, then purl skipped st, sl both sts from needle together, k 2, repeat from * across row, end k 1.

Repeat Rows 1 and 2 for Pattern Stitch.

125. Any number of stitches.

Row 1: * K 2nd st, k first st, repeat from * across row.

Row 2: P 1, * p 2nd st, p first st, repeat from * across row, end p 1.

Repeat Rows 1 and 2 for Pattern Stitch.

126. Multiple of 5 stitches plus 3.

Row 1: * K 1, p 1, k 1, p 2, repeat from * across row, end k 1, p 1, k 1.

Row 2: * P 1, k 1, p 1, k 2, repeat from * across row, end p 1, k 1, p 1.

Row 3: Repeat Row 1.

Row 4: * P 1, k 1, p 1, k 2 tog and hold on left needle, k the first st, take off needle and repeat from * across row, end p 1, k 1, p 1.

Repeat Rows 1-4 for Pattern Stitch.

127. Multiple of 8 stitches.
Row 1: * P 5, k 3, repeat from * across row.
Rows 2, 4: * P 3, k 5, repeat from * across row.
Row 3: * P 5, sl 1, k 2, yo, psso, repeat from * across row.
Repeat Rows 1-4 for Pattern Stitch.

128. Multiple of 8 stitches plus 4.
Rows 1, 3: K 4, * p 4, k 4, repeat from * across row.
Row 2: P 4, * (sl 1 yib, k 1, yo, pass sl st over k st and yo) 2 times, p 4, repeat from * across row.
Repeat Rows 1-3 for Pattern Stitch.

129. Multiple of 5 stitches plus 2.
Row 1: P 2, * sl 1, k 2, psso, p 2, repeat from * across row.
Row 2: K 2, * p 1, yo, p 1, k 2, repeat from * across row.
Row 3: P 2, * k 3, p 2, repeat from * across row.
Row 4: K 2, * p 3, k 2, repeat from * across row.
Repeat Rows 1-4 for Pattern Stitch.

130. Multiple of 5 stitches plus 2.

Row 1: P 1, * skip 2 sts, k the 3rd st (do not drop from needle), k the 2 skipped sts, and drop the 3rd st from needle (cable made), p 2, repeat from * across row, end make 1 cable, p 1.

Row 2: K 1, * p 3, k 2, repeat from * across row, end p 3, k 1.

Row 3: P 1, * k 3, p 2, repeat from * across row, end k 3, p 1.

Row 4: Repeat Row 2.

Repeat Rows 1-4 for Pattern Stitch.

131. Multiple of 6 stitches.

Row 1: Purl.

Row 2: Knit.

Row 3: Purl.

Row 4: K 3, * sl 3 sts to dpn, hold in back of work, k 3, k 3 from dpn, repeat from * across row, end k 3.

Row 5: Purl.

Row 6: Knit.

Row 7: Purl.

Row 8: * Sl 3 to dpn, hold in front of work, k 3, k 3 from dpn, repeat from * across row.

Repeat Rows 1-8 for Pattern Stitch.

132. Multiple of 8 stitches plus 2.

Row 1: P 2, * k 6, p 2, repeat from * across row.

Row 2: K 2, * p 6, k 2, repeat from * across row.

Row 3: Repeat Row 1.

Row 4: Repeat Row 2.

Row 5: P 2, * sl 3 to dpn, hold in front, k next 3 sts, k 3 sts frm dpn, p 2, repeat from * across row.

Row 6: Repeat Row 2.

Row 7: Repeat Row 1.

Row 8: Repeat Row 2.

133. Multiple of 4 stitches plus 1.
Rows 1,3: Knit.
Rows 2,4: Purl.
Row 5: * P 3, (k 1, p 1, k 1) in next st, repeat from * across row, end p 3.
Rows 6,8: * K 3, p 3, repeat from * across row, end k 3.
Rows 7,9: * P 3, k 3, repeat from * across row, end p 3.
Row 10: * P 3 tog, k 3, repeat from * across row, end p 3 tog.

134. Multiple of 15 stitches plus 1.
Row 1: K 5, * p 1, k 4, repeat from * across row, end k 5.
Row 2: P 5, * k 1, p 4, repeat from * across row, end p 5.
Row 3: K 5, * p 1, k 4th st, hold on needle, k 1st, 2nd, 3rd sts, sl 4th st off, p 1, sl next st on holder, hold in front, k 3, k st on holder, repeat from * across row, end p 1, k 5.
Row 4: Repeat Row 2.
Row 5: Repeat Row 1.
Row 6: Repeat Row 2.
Row 7: Repeat Row 3.
Repeat Rows 1-7 for Pattern Stitch.

135. Multiple of 12 stitches plus 6.
Row 1: * P 2, k 2, p 2, k 6, repeat from * across row, end p 2.
Row 2: K 2, p 2, k 2, * p 6, k 2, p 2, k 2, repeat from * across row.
Rows 3,5: Repeat Row 1.
Rows 4,6: Repeat Row 2.
Row 7: * P 2, k 2, p 2, sl 3 sts to holder, hold in front, k 3, k 3 sts from holder, repeat from * across row.
Repeat Rows 2-7 for Pattern Stitch.

136. Multiple of 2 stitches plus 1.
Row 1: * K 2nd st left needle, k the first and drop both off needle (right twist), k in back of 2nd st on left needle, k the first st, drop both off needle (left twist), repeat from * across row.
Row 2: Purl.
Row 3: Knit.
Row 4: Sl 1, * p 2, yif sl 2, repeat from * across row, end p 2, sl 1.
Row 5: * Work 1 left twist, work a right twist, repeat from * across row.
Row 6: Purl.
Row 7: Knit.
Row 8: P 1, * sl 2, p 2, repeat from * across row, end sl 2, p 1.
Repeat Rows 1-8 for Pattern Stitch.

137. Multiple of 8 stitches.
Rows 1,2,3,4: * K 4, p 4, repeat from * across row.
Row 5: * P 4, sl next 2 sts on to cable needle and leave at front of work, k 2, p 2 from cable needle, repeat from * across row.
Repeat Rows 2-5 for Pattern Stitch.

Rib
Stitch Patterns

Rib patterns are designed for a fitted, hugged look. They are simple to knit, with a multitude of variations from which to choose. Begin with the simple K 1, p 1 rib—an ideal stitch pattern for sleeve cuffs. Work your way up to an all-rib dress, K 5, p 1.

Try any of the rib patterns for sweater or sleeve bindings, contrasting the edges with a wide-ribbed hemline or close-knitted ribs climbing all the way up the sleeves.

138. Multiple of 3 stitches plus 1.
Row 1: * K 3, sl 1, repeat from * across row.
Row 2: Purl.
Repeat Rows 1 and 2 for Pattern Stitch.

139. R.P. Reversible Pattern.
Multiple of 5 stitches.
Row 1: * P 2, k 1, sl 1, k 1, repeat from * across row.
Row 2: * P 3, k 2, repeat from * across row.
Repeat Rows 1 and 2 for Pattern Stitch.

140. R.P. Reversible Pattern.
Multiple of 3 stitches.
Row 1: * K 2, p 1, repeat from * across row.
Repeat Row 1 for Pattern Stitch.

141. Multiple of 6 stitches.
Row 1: P 2, * k 2, p 4, repeat from * across row, end k 2, p 2.
Row 2: K 2, * p 2, k 4, repeat from * across row, end p 2, k 2.
Repeat Rows 1 and 2 for Pattern Stitch.

142. Multiple of 3 stitches plus 1.
Row 1: P 1, * skip next st, knit in next st thru front lp and keep on left
needle, k the skipped st, drop both from left needle, p 1, repeat
from * across row, end p 1.
Row 2: K 1, * p 2, k 1, repeat from * across row, end k 1.
Repeat Rows 1 and 2 for Pattern Stitch.

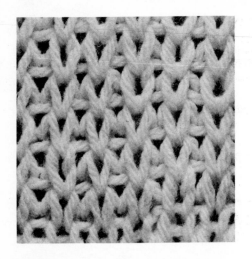

143. Even number of stitches.
Row 1: * K 1, p 1, repeat from * across row.
Row 2: * K 1, p 1, k 1 in row below, p 1, repeat from * across row.
Repeat Rows 1 and 2 for Pattern Stitch.

144. Multiple of 6 stitches.
Row 1: * K 3, p 3, repeat from * across row, end p 3.
Row 2: * K 1, p 1, repeat from * across row, end p 1.
Repeat Rows 1 and 2 for Pattern Stitch.

145. Multiple of 3 stitches plus 2.
Row 1: Knit.
Row 2: P 2, * k 1 (in back of st), p 2, repeat from * across row.
Repeat Rows 1 and 2 for Pattern Stitch.

146. Multiple of 3 stitches plus 1.
Row 1: K 1, * k 2 tog, yo, k 1, repeat from * across row.
Row 2: Purl.
Repeat Rows 1 and 2 for Pattern Stitch.

147. R.P.
Multiple of 4 stitches.
Row 1: * Sl 1, yo, sl 1, k 2 tog, repeat from * across row.
Row 2: Purl.
Repeat Rows 1 and 2 for Pattern Stitch.

148. Multiple of 7 stitches plus 1.
Row 1: K 3, * k 2 tog—leave on left needle, k the first st, drop both sts
      from left needle, k 5, repeat from * across row, end k 3.
Row 2: P 3, * yif sl 2 sts, p 5, repeat from * across row, end p 3.
Repeat Rows 1 and 2 for Pattern Stitch.

149. Multiple of 5 stitches plus 2.
Row 1: K 2, p 3, k 2, repeat from * across row.
Row 2: P 2, * k 1, sl 1, k 1, p 2, repeat from * across row.
Repeat Rows 1 and 2 for Pattern Stitch.

150. Multiple of 6 stitches plus 2.
Row 1: * P 2, k 2 tog, yo, k 2, repeat from * across row, end p 2.
Row 2: K 2, * p 2 tog, yo, p 2, k 2, repeat from * across row.
Repeat Rows 1 and 2 for Pattern Stitch.

151. R.P.
Multiple of 4 stitches.
Row 1: * K 3, p 1, repeat from * across row.
Row 2: * K 2, p 1, k 1, repeat from * across row.
Repeat Rows 1 and 2 for Pattern Stitch.

152. R.P.
Multiple of 5 stitches plus 2.
Row 1: * P 2, k 1, p 1, k 1, repeat from * across row, end p 2.
Row 2: * K 2, p 3, repeat from * across row, end k 2.
Repeat Rows 1 and 2 for Pattern Stitch.

153. Multiple of 6 stitches.
Row 1: * K 3, p 3, repeat from * across row.
Row 2: Knit.
Repeat Rows 1 and 2 for Pattern Stitch.

154. Multiple of 6 stitches.
Row 1: * P 3, sl 1, k 1 yib, sl 1 yif, repeat from * across row.
Rows 2, 4: * P 3, k 3, repeat from * across row.
Row 3: * P 3, k 1, sl 1 yib, k 1, repeat from * across row.
Repeat Rows 1-3 for Pattern Stitch.

155. Multiple of 4 stitches.
Row 1: * K 2, yo, sl 1, k 1, psso, repeat from * across row.
Row 2: * P 2, yo, p 2 tog, repeat from * across row.
Repeat Rows 1 and 2 for Pattern Stitch.

156. Multiple of 6 stitches plus 3.
Row 1: * P 3, yo, sl 1, k 2 tog, psso, yo, repeat from * across row, end p 3.
Row 2: * K 3, p 3, repeat from * across row, end k 3.
Repeat Rows 1 and 2 for Pattern Stitch.

157. Multiple of 4 stitches plus 3.
Row 1: * K 2, p 2, repeat from * across row, end k 2, p 1.
Repeat Row 1 for Pattern Stitch.

158. Even number of stitches.
Row 1: K 1, * p 1, k 1 in row below, repeat from * across row, end p 1.
Repeat Row 1 for Pattern Stitch.

159. Multiple of 3 stitches.
Row 1: * K 2, p 1, repeat from * across row, end p 1.
Row 2: * K 1, p 2, repeat from * across row, end p 2.
Repeat Rows 1 and 2 for Pattern Stitch.

160. Multiple of 2 stitches.
Row 1: * K 1, p 1, repeat from * across row, end p 1.
Repeat Row 1 for Pattern Stitch.

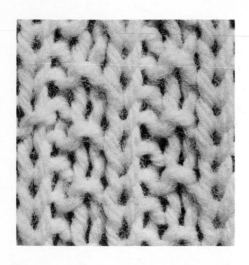

161. Multiple of 3 stitches.
Row 1: * K 2, p 1, repeat from * across row, end p 1.
Repeat Row 1 for Pattern Stitch.

162. Multiple of 4 stitches plus 1.
Row 1: * K 3, p 1, repeat from * across row, end p 1, k 1.
Repeat Row 1 for Pattern Stitch.

163. Multiple of 4 stitches.
Row 1: * K 1, yo, sl 1, k 1, p 1, repeat from * across row.
Row 2: * K 1, p 1, k 2 tog, p 1, repeat from * across row.
Repeat Rows 1 and 2 for Pattern Stitch.

164. Multiple of 4 stitches plus 3.
Row 1: K 3, * p 1, k 3, repeat from * across row.
Row 2: K 1, * p 1, k 3, repeat from * across row, end p 1, k 1.
Repeat Rows 1 and 2 for Pattern Stitch.

165. Multiple of 4 stitches plus 3.
Row 1: K 3, * sl 1 yif, k 3, repeat from * across row.
Row 2: K 1, * sl 1 yif, k 3, repeat from * across row, end sl 1, k 1.
Repeat Rows 1 and 2 for Pattern Stitch.

166. Multiple of 5 stitches plus 2.
Row 1: K 2, * p 3 tog, k 2, repeat from * across row.
Row 2: P 2, * yo, p 1, yo, p 2, repeat from * across row.
Repeat Rows 1 and 2 for Pattern Stitch.

167. Multiple of 2 stitches plus 1.
Row 1: Knit.
Row 2: * K 1, p 1, repeat from * across row, end k 1.
Repeat Rows 1 and 2 for Pattern Stitch.

168. Multiple of 8 stitches plus 4.
Row 1: * P 4, k 2 tog, yo, k 2, repeat from * across row, end p 4.
Row 2: * K 4, p 2 tog, yo, p 2, repeat from * across row, end k 4.
Repeat Rows 1 and 2 for Pattern Stitch.

169. Multiple of 4 stitches plus 3.
Row 1: P 1, * k 3, p 1, repeat from * across row, end k 2.
Row 2: P 2, * k 1, p 3, repeat from * across row, end k 1.
Row 3: Repeat Row 1.
Row 4: P 2 tog, * yo, k 1, yo, p 3 tog, repeat from * across row, end yo, k 1.
Row 5: K 2, * p 1, k 3, repeat from * across row, end p 1.
Row 6: K 1, * p 3, k 1, repeat from * across row, end p 2.
Row 7: Repeat Row 5.
Row 8: K 1, yo, * p 3 tog, yo, k 1, yo, repeat from * across row, end p 2 tog.
Repeat Rows 1-8 for Pattern Stitch.

170. Multiple of 12 stitches.
Rows 1,3: K 2, * p 2, k 4, repeat from * across row, end p 2, k 2.
Rows 2,4: P 2, * k 2, p 4, repeat from * across row, end k 2, p 2.
Rows 5,7: K 1, * p 4, k 2, repeat from * across row, end p 4, k 1.
Rows 6,8: P 1, * k 4, p 2, repeat from * across row, end k 4, p 1.
Repeat Rows 1-8 for Pattern Stitch.

171. Multiple of 12 stitches plus 7.
Rows 1,3: K 2, * p 3, k 3, repeat from * across row, end p 3, k 2.
Row 2: P 2, * k in back of next 3 sts, p 3, repeat from * across row, end k in back of sts 3 times, p 2.
Row 4: P 2, * yo, sl 1, k 2 tog, psso, yo, p 3, repeat from * across row, end yo, p 2.
Repeat Rows 1-4 for Pattern Stitch.

172. Multiple of 8 stitches plus 1.
Row 1: P 3, * k 3, p 5, repeat from * across row, end p 3.
Row 2: K 4, * sl 1, k 7, repeat from * across row, end k 4.

173. Multiple of a stitch plus 3.
Row 1: Knit.
Row 2: Purl.
Row 3: * K 3, sl 1, repeat from * across row, end k 3.
Row 4: * P 3, sl 1, repeat from * across row, end p 3.
Repeat Rows 1-4 for Pattern Stitch.

174. Multiple of 2 stitches.
Rows 1,3: * Sl 1, k 1, yo, psso, repeat from * across row.
Rows 2,4,6: Purl.
Row 5: Knit.
Repeat Rows 1-5 for Pattern Stitch.

175. Multiple of 5 stitches plus 2.
Row 1: * K 2, p 1, k 1, p 1, repeat from * across row, end k 2.
Row 2: P 3, * k 1, p 4, repeat from * across row, end p 3.
Repeat Rows 1-2 for Pattern Stitch.

Lace
Stitch Patterns

Here's a chance to knit something ultra-elegant and easy too. These fragile, delicate looking patterns make sensational evening dresses and skirts. A lace trim will vamp up a simple dress.

These patterns can reflect years of tradition and nostalgia or a contemporary effect, as you wish. Work large patterns for capes, shawls, gowns and carriage covers.

A word of caution: Lace Pattern knits tend to stretch, so double check your stitch gauge every now and then.

These exquisitely webbed and balanced patterns lend themselves to invention. Invent a row, using lots of yarn overs, purl the next row, repeat the first row. Your own lace pattern!

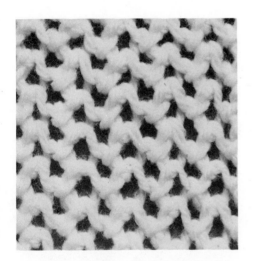

176. Even number of stitches.
Row 1: K 1, * yo, p 2 tog, repeat from * across row, end k 1.
Repeat Row 1 for Pattern Stitch.

177. Multiple of 6 stitches plus 5.
Row 1: K 1, * yo, k 3 tog, yo, k 3, repeat from * across row, end k 4.
Row 2: Purl.
Row 3: K 4, * yo, k 3 tog, yo, k 3, repeat from * across row, end k 1.
Row 4: Purl.
Repeat Rows 1-4 for Pattern Stitch.

178. Multiple of 6 stitches plus 4.
Row 1: K 2, * yo, sl 1, k 1, psso, k 1, k 2 tog, yo, k 1, repeat from * across row, end k 2.
Row 2: Purl.
Row 3: K 3, * yo, sl 1, k 2 tog, psso, yo, k 3, repeat from * across row.
Row 4: Purl.
Repeat Rows 1-4 for Pattern Stitch.

179. Even number of stitches.
Row 1: K 1, * yo, k 1, repeat from * across row, end k 1.
Row 2: K 1, purl across row to last st, end k 1.
Row 3: K 1, * k 2 tog, repeat from * across row, end k 1.
Rows 4,5: K 1, * yo, k 2 tog, repeat from * across row, end k 1.
Rows 6,7: Knit.
Repeat Rows 1-7 for Pattern Stitch.

180. Multiple of 4 stitches plus 1.
Row 1: K 1, * yo, sl 1, k 2 tog, psso, yo, k 1, repeat from * across row.
Row 2: K 1, * p 3, k 1, repeat from * across row.
Row 3: Knit.
Row 4: Repeat Row 2.
Repeat Rows 1-4 for Pattern Stitch.

181. Multiple of 4 stitches plus 1.
Row 1: Purl.
Row 2: K 2 tog, * (k 1 yo, k 1) in same st, sl 1, k 2 tog, psso, repeat from *
across row, end (k 1, yo, k 1) in same st, sl 1, k 1, psso.
Repeat Rows 1 and 2 for Pattern Stitch.

182. Multiple of 9 stitches plus 4.
Rows 1,3: Purl.
Row 2: K 3, * yo, k 2, k 2 tog, k 2 tog, yo, k 1, repeat from * across row, end
k 1.
Row 4: K 2, * yo, k 2, k 2 tog, k 2 tog, yo, k 1, repeat from * across row, end
k 2.
Repeat Rows 1-4 for Pattern Stitch.

183. Multiple of 6 stitches plus 3.
Row 1: K 2, * yo, sl 1, k 1, psso, k 1, k 2 tog, yo, k 1, repeat from * across
row, end k 2.
Row 2: Purl.
Row 3: K 3, * yo, sl 1, k 2 tog, psso, yo, k 3, repeat from * across
row.
Row 4: Purl.
Repeat Rows 1-4 for Pattern Stitch.

184. Multiple of 9 stitches plus 4.
Row 1: K 3, * yo, k 2, sl 2, k 1, psso, k 2 tog, k 2, yo, k 1, repeat from * across row, end k 2.
Row 2: Purl.
Row 3: K 2, * yo, k 2, sl 1, k 1, psso, k 2 tog, k 2, yo, k 1, repeat from * across row, end k 3.
Row 4: Purl.
Repeat Rows 1-4 for Pattern Stitch.

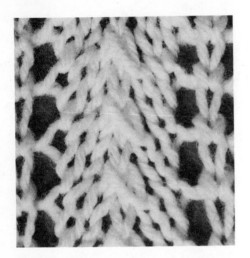

185. Multiple of 8 stitches plus 1.
Row 1: Purl.
Row 2: K 1, * yo, k 2, sl 1, k 2 tog, psso, k 2, yo, k 1, repeat from * across row.
Repeat Rows 1 and 2 for Pattern Stitch.

186. Multiple of 8 stitches plus 1.
Row 1 and odd-numbered rows: Purl.
Row 2: K 1, * k 1, k 2 tog, yo, k 1, yo, k 2 tog, k 2, repeat from * across row.
Row 4: K 1, * k 2 tog, yo, k 3, yo, k 2 tog, k 1, repeat from * across row.
Row 6: K 2 tog, * yo, k 5, yo, sl 1, k 2 tog, psso, repeat from * across row, end k 2 tog.
Row 8: K 1, * yo, k 2 tog, k 3, k 2 tog, yo, k 1, repeat from * across row.
Row 10: K 1, * k 1, yo, k 2 tog, k 1, k 2 tog, yo, k 2, repeat from * across row.
Row 12: K 1, * k 2, yo, sl 1, k 2 tog, psso, yo, k 3, repeat from * across row.
Repeat Rows 1-12 for Pattern Stitch.

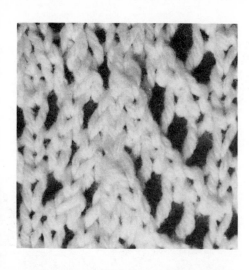

187. Multiple of 10 stitches plus 1.
Rows 1,3: Purl.
Row 2: K 1, * yo, k 2 tog (2 times), k 1, k 2 tog, yo (2 times), k 1, repeat from * across row.
Row 4: K 2, * yo, k 2 tog, yo, sl 2, k 1, psso (2 over), yo, k 2 tog, yo, k 3, repeat from * across row, end k 2.
Repeat Rows 1-4 for Pattern Stitch.

188. Multiple of 4 stitches plus 2.
Row 1: K 2, * p 1, yo, p 2 tog, k 1, repeat from * across row, end k 1.
Repeat Row 1 for Pattern Stitch.

189. Multiple of 3 stitches plus 1.
Row 1: K 1, * yo, sl 1, k 1, psso, k 1, repeat from * across row.
Row 2: K 1, * yo, p 2 tog, k 1, repeat from * across row.
Repeat Rows 1 and 2 for Pattern Stitch.

190. Multiple of 7 stitches plus 2.
Rows 1,3: K 2, * p 5, k 2, repeat from * across row.
Row 2: P 2, * k 5, p 2, repeat from * across row.
Row 4: P 2, * k 2 tog, yo, k 1, yo, sl 1, k 1, psso, p 2, repeat from * across row.
Repeat Rows 1-4 for Pattern Stitch.

191. Multiple of 8 stitches plus 1.
Row 1: Knit.
Row 2 and even-numbered rows: Purl.
Row 3: K 3, * k 2 tog, yo, k 6, repeat from * across row, end k 4.
Row 5: K 2, * k 2 tog, yo, k 1, yo, sl 1, k 1, psso, k 3, repeat from * across row, end k 2.
Row 7: K 1, * k 2 tog, yo, k 3, yo, sl 1, k 1, psso, k 1, repeat from * across row.
Row 9: K 2 tog, * yo, k 1, yo, sl 1, k 2 tog, psso, repeat from * across row, end sl 1, k 1, psso.
Rows 10, 11, 12: Knit .
Repeat Rows 3-12 for Pattern Stitch.

192. Multiple of 8 stitches plus 1.
Row 1: * k 1, yo, k 2, sl 1, k 2 tog, psso, k 2, yo, * end k 1.
Row 2: Purl.
Repeat Rows 1 and 2 for Pattern Stitch.

193. Multiple of 12 stitches plus 8.
Row 1: K 8, * k 2 tog, yo twice, k 2 tog, k 8, repeat from * across row.
Row 2 and even-numbered rows: Purl.
Rows 3,7: K 6, * k 2 tog, yo twice, (k 2 tog) twice, yo twice, k 2 tog, k 4, repeat from * across row, end k 6.
Rows 5,9: Repeat Row 1.
Row 11: K 2, * k 2 tog, yo twice, k 2 tog, k 8, repeat from * across row, end k 2.
Row 13: * K 2 tog, yo twice, (k 2 tog) twice, yo twice, k 2 tog, k 4, repeat from * across row, end k 2 tog, yo twice, (k 2 tog) twice, yo twice, k 2 tog.
Rows 15, 19: Repeat Row 11.
Row 17: Repeat Row 13.
Row 18: Repeat Row 2.
Repeat Rows 1-18 for Pattern Stitch.

194. Multiple of 3 stitches plus 4.
Row 1: K 2, * sl 1, k 2 tog, psso, yo (twice), repeat from * across row, end k 2.
Row 2: K 2, * (p 1, k 1) in yo, p 1, repeat from * across row, end k 2.
Row 3: Knit.
Repeat Rows 1-3 for Pattern Stitch.

195. Multiple of 7 stitches.
Row 1: Purl.
Row 2: * K 1, k 2 tog, yo, k 1, yo, k 2 tog, k 1, repeat from * across row.
Row 3: Purl.
Row 4: * K 2 tog, yo, k 3, yo, k 2 tog, repeat from * across row.
Repeat Rows 1-4 for Pattern Stitch.

196. Multiple of 12 stitches plus 5.
Row 1 and odd-numbered rows: Purl.
Rows 2, 4: K 2, * k 1, yo, k 3, k 2 tog, k 1, sl 1, k 1, psso, k 3, yo, repeat from * across row, end k 3.
Rows 6, 8: K 2, * k 1, sl 1, k 1, psso, k 3, yo, k 1, yo, k 3, k 2 tog, repeat from * across row, end k 4.
Repeat Rows 1-8 for Pattern Stitch.

197. Multiple of 4 stitches plus 1.
Row 1: K 1, * yo, sl 1, p 2 tog, yib, pass sl 1 over the p 2 tog, yo, k 1, repeat from * across row.
Row 2: K 1, * p 3, k 1, repeat from * across row.
Repeat Rows 1 and 2 for Pattern Stitch.

198. Multiple of 3 stitches.
Row 1: * Yo, sl 1, k 2, psso, repeat from * across row.
Row 2: Purl.
Repeat Rows 1 and 2 for Pattern Stitch.

199. Multiple of 7 stitches plus 2.
Row 1: K 1, * (k 2 tog, yo) twice, k 1, (yo, k 2 tog in back of sts) twice, repeat from * across row, end k 1.
Row 2: K 1, purl across row, end k 1.
Repeat Rows 1 and 2 for Pattern Stitch.

200. Multiple of 11 stitches plus 3.
Row 1: * K 3, yo, sl 1, k 2 tog, psso, yo, p 2, yo, sl 1, k 2 tog, psso, yo, repeat from * across row, end k 3.
Row 2: P 6, k 2, * p 9, k 2, repeat from * across row, end p 6.
Row 3: K 6, p 2, * k 9, p 2, repeat from * across row, end k 6.
Row 4: Repeat Row 2.
Repeat Rows 1-4 for Pattern Stitch.

201. Multiple of 8 stitches.
Row 1: Knit.
Row 2: Purl.
Row 3: * K 6, yo, k 2 tog, repeat from * across row.
Row 4: Knit.
Row 5: Knit.
Row 6: Purl.
Row 7: K 2, * yo, k 2 tog, k 6, repeat from * across row, end k 4.
Row 8: Knit.
Repeat Rows 1-8 for Pattern Stitch.

202. Even number of stitches.
Row 1: Knit.
Row 2: * K 2 tog (hold on needle, knit the first st, drop both from needle), repeat from * across row.
Row 3: Knit.
Row 4: Repeat Row 2.
Row 5: Knit.
Row 6: * K 2 tog, hold on needle, yo, knit the first st, drop both off needle, repeat from * across row.
Row 7: Knit across row, dropping the yo's off needle.
Repeat Rows 1-7 for Pattern Stitch.

203. Multiple of 12 stitches plus 6.
Row 1: * K 2 tog, yo, k 2, k 2 tog, p 6, repeat from * across row.
Row 2: * P 6, k 6, repeat from * across row.
Repeat Rows 1 and 2 for Pattern Stitch.

204. Multiple of 8 stitches plus 1.
Rows 1,2,3,4: * K 1, p 1, repeat from * across row, end k 1.
Rows 5,6: * K 1, yo, sl 1, k 1, psso, k 3, k 2 tog, yo, repeat from * across row, end k 1.
Repeat Rows 1-6 for Pattern Stitch.

205. Multiple of 6 stitches plus 1.
Row 1: * P 1, p 2 tog, yo, p 1, yo, p 2 tog, repeat from * across row, end p 1.
Rows 2,4: Purl.
Row 3: Knit.
Repeat Rows 1-4 for Pattern Stitch.

206. Multiple of 8 stitches plus 1.
Row 1: K 3, * yo, sl 1, k 2 tog, psso, yo, k 5, repeat from * across row, end yo, sl 1, k 2 tog, psso, yo, k 3.
Row 2 and even-numbered rows: Purl.
Row 3: K 2 tog, k 1, * yo, k 3, yo, k 1, sl s, k 2 tog, psso, k 1, repeat from * across row, end psso, k 1, yo, k 3, yo, k 1, sl 1, k 1.
Row 5: K 2 tog, * yo, k 5, yo, sl 1, k 2 tog, psso, repeat from * across row, end yo, k 5, yo, k 2 tog.
Row 7: K 2, * yo, k 1, sl 1, k 2 tog, psso, k 1, yo, k 3, repeat from * across row, end k 2.
Row 8: Purl.
Repeat Rows 1-8 for Pattern Stitch.

207. Multiple of 4 stitches.
Row 1: * K 3, p 1, repeat from * across row.
Row 2,4: * K 2, p 3, repeat from * across row.
Row 3: * Yo, sl 1 as if to purl, p 2 tog, psso, yo, p 1, repeat from * across row.
Repeat Rows 1-4 for Pattern Stitch.

208. Multiple of 6 stitches plus 1.
Row 1: * K 1, yo, sl 1, k 1, psso, k 1, k 2 tog, yo, repeat from * across row, end k 1.
Row 2: Purl.
Row 3: K 2, * yo, sl 1, k 2 tog, psso, yo, k 3 repeat from * across row, end k 2.
Repeat Rows 1-3 for Pattern Stitch.

209. Multiple of 2 stitches.
Rows 1,3,5,7: * Yo, k 2 tog, repeat from * across row.
Rows 2,4,6: * Yo, p 2 tog, repeat from * across row.
Rows 8,9,10,11: Knit.
Repeat Rows 1-11 for Pattern Stitch.

210. Multiple of 6 stitches plus 1.
Row 1: K 1, * yo, k 2 tog, k 1, k 2 tog, yo, k 1, repeat from * across row.
Rows 2,4,6,8: Purl.
Row 3: K 1, * yo, k 1, p 3 tog, k 1, yo, k 1, repeat from * across row.
Row 5: K 1, * k 2 tog, yo, k 1, yo, k 2 tog, k 1, repeat from * across row.
Row 7: P 2 tog, * (k 1, yo) twice, k 1, p 3 tog, repeat from * across row, end p 2 tog.
Repeat Rows 1-7 for Pattern Stitch.

211. Multiple of 4 stitches plus 2.

Row 1: K 1, * p 3 tog, (k 1, p 1, k 1) in next st, repeat from * across row, end k 1.

Rows 2,4: Purl.

Row 3: K 2, * (k 1, p 1, k 1) in next st, p 3 tog, repeat from * across row, end k 1.

Row 5: K, wrapping yarn 3 times around needle for each st.

Row 6: P, drop extra yarn off needle.

Diamond and Diagonal

Stitch Patterns

These patterns combine pure line and texture. Among the group you will find a network of open and shut diamonds that criss-cross. Raised diamonds on a deep surface produce a three-dimensional effect.

The patterns are strong, bold and sturdy, yet are not stiff in texture. They may appear a trifle complicated, but they are a breeze to work.

Add some embroidery or a flower to the center of each diamond. The diagonal-type patterns are perfect for skirts cut on the bias.

Experiment with different kinds of motions. Wavy, staccato, swirling, spiraling. These ribbon-like patterns have fluid overlapping lines that are ideal for sweaters, dresses, suits and coats.

212. Multiple of 3 stitches plus 2.
Row 1: Purl.
Row 2: K 1, * yo, sl 1, k 2, psso, repeat from * across row, end k 1.
Row 3: Purl.
Row 4: * Sl 1, k 2, psso, yo, repeat from * across row, end k 2.
Repeat Rows 1-4 for Pattern Stitch.

213. Multiple of 4 stitches plus 2.
Row 1: K 2, * k into the 2nd st on left needle, hold loop on left needle, k first st on left needle, k 2, repeat from * across row.
Row 2: Purl.
Row 3: K 4, repeat from * of Row 1 ending k 4.
Row 4: Purl.
Repeat Rows 1-4 for Pattern Stitch.

214. Multiple of 4 stitches plus 2.
Row 1: * K 2, p 2, repeat from * across row, end k 2.
Row 2: K 1, * p 2, k 2, repeat from * across row, end p 1.
Row 3: * P 2, k 2, repeat from * across row, end p 2.
Row 4: P 1, * k 2, p 2, repeat from * across row, end k 1.
Repeat Rows 1-4 for Pattern Stitch.

215. Multiple of 4 stitches plus 1.
Rows 1, 3: K 1, * p 1, k 1, repeat from * across row.
Row 2: P 1, * sl 1, yib, k into front and back of next st, k 1, pass sl st over last 3 sts made, p 1, repeat from * across row.
Row 4: P 1, k 1, p 1, repeat from * of Row 2, end k 1, p 1.
Repeat Rows 1-4 for Pattern Stitch.

216. Multiple of 8 stitches.
Row 1: * P 1, k 7, repeat from * across row.
Rows 2, 8: * K 1, p 5, k 1, p 1, repeat from * across row.
Rows 3, 7: * K 2, p 1, k 3, p 1, k 1, repeat from * across row.
Rows 4, 6: * P 2, k 1, p 1, k 1, p 3, repeat from * across row.
Row 5: * K 4, p 1, k 3, repeat from * across row.
Repeat Rows 1-8 for Pattern Stitch.

217. Multiple of 4 stitches.
Row 1: * K 2, p 2, repeat from * across row.
Row 2: K 1, * p 2, k 2, repeat from * across row, end k 1.
Row 3: * P 2, k 2, repeat from * across row.
Row 4: P 1, * k 2, p 2, repeat from * across row, end p 1.
Repeat Rows 1-4 for Pattern Stitch.

218. Multiple of 2 stitches.
Row 1: Knit.
Row 2: P 1, * yo, p 2 tog, repeat from * across row, end p 1.
Row 3: K 2, * yo, k 2 tog, repeat from * across row.
Row 4: P 2, * yo, p 2 tog, repeat from * across row.
Row 5: K 1, * yo, k 2 tog, repeat from * across row, end k 1.
Repeat Rows 2-5 for Pattern Stitch.

219. Multiple of 2 stitches.
Row 1: * Sl 1, k 1, yo, psso, repeat from * across row.
Rows 2, 4: Purl.
Row 3: K 1, * sl 1, k 1, yo, psso, repeat from * across row, end k 1.
Repeat Rows 1-4 for Pattern Stitch.

220. Multiple of 3 stitches plus 1.
Row 1: * P 1, yo, p 2 tog, repeat from * across row, end p 1.
Row 2: K 1, * sl 1, k 2, psso, repeat from * across row.
Row 3: * P 2, yo, repeat from * across row, end k 1.
Row 4: * Sl 1, k 2, psso, repeat from * across row, end k 1.
Row 5: P 1, * yo, p 2, repeat from * across row.
Repeat Rows 2-5 for Pattern Stitch.

221. Multiple of 4 stitches.
Rows 1, 3: Knit.
Row 2: * Yo, p 2, psso, p 2, repeat from * across row.
Row 4: * P 2, yo, p 2, psso, repeat from * across row.
Repeat Rows 1-4 for Pattern Stitch.

222. Multiple of 4 stitches.
Row 1: K 1, * yo, k 3, psso first st over last 2 sts, repeat from * across row.
Row 2: Purl.
Repeat Rows 1 and 2 for Pattern Stitch.

223. Multiple of 3 stitches plus 1.
Row 1: K 1, * yo, k 2 tog, repeat from * across row, end k 1.
Row 2: Purl.
Row 3: K 2, * yo, k 2 tog, repeat from * across row.
Row 4: Purl.
Repeat Rows 1-4 for Pattern Stitch.

224. Multiple of 3 stitches.
Row 1: * K 1, yo, k 2 tog, repeat from * across row, end k 2 tog.
Row 2: Purl.
Repeat Rows 1 and 2 for Pattern Stitch.

225. Multiple of 8 stitches.
Knit 1 row, purl 2 rows (twice).
Rows 1, 9: * K 3, yo, sl 1, k 1, psso, k 3, repeat from * across row.
Row 2 and even-numbered rows: Purl.
Rows 3, 7: * K 2, (yo, sl 1, k 1, psso) twice, k 2, repeat from * across row.
Row 5: * K 1, (yo, sl 1, k 1, psso) 3 times, k 1, repeat from * across row.
Rows 10-14: Purl 2 rows, knit 1 row, purl 2 rows.
Repeat Rows 1-14 for Pattern Stitch.

226. Multiple of 9 stitches.
Row 1: * K 4, yo, sl 1, k 1, psso, k 3, repeat from * across row.
Row 2 and even-numbered rows: Purl.
Row 3: * K 2, k 2 tog, yo, k 1, yo, sl 1, k 1, psso, k 2, repeat from * across row.
Row 5: * K 1, k 2 tog, yo, k 3, yo, sl 1, k 1, psso, k 1, repeat from * across row.
Row 7: * K 2 tog, yo, k 5, yo, sl 1, k 1, psso, repeat from * across row.
Row 8: Purl.
Repeat Rows 1-8 for Pattern Stitch.

227. Multiple of 15 stitches.
Row 1: * P 2 tog, p 4, k 1, yo, k 1, yo, k 1, p 4, p 2 tog, repeat from * across row.
Row 2 and even-numbered rows: Purl.
Row 3: * P 2 tog, p 3, k 2, yo, k 1, yo, k 2, p 3, p 2 tog, repeat from * across row.
Row 5: * P 2 tog, p 2, k 3, yo, k 1, yo, k 3, p 2, p 2 tog, repeat from * across row.
Row 7: * P 2 tog, p 1, k 4, yo, k 1, yo, k 4, p 1, p 2 tog, repeat from * across row.
Row 9: * P 2 tog, k 5, yo, k 1, yo, k 5, p 2 tog, repeat from * across row.
Row 10: Purl.
Repeat Rows 1-10 for Pattern Stitch.

228. Multiple of 8 stitches.
Row 1: * P 1, k 3, repeat from * across row.
Row 2: * K 1, p 5, k 1, p 1, repeat from * across row, end p 1, k 1, p 3.
Row 3: * K 2, p 1, k 3, p 1, k 1, repeat from * across row.
Row 4: * P 2, k 1, p 1, k 1, p 3, repeat from * across row, end p 5, k 1, p 1.
Repeat Rows 1-4 for Pattern Stitch.

229. Multiple of 8 stitches plus 4.
Row 1: K 4, * p 4, k 4, repeat from * across row.
Row 2 and even-numbered rows: Purl.
Row 3: P 1, * k 4, p 4, repeat from * across row, end k 3.
Row 5: P 2, * k 4, p 4, repeat from * across row, end k 2.
Row 7: P 3, * k 4, p 4, repeat from * across row, end k 1.
Row 9: P 4, * k 4, p 4, repeat from * across row.
Row 11: K 1, * p 4, k 4, repeat from * across row, end p 3.
Row 13: K 2, * p 4, k 4, repeat from * across row, end p 2.
Row 15: K 3, * p 4, k 4, repeat from * across row, end p 1.
Row 16: Purl.
Repeat Rows 1-16 for Pattern Stitch.

230. Multiple of 6 stitches plus 2.
Row 1 and odd-numbered rows: Purl.
Row 2: * Yo, k 3, yo, sl 1, k 2 tog, psso, repeat from * across row, end k 2.
Row 4: * Yo, sl 1, k 1, psso, k 1, k 2 tog, yo, k 1, repeat from * across row, end yo, sl 1, k 1, psso.
Row 6: K 1, * yo, sl 1, k 2 tog, psso, yo, k 3, repeat from * across row, end k 4.
Row 8: * K 2 tog, yo, k 1, yo, sl 1, k 1, psso, k 1, repeat from * across row, end k 3.
Row 10: K 4, * yo, sl 1, k 2 tog, psso, yo, k 3, repeat from * across row, end k 1.
Repeat Rows 3-10 for Pattern Stitch.

231. Multiple of 10 stitches.
Row 1 and odd-numbered rows: Purl.
Row 2: K 3, * yo, sl 1, k 2 tog, psso, yo, k 7, repeat from * across row, end k 4.
Row 4: K 2 tog, k 2, * yo, k 1, yo, k 2, sl 1, k 1, psso, k 1, k 2 tog, k 2, repeat from * across row, work last 6 sts-yo, k 1, yo, k 2, sl 1, k 1, psso, k 1.
Row 6: * K 2 tog, k 1, yo, k 3, yo, k 1, sl 1, k 1, psso, k 1, repeat from * across row.
Row 8: K 2 tog, * yo, k 5, yo, sl 1, k 1, psso, k 1, k 2 tog, repeat from * across row, work last 8 sts-yo, k 5, yo, sl 1, k 1, psso, k 1.
Row 10: K 1, yo, * k 7, yo, sl 1, k 2 tog, psso, yo, repeat from * across row, work last 9 sts-k 7, yo, sl 1, k 1, psso.
Row 12: K 1, * yo, k 2, sl 1, k 1, psso, k 1, k 2 tog, k 2, yo, k 1, repeat from * across row.
Row 14: K 2 tog, * yo, k 1, sl 1, k 1, psso, k 1, k 2 tog, k 1, yo, k 3, repeat from * across row, end k 2.
Row 16: K 2, * yo, sl 1, k 2, psso, k 1, k 2 tog, yo, k 5, repeat from * across row, end k 3.
Repeat Rows 1-16 for Pattern Stitch.

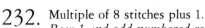

232. Multiple of 8 stitches plus 1.
Row 1 and odd-numbered rows: Purl.
Row 2: K 1, * yo, sl 1, k 1, psso, k 3, k 2 tog, yo, k 1, repeat from * across row.
Row 4: K 2, * yo, sl 1, k 1, psso, k 1, k 2 tog, yo, k 3, repeat from * across row, end yo, k 2.
Row 6: K 3, * yo, sl 1, k 2 tog, psso, yo, k 5, repeat from * across row, end yo, k 3.
Row 8: K 2, * k 2 tog, yo, k 1, yo, sl 1, k 1, psso, k 3, repeat from * across row, end k 2.
Row 10: K 1, * k 2 tog, yo, k 3, yo, sl 1, k 1, psso, k 1. Repeat from * across row.
Row 12: K 2 tog, * yo, k 5, yo, sl 1, k 2 tog, psso, repeat from * across row, end yo, sl 1, k 1, psso.
Repeat Rows 1-12 for Pattern Stitch.

233. Multiple of 11 stitches plus 6.
Row 1: * K 6, k 2 tog, yo, k 1, yo, sl 1, k 1, psso, repeat from * across row, end k 6.
Row 2 and even-numbered rows: Purl.
Row 3: K 5, * k 2 tog, yo, k 3, yo, sl 1, k 1, psso, k 4, repeat from * across row, end k 5.
Row 5: K 4, * k 2 tog, yo, k 5, yo, sl 1, k 1, psso, k 2, repeat from * across row, end k 4.
Row 7: K 5, * yo, sl 1, k 1, psso, k 3, k 2 tog, yo, k 4, repeat from * across row, end k 5.
Row 9: K 6, * yo, sl 1, k 1, psso, k 1, k 2 tog, yo, k 6, repeat from * across row.
Row 11: K 7, * yo, sl 1, k 2 tog, psso, yo, k 8, repeat from * across row, end k 7.
Row 12: Purl.
Repeat Rows 1-12 for Pattern Stitch.

234. Multiple of 8 stitches.
Notes: Back Cross (BC): Sl 1 st to double pointed needle and hold in back, k 1, p the st from the dpn.
Front Cross (FC): Sl 1 st to dpn and hold in front, p 1, k the st from the dpn.
Back Knit Cross (BKC): Sl 1 st to dpn and hold in back, k 1, k the st from dpn.
Front Knit Cross (FKC): Sl 1 st to dpn and hold in front, k 1, k the st from dpn.

Row 1: P 3, BKC, * p 6, BKC, repeat from * across row, end p 3.
Row 2 and even-numbered rows: Knit all the k sts, and purl all the p sts.
Row 3: P 2, * BC, FC, p 4, repeat from * across row, end p 2.
Row 5: P 1, * BC, p 2, FC, p 2, repeat from * across row, end p 1.
Row 7: * BC, p 4, FC, repeat from * across row.
Row 9: K 1, * p 6, FKC, repeat from * across row, end p 6, k 1.
Row 11: * FC, p 4, BC, repeat from * across row.
Row 13: P 1, * FC, p 2, BC, p 2, repeat from * across row, end p 1.
Row 13: P 1, * FC, p 2, BC, p 2, repeat from * across row, end p 1.
Row 15: P 2, * FC, BC, p 4, repeat from * across row, end p 2.
Row 16: Repeat Row 2.
Repeat Rows 1-16 for Pattern Stitch.

235. Multiple of 11 stitches plus 6.
Row 1: * K 6, k 2 tog, yo, k 1, yo, sl 1, k 1, psso, repeat from * across row, end k 6.
Row 2 and even-numbered rows: Purl.
Row 3: K 5, * k 2 tog, yo, k 3, yo, sl 1, k 1, psso, k 4, repeat from * across row, end k 5.
Row 5: K 4, * k 2 tog, yo, k 5, yo, sl 1, k 1, psso, k 2, repeat from * across row, end k 4.
Row 7: K 5, * yo, sl 1, k 1, psso, k 3, k 2 tog, yo, k 4, repeat from * across row, end k 5.
Row 9: K 6, * yo, sl 1, k 1, psso, k 1, k 2 tog, yo, k 6, repeat from * across row.
Row 11: K 7, * yo, sl 1, k 2 tog, psso, yo, k 8, repeat from * across row, end k 7.
Row 12: Purl.
Repeat Rows 1-12 for Pattern Stitch.

236. Multiple of 8 stitches.
Row 1: * P 7, k 1, repeat from * across row.
Row 2: * P 2, k 6, repeat from * across row.
Row 3: * P 5, k 3, repeat from * across row.
Row 4: * P 4, k 4, repeat from * across row.
Row 5: * P 3, k 5, repeat from * across row.
Row 6: * P 6, k 2, repeat from * across row.
Repeat Rows 1-6 for Pattern Stitch.

237. Multiple of 4 stitches plus 2.
Row 1: P 2, * k 2, p 2, repeat from * across row.
Row 2: K 2, * p 2, k 2, repeat from * across row.
Row 3: P 2, * k 2 tog, k first st again, p 2, repeat from * across row.
Row 4: Repeat Row 2.
Row 5: Repeat Row 2.
Row 6: Repeat Row 1.
Row 7: * K 2 tog and k first st again, p 2, repeat from * across row, end k 2 tog, k first st again.
Row 8: Repeat Row 1.
Repeat Rows 1-8 for Pattern Stitch.

238. Multiple of 4 stitches plus 1.
Row 1: P 1, * yib, sl 3, yif, p 1, repeat from * across row.
Row 2: Knit.
Row 3: Purl.
Row 4: K 2, * under lp below and on next st tog, k 3, repeat from * across row, end k 2.
Row 5: P 3, * yib, sl 3, yif, p 1, repeat from * across row, end p 3.
Row 6: Knit.
Row 7: Purl.
Row 8: K 4, * under lp below and st as before, k 3, repeat from * across row, end k 4.
Repeat Rows 1-8 for Pattern Stitch.

239. Multiple of 3 stitches.
Row 1: * K 2 tog, do not drop off needle, k first st, k 1, repeat from * across row.
Row 2: Purl.
Row 3: * K 1, k 2 tog, do not drop off needle, k first st, repeat from * across row.
Row 4: Purl.
Repeat Rows 1-4 for Pattern Stitch.

240. Multiple of 8 stitches plus 7.
Row 1: * K 7, p 1, repeat from * across row, end k 7.
Row 2: Purl.
Row 3: * P 1, k 7, repeat from * across row, end p 1, k 6.
Row 4: Purl.
Row 5: K 1, * p 1, k 7, repeat from * across row, end p 1, k 5.
Row 6: Purl.
Row 7: K 2, * p 1, k 3, k 5 sts into next st (popcorn made), k 3, repeat from * across row, end p 1, k 4.
Row 8: P 8, * p 5 tog, p 7, repeat from * across row, end p 5 tog, p 6.
Row 9: K 3, * p 1, k 7, repeat from * across row, end p 1, k 3.
Row 10: Purl.
Row 11: K 4, * p 1, k 7, repeat from * across row, end p 1, k 2.
Row 12: Purl.
Row 13: K 5, * p 1, k 7, repeat from * across row, end p 1, k 1.
Row 14: Purl.
Row 15: K 6, * p 1, k 3, k 5 sts into next st, k 3, repeat from * across row, end p 1.
Row 16: P 4, * p 5 tog, p 7, repeat from * across row, end p 10.
Repeat Rows 1-16 for Pattern Stitch.

Textured
Stitch Patterns

The raised three-dimensional quality of these patterns is terrific for children's wear. "Touchable" garments prove irresistible to little fingers, providing never ending fascination.

Moreover, these patterns work up to materials with lots of weight and substance without heavy bulkiness.

The variety is endless—choose from a field of soft and spongy patterns, thick and deep, grained and uneven, crunchy...pebbled...nubby...all for active, exciting sportswear designs.

241. Multiple of 10 stitches plus 9.
Rows 1,3,5,7,9: K 2, * sl 5 yif, k 5, repeat from * across row, end sl 5, k 2.
Rows 2,4,6,8: Purl.
Row 10: P 4, * on the next st (center of the slipped group) insert right needle down the 5 loose strands, bring needle up and put the 5 loose strands to left needle, p the 5 strands and the next st together as one st, p 9, repeat from * across row, end p 4.
Rows 11,13,15,17,19: K 7, * sl 5 yif, k 5, repeat from * across row, end sl 5, k 7.
Rows 12,14,16,18: Purl.
Row 20: P 9, * (see Row 10), p 9, repeat from * across row.
Repeat Rows 1-20 for Pattern Stitch.

242. Multiple of 12 stitches plus 1.
Row 1: Purl.
Row 2: Knit.
Rows 3,5: P 5, * k 3 in back lp, p 9, repeat from * across row, end p 5.
Rows 4,6: K 5, * p 3, k 9, repeat from * across row, end k 5.
Rows 7,9: P 2, * k 9 in back lp, p 3, repeat from * across row, end p 2.
Rows 8,10: K 2, * p 9, k 3, repeat from * across row, end k 2.
Rows 11,13: Repeat Rows 3 and 5.
Rows 12,14: Repeat Rows 4 and 6.
Row 15: Purl.
Row 16: Knit.
Repeat Rows 1-16 for Pattern Stitch.

243. Multiple of 6 stitches.
Rows 1-3: * K 3, p 3, repeat from * across row.
Row 4: Knit.
Row 5: Purl.
Row 6: Knit.
Rows 7-9: * K 3, p 3, repeat from * across row.
Row 10: Purl.
Row 11: Knit.
Row 12: Purl.
Repeat Rows 1-12 for Pattern Stitch.

244. Multiple of 4 stitches plus 1.
Row 1: K 1, * yo, k 3, yo, k 1, repeat from * across row.
Row 2: P 2, * p 3 tog, p 3, repeat from * across row, end p 2.
Row 3: Purl.
Row 4: Knit.
Repeat Rows 1-4 for Pattern Stitch.

245. Multiple of 3 stitches plus 1.
Row 1: P 3, popcorn in next st (k in back, k in front, k in back, k in front, k in back of next st-5 sts in one), * p 3, popcorn in next st, repeat from * across row, end p 3.
Row 2: K 3, to close popcorn (* sl next 5 sts-one at a time, bind off each st over the first st on right-hand needle, knit in back lp of next st), k 2, repeat from * across row, end k 2.
Row 3: Purl.
Row 4: Knit.
Repeat Rows 1-4 for Pattern Stitch.

246. Multiple of 2 stitches plus 1.
Row 1: K 1, * sl 1, k 1, yo, psso, repeat from * across row.
Row 2: Knit.
Repeat Rows 1 and 2 for Pattern Stitch.

247. Multiple of 3 stitches.
Row 1: * K 3, slip the same 3 stitches onto left needle and purl each one, repeat from * across row.
Row 2: Knit.
Repeat Rows 1 and 2 for Pattern Stitch.

248. Even number of stitches.
Row 1: Purl.
Row 2: Knit.
Row 3: K 2, * sl 1, k 1, repeat from * across row.
Row 4: * K 1, yif sl 1, repeat from * across row, end k 2.
Row 5: K 1, * yo, k 2 tog, repeat from * across row, end k 1.
Row 6: Purl.
Repeat Rows 1-6 for Pattern Stitch.

249. Multiple of 4 stitches plus 1.
Rows 1, 3: Knit.
Row 2: K 1, * p 3 tog, yo, purl the same sts together again, k 1, repeat from * across row.
Row 4: K 1, p 1, k 1, * p 3 tog, yo, purl same 3 sts together again, k 1, repeat from * across row, end p 1, k 1.
Repeat Rows 1-4 for Pattern Stitch.

250. Multiple of 6 stitches plus 1.
Rows 1,3,6: K 2, * p 3, k 3, repeat from * across row, end k 2.
Rows 2,5,7: P 2, * k 3, p 3, repeat from * across row, end p 2.
Row 4: K 2, * yo, sl 1, k 2 tog, psso, yo, k 3, repeat from * across row, end psso, yo, k 2.
Row 8: K 2 tog, * yo, k 3, yo, sl 1, k 2 tog, psso, repeat from * across row, end yo, k 2 tog.
Repeat Rows 1-8 for Pattern Stitch.

251. Multiple of 4 stitches plus 3.
Row 1: K 2, * p 3 tog (knit them, purl them), k 1, repeat from * across row, end k 1.
Row 2: Purl.
Repeat Rows 1 and 2 for Pattern Stitch.

252. Multiple of 4 stitches plus 2.
Row 1: * K 2, p 2, repeat from * across row, end k 2.
Row 2: P 2, * sl 2 yif, p 2, repeat from * across row.
Repeat Rows 1 and 2 for Pattern Stitch.

253. Multiple of 6 stitches plus 4.
Rows 1,3,5,7,9: * K 4, p 2, repeat from * across row, end k 4.
Row 2 and even-numbered rows: Purl.
Rows 11,13,17,19: K 1, * p 2, k 4, repeat from * across row, end p 2, k 1.
Row 20: 1 Purl.
Repeat Rows 1-20 for Pattern Stitch.

254. Multiple of 6 stitches.
Rows 1,3: * K 4, p 2, repeat from * across row.
Row 2 and even-numbered rows: K the purl sts, p the knit sts.
Rows 5,7: * K 2, p 2, k 2, repeat from * across row, end p 2.
Rows 9,11: * P 2, k 4, repeat from * across row.
Repeat Rows 1-11 for Pattern Stitch.

255. Multiple of 4 stitches.
Row 1: * (K 1, yo, k 1) in same st, p 3 tog, repeat from * across row.
Row 2: * P 1, k 3, repeat from * across row.
Row 3: * P 3 tog, (k 1, yo, k 1) in same st, repeat from * across row.
Row 4: * K 3, p 1, repeat from * across row.
Repeat Rows 1-4 for Pattern Stitch.

256. Odd number of stitches.
Rows 1,3: Purl.
Row 2: * K 2, (yo and pull last st over yo) 4 times, repeat from * across row, end k 1.
Repeat Rows 1-3 for Pattern Stitch.

257. R.P.
Multiple of 4 stitches plus 1.
Row 1: P 1, * k 1, sl 1 yif, k 1, p 1, repeat from * across row.
Row 2: K 1, * sl 1 yib, p 1, sl 1 yib, k 1, repeat from * across row.
Repeat Rows 1 and 2 for Pattern Stitch.

258. Multiple of 4 stitches.
Row 1: Purl.
Row 2: * (K 1, p 1, k 1) in next st, sl 1, k 2 tog, psso, repeat from * across row.
Row 3: Purl.
Row 4: * Sl 1, k 2 tog, psso, (k 1, p 1, k 1) in next st, repeat from * across row, end k 1.
Repeat Rows 1-4 for Pattern Stitch.

259. Smocking Pattern. Multiple of 6 stitches.
Row 1: * K 5, p 1, repeat from * across row, end p 1.
Row 2: * K 1, p 5, repeat from * across row, end p 5.
Thread tapestry needle with single strand of yarn, use the same color or a contrasting color yarn.
Row 1: Hold work with purl side facing; begin at bottom left corner and work across one row. Skip first purl ridge, * join next 2 purl ridges with an overcast st, repeat from * across row.
Row 2: Skip 7 rows, and join first 2 purl ridges, * join next 2 ridges, repeat from * across row.
Repeat Rows 1 and 2 for smocking.

Finished piece looks like the diagram—purl ridges become a diamond or honeycomb pattern.
Dotted lines indicate yarn on wrong side of work.

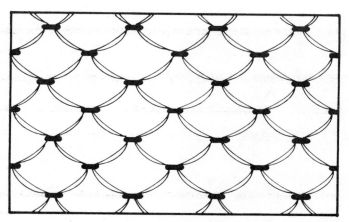

Finished piece looks like this—purl edges become diamond shaped.
Joined purl edges are worked with a contrasting color.

260. Multiple of 4 stitches plus 1.
Row 1: P 1, * yo, p 3, yo, p 1, repeat from * across row.
Row 2: K 2, * p 3 tog, k 3, repeat from * across row, end k 2.
Row 3: P 2, * yo, p 1, yo, p 3, repeat from * across row, end p 2.
Row 4: P 2 tog, * k 3, p 3 t g, repeat from * across row, end p 2 tog.
Repeat Rows 1-4 for Pattern Stitch.

261. Multiple of 3 stitches.
Row 1: * K 1, k next st—hold on left needle, yif purl the same st and the following st together.
Row 2: Purl.
Repeat Rows 1 and 2 for Pattern Stitch.

262. Any number of stitches.
Rows 1,3: K 2, * sl 2, k 1, sl 2, k 4, repeat from * across row, end k 2.
Rows 2,4: Purl.
Rows 5,7: P 2, * sl 2, k 1, sl 2, p 4, repeat from * across row, end p 2.
Rows 6,8: K 2, * p 5, k 4, repeat from * across row, end k 2.
Repeat Rows 1-8 for Pattern Stitch.

263. Multiple of 4 stitches.
Row 1: * K 2, yo, k 2 tog, repeat from * across row, end k 2 tog.
Row 2: Knit.
Row 3: Purl.
Row 4: Knit.
Repeat Rows 1-4 for Pattern Stitch.

264. Multiple of 3 stitches.
Row 1: * K 1, yo, k 2 tog, repeat from * across row.
Repeat Row 1 for Pattern Stitch.

265. Even number of stitches.
Row 1: * K 2, sl 2, repeat from * across row, end sl 2.
Row 2: * P 2, k 2, repeat from * across row, end k 2.
Row 3: * Sl 2, k 2, repeat from * across row, end k 2.
Row 4: * K 2, p 2, repeat from * across row, end p 2.
Repeat Rows 1-4 for Pattern Stitch.

266. Multiple of 3 stitches.
Row 1: Knit.
Row 2: * K 1, sl 2, repeat from * across row, end k 1.
Repeat Rows 1 and 2 for Pattern Stitch.

267. Multiple of 6 stitches plus 2.
Rows 1,3: * P 2, k 4, repeat from * across row, end p 2.
Rows 2,4: * K 2, p 4, repeat from * across row, end k 2.
Rows 5,7: * P 3, k 2, p 1, repeat from * across row, end p 3.
Rows 6,8: * K 3, p 2, k 1, repeat from * across row, end k 3.
Row 9: Purl.
Row 10: Knit.
Repeat Rows 1-10 for Pattern Stitch.

268. Multiple of 4 stitches plus 3.
Row 1: K 1, * k 1, p 3, repeat from * across row, end k 2.
Row 2: K 1, * p 2, k 2, repeat from * across row, end p 2.
Row 3: K 2, * p 1, k 3, repeat from * across row, end p 1.
Row 4: Purl.
Repeat Rows 1-4 for Pattern Stitch.

269. Multiple of 7 stitches plus 5.
Row 1: Knit.
Row 2: Purl.
Row 3: K 1, * k 3, p 4, repeat from * across row, end k 4.
Row 4: K 1, * p 3, k 4, repeat from * across row, end p 3, k 1.
Repeat Rows 1-4 for Pattern Stitch.

270. Even number of stitches
Rows 1-8: Work in stockinette stitch.
Row 9: Purl (right side).
Row 10: Knit.
Repeat Rows 1-10 for Pattern Stitch.
Fringe: Wind yarn around a 3 inch cardboard several times—cut open at one end. With crochet hook place one fringe in each loop of lower purl row of each purl ridge. Trim evenly.

271. Multiple of 3 stitches plus 1.
Row 1: P 1, * yif sl 2, yib pass 2 sl sts to left needle, yo, sl the same 2 sts to right needle, repeat from * across row.
Row 2: P 2, * p 2 tog, p 1, repeat from * across row, end p 1.
Repeat Rows 1 and 2 for Pattern Stitch.

272. Multiple of 4 stitches plus 3.

Row 1: Knit across row, wrap yarn twice around needle every 4th st, end k 3.

Row 2: K 3, * sl 1 (drop extra lp), k 3, repeat from * across row.

Row 3: P 3, * yif sl 3, p 3, repeat from * across row.

Row 4: K 3, * yib sl 1, k 3, repeat from * across row.

Row 5: K 1, * k 1 (wrap yarn twice around needle), k 3, repeat from * across row, end k 1 (yarn around needle twice), k 1.

Row 6: K 1, * sl 1, k 3, repeat from * across row, end sl 1, k 1.

Row 7: P 1, * yif sl 1, p 3, repeat from * across row, end sl 1, p 1.

Row 8: K 1, * yib sl 1, k 3, repeat from * across row, end sl 1, k 1.

Repeat Rows 1-8 for Pattern Stitch.

273. Odd number of stitches.

Row 1: Knit.

Row 2: Purl.

Row 3: Knit.

Row 4: K 1, * yo, k 2, psso (yo over last 2 sts), repeat from * across row.

Repeat Rows 1-4 for Pattern Stitch.

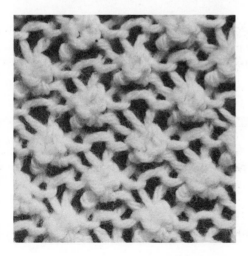

274. Multiple of 4 stitches.

Row 1: * (K 1, p 1, k 1) into first st, p 3 tog, repeat from * across row.

Rows 2,4: Purl.

Row 3: * P 3 tog, (k 1, p 1, k 1) into next st, repeat from * across row.

Repeat Rows 1-4 for Pattern Stitch.

275. Multiple of 3 stitches plus 1.
Row 1: K 1, purl across row, end k 1.
Row 2: K 1, * (k 1, p 1) in next st, p 2 tog, repeat from * across row, end k 1.
Row 3: Repeat Row 1.
Row 4: K 1, * p 2 tog, (k 1, p 1) in next st, repeat from * across row, end k 1.
Repeat Rows 1-4 for Pattern Stitch.

276. Multiple of 10 stitches plus 7.
Row 1: P 2, * k 3, p 2, repeat from * across row, end p 2.
Row 2 and all wrong-side rows: K 2, * p 3, k 2, repeat from * across row, end k 2.
Row 3: P 2, * yo, k 3, psso (yarn over the k 3), p 2, k 3, p 2, repeat from * across row, end yo, k 3, psso, p 2.
Repeat Rows 1-3 for Pattern Stitch.

277. R. P.
Multiple of 3 stitches plus 2.
Row 1: * P 2, k 1, repeat from * across row, end p 2.
Row 2: * K 2, p 1, repeat from * across row, end k 2.
Row 3: Knit.
Row 4: Purl.
Repeat Rows 1-4 for Pattern Stitch.

278. Multiple of 5 stitches plus 4.
Row 1: * K 4, yo, repeat from * across row, end k 4.
Row 2: * K 4, sl 1, repeat from * across row, end k 4.
Row 3: P 4, yif sl 1, repeat from * across row, end p 4.
Row 4: * K 4, sl 1, repeat from * across row, end k 4.
Row 5: Repeat Row 3.
Row 6: Repeat Row 4.
Row 7: Knit.
Repeat Rows 2-7 for Pattern Stitch.

279. R. P. Reversible Pattern.
Multiple of 3 stitches plus 2.
Row 1: * K 2, p 1, repeat from * across row, end k 2.
Row 2: * P 2, k 1, repeat from * across row, end p 2.
Row 3: Repeat Row 1.
Row 4: * P 2, rip down next st for 2 rows, pick up lp from ripped st and knit it, repeat from * across row, end p 2.
Repeat Rows 1-4 for Pattern Stitch.

280. R.P. Reversible Pattern.
Even number of stitches.
Row 1: * K 2, p 2, repeat from * across row, end k 2.
Row 2: * P 2, k 2, repeat from * across row, end p 2.
Rows 3, 4: Repeat Rows 1 and 2.
Rows 5, 6: Knit.
Repeat Rows 1-6 for Pattern Stitch.

281. Multiple of 6 stitches plus 1.
Rows 1,3,5: * K 1, k 2 tog, yo, k 1, yo, k 2 tog, repeat from * across row, end k 1.
Rows 2,4,6: Purl.
Row 7: Knit.
Row 8: Purl.
Repeat Rows 1-8 for Pattern Stitch.

282. Multiple of 6 stitches.
Rows 1-4: * K 3, p 3, repeat from * across row, end p 3.
Rows 5-8: * P 3, k 3, repeat from * across row, end k 3.
Repeat Rows 1-8 for Pattern Stitch.

283. Even number of stitches.
Row 1: * K 3, p 3, repeat from * across row, end p 3.
Row 2: * P 3, k 3, repeat from * across row, end k 3.
Repeat Rows 1 and 2 for Pattern Stitch.

284. Even number of stitches.
Row 1: * Yo, sl 1, k 1, psso, repeat from * across row, end psso.
Repeat Row 1 for Pattern Stitch.

285. Multiple of 3 stitches.
Row 1: Knit.
Row 2: * K 3 tog, keep sts on left needle, k 1, (knit 2 tog thru back lp), repeat from * across row.
Row 3: Purl.
Row 4: Knit.
Repeat Rows 1-4 for Pattern Stitch.

286. Any number of stitches.
Row 1: Knit.
Row 2: Knit.
Row 3: Purl.
Row 4: Knit.
Row 5: Purl.
Row 6: Purl.
Row 7: Knit.
Row 8: Purl.
Row 9: Purl.
Row 10: Knit.
Row 11: Purl.
Row 12: Knit.
Row 13: Purl.
Row 14: Knit.
Row 15: Purl.
Row 16: Purl.
Repeat Rows 2-16 for Pattern Stitch.

287. Even number of stitches.
Row 1: Knit.
Row 2: * K 2 tog, hold on needle, k the first st, drop both from needle, repeat from * across row.
Row 3: Knit.
Row 4: Repeat Row 2.
Row 5: Knit.
Row 6: * K 2 tog, hold on needle, yo, k the first st, drop both from needle, repeat from * across row.
Row 7: K across row, dropping yo's off needle.
Repeat Rows 1-7 for Pattern Stitch.

288. Multiple of 6 stitches plus 1.
Rows 1,7: Purl.
Rows 2,8: Knit.
Rows 3,5: K 1, * yif sl 2, yib k4, repeat from * across row.
Rows 9,11: * K 4, yif sl 2, repeat from * across row, end k 1.
Rows 4,6,10,12: P, slip the slipped sp of previous row.

289. Multiple of 4 stitches.
Row 1: * K 2, p 2nd st and hold on needle, p 1 st and drop from needle, repeat from * across row, end k 2.

290. *Row 1:* K 1, * yo, k 2 tog, repeat from * across row, ending yo, K 2 tog.
Row 2: Knit across row, k in back of yo's.
Row 3: K 1, yo, k 1, * yo, k 2 tog, repeat from * across row, end k 1, k 2 tog.
Row 4: Knit.
Repeat Rows 1-4 for Pattern Stitch.

Baroque
Stitch Patterns

These patterns are ornate and somewhat irregular in design, but they can create a mysterious, old-time feeling or be worked into a fresh, contemporary look.

The lacy, curly motifs make effective garment touches and finishes as well as overall designs. They are ideal as flounce and yoke combinations on children's dresses. Or ladies' evening capes and shawls. Try these unique patterns as separate panel inserts for blousy shapes, evening gowns or long at-home skirts.

Although Baroque Patterns may appear complex, they should cause no knitting anxieties. Just keep a pencil handy to check off rows as finished.

291.
R.P.
Multiple of 6 stitches.
Row 1: * P 2, yo, sl 1, k 1, psso, k 2 tog, repeat from * across row, end yo, p 2.
Row 2: * K 2, p 4, repeat from * across row, end k 2.
Row 3: * P 2, k 4, repeat from * across row, end p 2.
Row 4: Repeat Row 2.
Repeat Rows 1-4 for Pattern Stitch.

292.
Multiple of 6 stitches plus 2.
Row 1 and odd-numbered rows: Purl.
Rows 2,4,6: * Sl 1, k 1, psso, k 2, yo, k 2, repeat from * across row, end k 2.
Rows 8,10,12: K 1, * k 2, yo, k 2 tog, repeat from * across row, end k 1.
Repeat Rows 1-12 for Pattern Stitch.

293.

Multiple of 7 stitches plus 4.

Row 1: K 2, * yo, sl 1, k 1, psso, k 5, repeat from * across row, end yo, k 2 tog.

Row 2 and even-numbered rows: Purl.

Row 3: K 2, * yo, k 1, sl 1, k 1, psso, k 4, repeat from * across row, end yo, k 2 tog.

Row 5: K 2, * yo, k 2, sl 1, k 1, psso, k 3, repeat from * across row, ending yo, k 2 tog.

Row 7: K 2, * yo, k 3, sl 1, k 1, psso, k 2, repeat from * across row, ending yo, k 2 tog.

Row 9: K 2, * yo, k 4, sl 1, k 1, psso, k 1, repeat from * across row, end yo, k 2 tog.

Row 11: K 2, * yo, k 5, sl 1, k 1, psso, repeat from * across row, end yo, k 2 tog.

Row 12: Purl.

Repeat Rows 1-12 for Pattern Stitch.

294.

Multiple of 7 stitches plus 3.

Row 1: K 2, * yo, sl 1, k 2 tog, psso, yo, k 4, repeat from * across row, end k 5.

Row 2 and even-numbered rows: Purl.

Row 3: Repeat Row 1.

Row 5: K 5, * yo, sl 1, k 2 tog, psso, yo, k 4, repeat from * across row, end yo, k 2.

Row 7: K 5, * yo, sl 1, k 2 tog, psso, yo, k 4, repeat from * across row, end yo, k 2.

Row 8: Purl.

Repeat Rows 1-8 for Pattern Stitch.

295.

Multiple of 8 stitches plus 5.

Row 1 and odd-numbered rows: Purl.

Row 2: K 2, sl 1, k 1, psso, yo, k 1, yo, k 2 tog, k 3, repeat from * across row, end k 1.

Row 4: K 5, * yo, sl 2, k 1, pass 2 over, yo, k 5, repeat from * across row.

Row 6: Repeat Row 2.

Row 8: Sl 1, k 1, psso, yo, k 1, yo, k 2 tog, * k 3, sl 1, k 1, psso, yo, k 1, yo, k 2 tog, repeat from * across row.

Row 10: Repeat Row 2.

Row 12: Repeat Row 8.

Repeat Rows 1-12 for Pattern Stitch.

296. Multiple of 6 stitches plus 1.
Row 1 and odd-numbered rows: Purl.
Rows 2,4,6: K 1, * yo, sl 1, k 1, psso, k 1, k 2 tog, yo, k 1, repeat from * across row.
Row 8: K 2, * yo, sl 1, k 2 tog, psso, yo, k 3, repeat from * across row, end k 2.
Row 10: K 1, * k 2 tog, yo, k 1, yo, sl 1, k 1, psso, k 1, repeat from * across row.
Row 12: K 2 tog, * yo, k 3, yo, sl 1, k 2 tog, psso, repeat from * across row, end yo, k 3, yo, sl 1, k 1, psso.
Repeat Rows 1-12 for Pattern Stitch.

297. Multiple of 10 stitches plus 1.
Row 1: K 1, * yo, k 2 tog, k 5, k 2 tog, yo, k 1, repeat from * across row.
Row 2: P 1, * p 1, yo, p 2 tog, k 3, p 2 tog, yo, p 2, repeat from * across row.
Row 3: K 1, * k 2, yo, k 2 tog, k 1, k 2 tog, yo, k 3, repeat from * across row.
Row 4: K 1, * k 2, p 1, yo, p 3 tog, yo, p 1, k 3, repeat from * across row.
Row 5: K 1, * k 2, k 2 tog, yo, k 1, yo, k 2 tog, k 3, repeat from * across row.
Row 6: K 1, * k 1, p 2 tog, yo, p 3, yo, p 2 tog, k 2, repeat from * across row.
Row 7: K 1, * k 2 tog, yo, k 5, yo, k 2 tog, k 1, repeat from * across row.
Row 8: P 2 tog, * yo, p 1, k 5, p 1, yo, p 3 tog, repeat from * across row, end p 2 tog.
Repeat Rows 1-8 for Pattern Stitch.

298. Multiple of 8 stitches plus 5.
Row 1: K 1, * yo, sl 1, k 2 tog, psso, yo, k 1, repeat from * across row.
Rows 2,4,6: K 1, purl across row, end k 1.
Rows 3,5: K 1, * yo, sl 1, k 2 tog, psso, yo, k 5, repeat from * across row, end yo, k 1.
Row 7: K 1, * k 3, yo, k 2 tog, k 1, k 2 tog, yo, repeat from * across row, end k 4.
Row 8: Repeat Row 2.
Repeat Rows 1-8 for Pattern Stitch.

299. Multiple of 7 stitches plus 3.

Row 1: K 2, * yo, sl 1, k 2 tog, psso, yo, k 4, repeat from * across row, end k 5.

Rows 2,4,6: Purl.

Row 3: Repeat Row 1.

Row 5: K 5, * yo, sl 1, k 2 tog, psso, yo, k 4, repeat from * across row, end yo, k 2.

Row 7: Repeat Row 5.

Row 8: Purl.

Repeat Rows 1-8 for Pattern Stitch.

300. Multiple of 10 stitches plus 6.

Row 1: K 6, * yo, k 1, yo twice, k 1, yo 3 times, k 1, yo twice, k 1, yo, k 6, repeat from * across row.

Row 2: Knit (drop all yo's).

Rows 3,4: Knit.

Row 5: K 1, * yo, k 1, yo twice, k 1, yo 3 times, k 1, yo twice, k 1, yo, k 6, repeat from * across row, end k 1.

Row 6: Repeat Row 2.

Rows 7,8: Knit.

Repeat Rows 1-8 for Pattern Stitch.

301. Multiple of 12 stitches.

Row 1: K 1, * yo, k 2 tog, k 5, k 2 tog, yo, k 1 repeat from * across row, end k 1.

Row 2 and even-numbered rows: Purl.

Row 3: K 2, * yo, k 2 tog, k 3, k 2 tog, yo, k 3, repeat from * across row, end yo, k 2.

Row 5: K 5, * yo, k 2 tog, k 1, k 2 tog, yo, k 5, repeat from * across row, end yo, k 1.

Row 7: K 4, * yo, sl 1, k 2 tog, psso, yo, k 7, repeat from * across row, end yo, k 4.

Row 8: Purl.

Repeat Rows 1-8 for Pattern Stitch.

302. Multiple of 10 stitches plus 1.
Rows 1,3: Purl.
Row 2: K 1, * yo, k 3, sl 1, k 2 tog, psso, k 3, yo, k 1, repeat from * across row.
Row 4: P 1, * k 1, yo, k 2, sl 1, k 2 tog, psso, k 2, yo, k 1, p 1, repeat from * across row.
Rows 5,7: K 1, * p 9, k 1, repeat from * across row.
Row 6: P 1, * k 2, yo, k 1, sl 1, k 2 tog, psso, k 1, yo, k 2, p 1, repeat from * across row.
Row 8: P 1, * k 3, yo, sl 1, k 2 tog, yo, k 3, p 1, repeat from * across row.
Repeat Rows 1-8 for Pattern Stitch.

303. Multiple of 6 stitches plus 1.
Row 1 and odd-numbered rows: Purl.
Row 2: K 3, * yo, sl 1, k 1, psso, k 4, repeat from * across row, end yo, sl 1, k 1, psso, k 2.
Row 4: K 1, * k 2 tog, yo, k 1, yo, sl 1, k 1, psso, k 1, repeat from * across row.
Row 6: K 2 tog, yo, * k 3, yo, sl 1, k 2 tog, psso, yo, repeat from * across row, end k 3, yo, sl 1, k 1, psso.
Rows 8,10: K 1, * yo, sl 1, k 1, psso, k 1, k 2 tog, yo, k 1, repeat from * across row.
Repeat Rows 1-10 for Pattern Stitch.

304. Multiple of 12 stitches.
Row 1: Yo, k 4, * sl 1, k 2 tog, psso, k 4, yo, k 1, yo, k 4, repeat from * across row, end sl 1, k 2 tog, psso, k 4, yo, k 1.
Row 2 and even-numbered rows: Purl.
Row 3: K 1, yo, k 3, * sl 1, k 2 tog, psso, k 3, yo, k 3, yo, k 3, repeat from * across row, end sl 1, k 2 tog, psso, k 3, yo, k 2.
Row 5: K 2, yo, k 2, * sl 1, k 2 tog, psso, k 2 tog, yo, k 5, yo, k 2, repeat from * across row, end sl 1, k 2 tog, psso, k 2, yo, k 3.
Row 7: K 3, yo, k 1, * sl 1, k 2 tog, psso, k 1, yo, k 7, yo, k 1, repeat from * across row, end k 4.
Row 9: K 2 tog, k 3, yo, * k 1, yo, k 4, sl 1, k 2 tog, psso, k 4, yo, repeat from * across row, end sl 1, k 1, psso.
Row 11: K 2 tog, k 2, yo, * k 3, yo, k 3, sl 1, k 2 tog, psso, k 3, yo, repeat from * across row, end, sl 1, k 1, psso.
Row 13: K 2 tog, k 1, yo, * k 5, yo, k 2, sl 1, k 2 tog, psso, k 2, yo, repeat from * across row, end sl 1, k 1, psso.
Row 14: Purl.
Repeat Rows 1-14 for Pattern Stitch.

305. Multiple of 4 stitches.
Row 1: P 2, * yo, p 4 tog, repeat from * across row, end p 2.
Row 2: K 2, * k 1, (k 1, p 1, k 1) in yo of previous row, repeat from * across row, end k 2.
Row 3: Knit.
Repeat Rows 1-3 for Pattern Stitch.

306. Multiple of 4 stitches plus 1.
Row 1: K 2, * yo, k 1, k 2 tog, k 1, repeat from * across row, end k 2 tog.
Row 2 and even-numbered rows: Purl.
Rows 3,5: Repeat Row 1.
Row 7: * K 2 tog, k 1, yo, k 1, repeat from * across row, end k 1.
Rows 9,11: Repeat Row 7.
Row 12: Purl.
Repeat Rows 1-12 for Pattern Stitch.

307. Multiple of 18 stitches.
Row 1: Knit.
Row 2: Purl.
Row 3: * K 2 tog (3 times), yo, k 6, k 2 tog (3 times), repeat from * across row.
Row 4: Knit.
Repeat Rows 1-4 for Pattern Stitch.

308. Multiple of 8 stitches plus 1.

Row 1: K 1, * yo, k 2, sl 1, k 2 tog, psso, k 2, yo, k 1, repeat from * across row.

Row 2 and even-numbered rows: Purl.

Row 3: K 2, * yo, k 1, sl 1, k 2 tog, psso, k 1, yo, k 3, repeat from * across row, end k 2.

Row 5: K 3, * yo, sl 1, k 2 tog, psso, yo, k 5, repeat from * across row, end k 3.

Row 7: K 1, k 2 tog, k 1, * yo, k 1, yo, k 2, sl 1, k 2 tog, psso, k 2, repeat from * across row, end yo, k 1, yo, k 1, k 2 tog, k 1.

Row 9: K 1, k 2 tog, yo, k 3, yo, * k 1, sl 1, k 2 tog, psso, k 1, yo, k 3, yo, repeat from * across row, end k 2 tog, k 1.

Row 11: K 2 tog, yo, k 5, yo, * sl 1, k 2 tog, psso, yo, k 5, yo, repeat from * across row, end k last 2 sts tog.

Row 12: Purl.

Repeat Rows 1-12 for Pattern Stitch.

309. Multiple of 8 stitches plus 1.

Row 1: K 3, * yo, sl 1, k 2 tog, psso, yo, k 5, repeat from * across row, end yo, sl 1, k 2 tog, psso, yo, k 3.

Row 2 and even-numbered rows: Purl.

Row 3: K 2 tog, k 1, * yo, k 3, yo, k 1, sl 1, k 2 tog, psso, k 1, repeat from * across row, end yo, k 3, yo, k 1, k 2 tog.

Row 5: K 2 tog, * yo, k 5, yo, sl 1, k 2 tog, psso, repeat from * across row, end yo, k 5, yo, k 2 tog.

Row 7: K 2, * yo, k 1, sl 1, k 2 tog, psso, k 1, yo, k 3, repeat from * across row, end k 2.

Row 8: Purl.

Repeat Rows 1-8 for Pattern Stitch.

310. Even number of stitches.

With Color A, Knit one row.

Row 1: Color B, K 1, * k 1, yib sl 1, repeat from * across row, end k 1.

Row 2: B, K 1, * yif sl 1, k 1, repeat from * across row, end k 1.

Row 3: A, K 1, * yib sl 1, k 1, repeat from * across row, end k 1.

Row 4: A, K 1, * k 1, yif sl 1, repeat from * across row, end k 1.

Repeat Rows 1-4 for Pattern Stitch.

311. Multiple of 9 stitches.
Row 1: * K 2 tog, k 2, yo, k 1, yo, k 2, k 2 tog, repeat from * across row.
Rows 2,4: Purl.
Row 3: * K 2 tog, k 1, yo, k 3, yo, k 1, k 2 tog, repeat from * across row.
Row 5: * K 2 tog, yo, k 5, yo, k 2 tog, repeat from * across row.
Row 6: Purl.
Repeat Rows 1-6 for Pattern Stitch.

312. Multiple of 12 stitches plus 1.
Rows 1,2: Knit.
Row 3: K 5, * yo, sl 1, k 2 tog, psso, yo, k 9, repeat from * across row, end k 5.
Row 4: Purl.
Row 5: P 3, * k 2, yo, k 3, yo, k 2, p 5, repeat from * across row, end p 3.
Row 6: K 2 tog, * p 11, k 3 tog, repeat from * across row, end k 2 tog.
Row 7: Repeat Row 3.
Row 8: Knit.
Repeat Rows 1-8 for Pattern Stitch.

313. Multiple of 7 stitches plus 6.
Row 1: P 6, * yo, k 1, yo, p 6, repeat from * across row.
Row 2: * K 6, p 3, repeat from * across row, end k 6.
Row 3: P 6, * k 1, yo, k 1, yo, k 1, p 6, repeat from * across row.
Row 4: * K 6, p 5, repeat from * across row, end k 6.
Row 5: P 6, * k 2, yo, k 1, yo, k 2, p 6, repeat from * across row.
Row 6: * K 6, p 7, repeat from * across row, end k 6.
Row 7: P 6, * k 3, yo, k 1, yo, k 3, p 6, repeat from * across row.
Row 8: * K 6, p 9, repeat from * across row, end k 6.
Row 9: P 6, * sl 1, k 1, psso, k 5, k 2 tog, p 6, repeat from * across row.
Row 10: * K 6, p 7, repeat from * across row, end k 6.
Row 11: P 6, * sl 1, k 1, psso, k 3, k 2 tog, p 6, repeat from * across row.
Row 12: * K 6, p 5, repeat from * across row, end k 6.
Row 13: P 6, * sl 1, k 1, psso, k 1, k 2 tog, p 6, repeat from * across row.
Row 14: * K 6, p 3, repeat from * across row, end k 6.
Row 15: P 6, * sl 1, k 2 tog, psso, p 6, repeat from * across row.
Rows 16,18,20: Knit. *Rows 17,19:* Purl.
Repeat Rows 1-20 for Pattern Stitch.

314. Multiple of 8 stitches.

Row 1: * K 1, yo, k 2, sl 1, k 2 tog, psso, k 2, yo, repeat from * across row, end k 1.

Row 2 and even-numbered rows: Purl.

Row 3: K 2, * yo, k 1, sl 1, k 2 tog, psso, k 1, yo, k 3, repeat from * across row, end k 2.

Row 5: K 3, * yo, sl 1, k 2 tog, psso, yo, k 5, repeat from * across row, end k 3.

Row 6: Purl.

Repeat Rows 1-6 for Pattern Stitch.

315. Multiple of 13 stitches plus 2.

Row 1: * P 2, (k 1, yo) 10 times, k 1, repeat from * across row, end p 2.

Row 2: * K 2, p 2 tog, p 17, p 2 tog, repeat from * across row, end k 2.

Row 3: * P 2, sl 1, k 1, psso, k 15, k 2 tog, repeat from * across row, end p 2.

Row 4: * K 2, p 2 tog, p 13, p 2 tog, repeat from * across row, end k 2.

Row 5: * P 2, sl 1, k 1, psso, k 11, k 2 tog, repeat from * across row, end p 2.

Row 6: * K 2, p 2 tog, p 9, p 2 tog, repeat from * across row, end k 2.

Repeat Rows 1-6 for Pattern Stitch.

316. Multiple of 10 stitches plus 5.

Rows 1,3,9,11: Knit.

Rows 2,4,6,8,10,12: Purl.

Row 5: K 5, * insert needle into a st 5 rows below 3rd st from left needle and pull up a lp, k 5, pull up a lp from the same st below, k 5, repeat from * across row.

Row 6: P 4, * p 2 tog, p 5, p 2 tog, p 3, repeat from * across row, end p 4.

Row 7: K 7, * pull up a lp from st below where loops were made in row 5, place on left needle and k thru back lp and front of next st tog, k 9, repeat from * across row, end k 7.

Repeat Rows 5-12 for Pattern Stitch.

317. Multiple of 6 stitches plus 1.
Row 1: K 1, * yo, k 2 tog, k 1, k 2 tog, yo, k 1, repeat from * across row.
Rows 2,4: Purl.
Row 3: K 1, * yo, k 1, p 3 tog, k 1, yo, k 1, repeat from * across.

318. Multiple of 5 stitches plus 2.
Row 1: K 2, * yo, k 1, repeat from * across row, end k 2.
Row 2: P 2, * drop yo, p 1, repeat from * across row, end p 2.
Row 3: K 1, * sl 2, k 2 tog, pass 2 sl sts over last st, (k 1, p 1, k 1, p 1) in next st, repeat from * across row, end k 1.
Rows 4,5,6: Purl.
Repeat Rows 1-6 for Pattern Stitch.

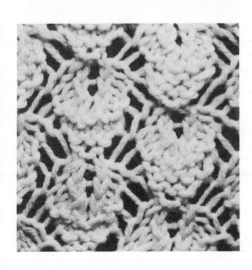

319. Multiple of 12 stitches.
Row 1: * Sl 1, k 1, psso, k 3, yo, p 2, yo, k 3, k 2 tog, repeat from * across row.
Row 2: * P 2 tog, p 2, yo, k 4, yo, p 2, p 2 tog, repeat from * across row.
Row 3: * Sl 1, k 1, psso, k 1, yo, k 6, yo, k 1, k 2 tog, repeat from * across row.
Row 4: * P 2 tog, yo, k 8, yo, p 2 tog, repeat from * across row.
Row 5: * P 1, yo, k 3, k 2 tog, sl 1, k 1, psso, k 3, yo, p 1, repeat from * across row.
Row 6: * k 2, yo, p 2, p 2 tog, p 2 tog, p 2, yo, k 2, repeat from * across row.
Row 7: * P 3, yo, k 1, k 2 tog, sl 1, k 1, psso, k 1, yo, p 3, repeat from * across row.
Row 8: * K 4, yo, p 2 tog, p 2 tog, yo, k 4, repeat from * across row.
Repeat Rows 1-8 for Pattern Stitch

Crochet

Afghan
Stitch Patterns

This type of stitch has amazing body. It is sturdy and durable, and can be depended upon to hold its original shape for a long time. Afghan Crochet patterns resist spreading, which is an important consideration if you are going to make a jacket, coat or closely fitted garment. These stitches are also appropriate for making afghans because the stitches lie close together, providing extra warmth.

The stitches will be flat rather than textured like popcorn and cluster stitches which have raised designs. Because of this flatness, it is very easy to apply embroidered designs after the item has been completed. Pillows are great fun to make in Afghan Crochet, and they really hold up after many cleanings or washings. You might want to experiment by using an Afghan pattern and weaving with tapestry needle for an unusual look (See Pattern 337).

320. *Row 1:* Hold all lps on hook, sk first ch, pull up lp in each ch across, end yo and pull thru 1 lp, * yo and pull thru 2 lps, repeat from * across to last lp on hook.

Row 2: Hook under 1 vertical bar and next horizontal bar and pull up lp and work same in each st across. Work off lps as before.

Repeat Row 2 for Pattern Stitch.

321. *Row 1:* Hold all lps on hook, sk first ch, pull up lp in each st across row, end yo, pull thru 1 lp, * yo and thru 2 lps, repeat from * across row to within last lp on hook.

Row 2: Hook into center of horizontal bars, pull up lp in each st across row. End and work off as before.

Repeat Row 2 for Pattern Stitch.

322. *Row 1:* See Pat. No. 320.
Row 2: Dc (hold back last lp on hook) under each horizontal bar across row. Work lps off as before.
Row 3: Pull up lp under each horizontal bar across row, work lps off as before.
Repeat Rows 2 and 3 for Pattern Stitch.

323. *Row 1:* See Pat. No. 320.
Row 2: In center of 2 vertical bars, pull up lp, yo and thru lp, pull up lp, yo and thru lp in center of each 2 vertical sts across. Work lps off as before.
Repeat Row 2 for Pattern Stitch.

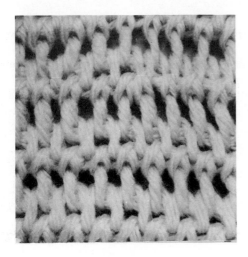

324. *Row 1:* See Pat. No. 320.
Row 2: Sk 1, * sc under each horizontal bar, repeat from * across row, work lps off as before.
Row 3: Sk 1, pull up lp in sp between each sc. Work lps off as before.

325. *Row 1:* Keep all lps on hook, sk first ch, pull up lp in each ch across, yo, pull thru first lp, * yo, pull thru next 2 lps, repeat from * across.

Row 2: Sk first bar, pull up lp under next bar and in each bar across, work lps off as before.

Repeat Row 2 for Pattern Stitch.

326. *Row 1:* Keep all lps on hook, sk first ch from hook, (lp on hook) in first st, pull up lp in each ch across, yo and pull thru first lp, * yo and pull thru next 2 lps, repeat from * across to within last lp.

Row 2: Keep all lps on hook, sk first bar, pull up lp under next bar and under each bar across. Work off lps as before.

Repeat Row 2 for Pattern Stitch.

327. *Row 1:* Hold all lps on hook, sk first ch, pull up lp in each ch across row, end yo and pull thru 1 lp, * yo and pull thru 2 lps, repeat from * across to within last lp on hook.

Row 2: Hook into each top horizontal bar, pull up lp in each st across. Work off lps as before.

Repeat Row 2 for Pattern Stitch.

328. *Row 1:* See Pat. No. 320.
Row 2: Dc in top of each st across row (hold lp of each st on hook). Work off as before.
Row 3: Sk 1, pull up lp between each dc, work lps off as before.
Repeat Rows 2 and 3 for Pattern Stitch.

329. *Row 1:* See Pat. No. 320.
Row 2: Insert hook from back to front in first sp, pull up lp, working from back to front, pull up lp in each sp across. Work off as before.
Repeat Row 2 for Pattern Stitch.

330. *Row 1:* See Pat. No. 320.
Row 2: Pull up lp in first sp and take off hook, twist around with fingers and replace on hook, repeat in each sp across, work off as before.
Repeat Rows 1 and 2 for Pattern Stitch.

331. *Row 1:* See Pat. No. 320.
Row 2: Hook into each vertical bar on wrong side, pull up lp, yo and thru 2 lps. Work off each lp as before. Ch 1.
Repeat Row 2 for Pattern Stitch.

332. *Row 1:* See Pat. No. 320.
Row 2: In first st (2 dc, dc and pull up lp and thru all 3 dc), * dc in next 3 sps, in next st (2 dc, dc and pull lp thru all dcs), repeat from * across, end dc in last 3 sps. Work off lps as before.
Row 3: Dc between vertical bars, hold last lp of each dc on hook. Work lps off as before.
Repeat Rows 2 and 3 for Pattern Stitch.

333. *Row 1:* Sk 3 chs, * hdc in next ch, sc in next ch, repeat from * across, end sc in last ch, ch 1, turn.
Row 2: Sk 1, pull up lp in top of each st across. Work off: yo and thru 1 lp, * yo and thru 2 lps, repeat from * across, end ch 1. Do not turn.
Row 3: Sk 1, * hdc in next st, sc in next st, repeat from * across row, end ch 1, turn.
Repeat Rows 2 and 3 for Pattern Stitch.

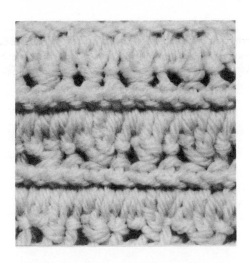

334. *Row 1:* See Pat. No. 320.
Row 2: In each sp, * pull up lp, yo and thru lp, yo and thru lp, in same st pull up lp, yo and thru lp, yo and thru 2 lps, in next sp, pull up lp, yo and thru lp, yo and thru all lps, repeat from * across. Work off lps as before.
Repeat Rows 1 and 2 for Pattern Stitch.

335. *Row 1:* See Pat. No. 320.
Row 2: (Hold on hook last lp of each hdc, work hdc under horizontal bar in each st across). Work off lps as before.
Row 3: Sk first st, pull up lp under bar between each hdc, work off lps as before.
Repeat Rows 2 and 3 for Pattern Stitch.

336. *Row 1:* Sk 3 chs, dc in each ch across, ch 1, turn.
Row 2: Sk 1 st, pull up lp in each dc across row, pull up lp in turning ch. Work off: yo and thru 1 lp, * yo and thru 2 lps, repeat from * across row. Ch 2. Do not turn.
Row 3: Work 1 dc in each st across row, ch 1, turn.
Repeat Rows 2 and 3 for Pattern Stitch.

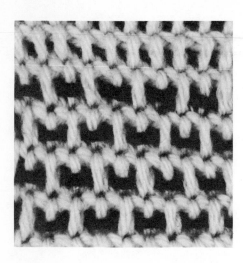

337. *Row 1:* See Pat. No. 320.
Row 2: Pull up lp in each st, work off lps as before.
Repeat Row 2 for Pattern Stitch.
Weaving: Thread tapestry needle or tie around a safety pin one or two strands of yarn and work over first st, * under next st, over next st, repeat from * across row. Be sure yarn is long enough to weave at least 2 rows before using another strand of yarn. Always end a row on the same side you started. Tack loose ends on wrong side. Use a back stitch and sew ends on wrong side.

338. *Row 1:* See Pat. No. 320.
Row 2: Insert hook (under each vertical bar and thru center of next horizontal bar, pull up lp, yo and thru lp) across row. Work off lps as before.
Row 3: Insert hook under each vertical bar, pull up lp (hold lps on hook), work off as before.
Repeat Rows 2 and 3 for Pattern Stitch.

Lace
Stitch Patterns

These are exquisite crochets of delicate, open-work patterns. It is easy to make many of these classical "old-fashioned" patterns into something new. Choose bright and cheery colors which will show off the airy, filigree textures of the design. A word of caution: Lace stitches tend to loosen up and stretch, so always be sure your stitch gauge is correct.

Choose Lace Crochets for their special ornamental quality. Shawls, sweaters and party dresses show off these lovely designs. The lighter weight yarns are especially good for Lace Patterns, for they emphasize their beauty and delicacy.

Although Lace patterns may look more complicated than some of the other designs, don't be hesitant about trying them. They are really just as simple to stitch and usually require about the same amount of time.

339. Multiple of 3 stitches plus 2.

Row 1: 2 dc in 3rd ch from hook, * ch 2, sk 2, 2 dc in next ch, repeat from * across row. End 2 dc in last ch, ch 2, turn.

Row 2: Sk 1, hdc in next dc, * 2 hdc in ch-2 sp, hdc in next 2 dc, repeat from * across row. End ch 2, turn.

Row 3: Sk 1, 2 dc in next hdc, * ch 2, sk 3, 2 dc in next hdc, repeat from * across row. End ch 2, turn.

Repeat Rows 2 and 3 for Pattern Stitch.

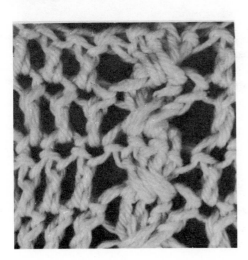

340. Multiple of 12 stitches plus 7.

Row 1: Dc in 4th ch from hook (counts as 2 dc), dc in each of next 2 chs, * sk next 2 chs, dc in next 2 chs; work over these two dc, work dc in first skipped ch, dc in 2nd skipped ch (4 cross stitches), dc in next 8 chs, repeat from * across, end last dc in last 4 chs, turn.

Row 2: Ch 3 (counts as 1 dc), sk first dc, dc in next 3 sts, * sk next 2 dc, dc in next 2 dc, work over these 2 dc, dc in first dc, dc in 2nd skipped dc, dc in next 8 dc, repeat from * across row. End last repeat with dc in last 4 dc, turn.

Repeat Row 2 for Pattern Stitch.

341. Multiple of 8 stitches plus 2.
Row 1: Dc in 4th ch from hook, dc in next ch, * ch 2, sk 2, dc in next st, ch 2, sk 2, 1 dc in next 3 sts, repeat from * across row, end ch 3, turn.
Row 2: 1 dc in next 2 dc, * ch 2, dc in next dc, ch 2, 1 dc in next 3 dc, repeat from * across row, work last dc in last ch, ch 3, turn.
Repeat Row 2 for Pattern Stitch.

342. Multiple of 7 stitches plus 1.
Row 1: Dc in 4th ch from hook, * sk next 2 chs, work dc in next st, ch 2, dc in same st (V st), sk next 2 chs, dc in each of next 2 chs, repeat from * across row.
Row 2: Ch 3 (counts as 1 dc), dc in next st, * dc in ch-2 sp of V st (shell made), dc in each of next 2 dc, repeat from * across row. End dc in dc, and dc in top of turning ch.
Row 3: Ch 3 (counts as 1 dc), dc in next dc, * V st of dc, ch 2, dc in center dc of shell, dc in next 2 dc, repeat from * across row, turn.
Repeat Rows 2 and 3 for Pattern Stitch.

343. Multiple of 6 stitches plus 3.
Row 1: Sk 2 chs, dc in next ch, * ch 1, 1 dc in next 3 sts, ch 2, 1 dc in next 3 sts, repeat from * across row, end ch 1, 2 dc, ch 3, turn.
Row 2: * (2 tr, ch 1, 2 tr) in ch-2 sp (1 tr, ch 2, 1 tr in ch-1 sp), repeat from * across row. End 1 tr in turning ch, ch 3, turn.
Repeat Row 2 for Pattern Stitch.

344. Multiple of 7 stitches plus 4.
Row 1: 3 dc in 3rd ch from hook, sk 2 chs, sc in next ch, * ch 3, sk 3, 3 dc in next ch, sk 2, sc in next ch, repeat from *, end 3 dc in last ch, ch 3, turn.
Row 2: 3 dc in first dc, * sc in ch 3 sp, ch 3, 3 dc in next dc, repeat from *, end sc in turning ch, ch 3, turn.
Repeat Row 2 for Pattern Stitch.

345. Multiple of 7 stitches plus 4.
Row 1: 1 dc in 2nd ch from hook, sk 2 chs, 3 dc in next st, * ch 3, sk 3, dc in next st, sk 2, 3 dc in next st, repeat from * across row, end ch 1, turn.
Row 2: 1 dc in first dc, 3 dc in next dc, * ch 3, 1 dc in ch-3sp, 3 dc in next dc, repeat from * across row, end ch 1, turn.
Repeat Row 2 for Pattern Stitch.

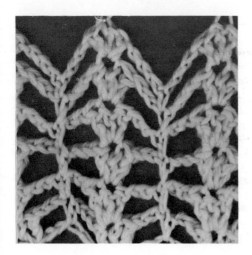

346. Multiple of 6 stitches plus 1.
Row 1: 3 dc (shell) in 3rd ch from hook, * ch 3, sk 2 chs, sc in next st, ch 3, sk 2 chs, shell in next st, repeat from * across row, end ch 3, turn.
Row 2: 2 dc in center of first shell, * ch 3, sc in sc, ch 3, shell in center of next shell, repeat from * across row, end ch 3, turn.
Repeat Row 2 for Pattern Stitch.

347. Multiple of 6 stitches plus 4.
Row 1: 2 dc, ch 1, 2 dc in 5th ch from hook, * ch 1, sk 2 chs, dc in next ch (post), ch 1, sk 2 chs, 2 dc, ch 1, 2 dc in next ch, repeat from * across row, end ch 1, sk 2 chs, dc in end st, ch 4, turn.
Row 2: * 2 dc, ch 1, 2 dc under ch-1 sp in center of next shell, ch 1, dc in next post, ch 1, repeat from * across row, end ch 1, dc in end st, ch 4, turn.
Repeat Row 2 for Pattern Stitch.

348. Multiple of 4 stitches.
Row 1: 1 sc in each ch across row, ch 3, turn (ch 3 counts as first dc and ch 1 sp).
Row 2: Sk next dc, 1 dc in next st, * ch 1, sk 1, dc in next st, repeat from * across row, end ch 1, turn.
Row 3: Sk first st, 1 sc in each st across row, ending 1 sc in top of 2nd st of turning ch, ch 1, turn.
Row 4: Repeat Row 1.
Row 5: Repeat Row 2.
Row 6: Repeat Row 3.
Repeat these 6 Rows for Pattern Stitch.

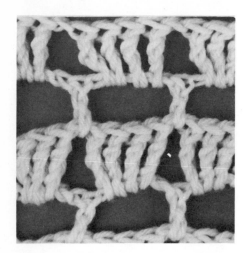

349. Multiple of 5 stitches plus 3.
Row 1: Tr in 4th ch from hook, 1 tr in next 2 chs, * ch 1, sk 1, tr in next 4 chs, repeat from * across row, end ch 4, turn.
Row 2: * dc in ch-1 sp of previous row, * ch 4, end 1 dc in turning ch, ch 4, turn.
Row 3: Work 3 tr in first ch-sp, * work 4 tr, ch 1, in each ch-lp across, repeat from * across row and end ch 4, turn.
Repeat Rows 2 and 3 for Pattern Stitch.

350. Multiple of 11 stitches.
Row 1: 1 sc in 2nd ch from hook and in each remaining ch, ch 6, turn.
Row 2: Sk 2 sc, work 1 tr in each of next 2 sc, * ch 2, sk 2 sc, work 1 tr in each of next 2 sc, repeat from * across row, ending sk 2 sc, 1 tr, ch 3, turn.
Row 3: In first ch-sp (yo, draw up lp in same sp) 3 times, yo and draw thru all lps on hook, ch 1 (puff st made), work another puff st, * ch 1, work 2 puff sts in next ch-2 sp, repeat from * across row, ending 2 puff sts in next ch-2 sp, repeat from * across row, ending 2 puff sts and 1 dc in last ch-6 sp, end ch 6, turn.
Row 4: Sk 2 puff sts, 2 tr in next sp, * ch 2, 2 tr in next sp, repeat from * across row, ending ch 2, 1 tr in ch-3 sp, ch 3, turn.
Repeat Rows 3 and 4 for Pattern Stitch.

351. Multiple of 4 stitches plus 1.
Row 1: (2 dc, ch 1, 2 dc) shell in 3rd ch from hook, * sk 3 chs, shell in next ch, repeat from * across row, end ch 3, turn.
Row 2: Dc in 2nd dc, * ch 1, dc in next 4 dc, repeat from * across row, end ch 3, turn.
Row 3: Shell in each ch-1 sp across row, ch 3, turn.
Repeat Rows 2 and 3 for Pattern Stitch.

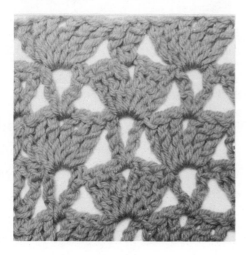

352. Multiple of 10 stitches plus 2.
Row 1: 1 tr in 6th ch from hook, * sk 4 chs, work (3 tr, ch 1, 3 tr) in next ch (shell), sk 4 chs, work (1 tr, ch 1, 1 tr) in next ch (V st), repeat from * across row, ending 1 V, ch 4, turn.
Row 2: Work 2 tr in first V sp (half shell), * work 1 V in sp of next shell, work 1 shell in sp of next V, repeat from * across row, ending 3 tr (half shell) instead of shell in last sp, ch 5, turn.
Row 3: Work 1 tr in first st, * work a shell in sp of next V, work a V in sp of next shell, repeat from * across row, ending with last V in top of turning ch, ch 4, turn.
Repeat Rows 2 and 3 for Pattern Stitch.

353. Multiple of 4 stitches plus 1.

Row 1: Sk first 3 chs, * make 1 sc, ch 3, sc in same st (group), ch 3, sk 3, repeat from * across row, end sc in last ch, turn.

Row 2: * ch 4, group in center ch of ch-3 sp, insert hook in front lp, sk 1 group, repeat from * across row, end ch 3, sc in last 3 ch-groups.

Repeat Row 2 for Pattern Stitch.

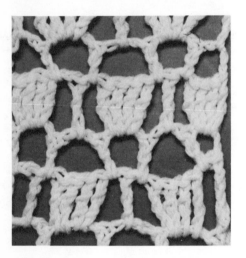

354. Multiple of 4 stitches plus 1.

Row 1: 1 dc in 7th ch from hook, * ch 3, sk 3 chs, 1 dc in next st, repeat from * across row, end ch 4, turn.

Row 2: Tr in first arch, * ch 1, 4 tr in next arch, ch 1, tr in next arch, repeat from * across, end ch 3, turn.

Row 3: Dc in first ch-sp, * ch 3, dc in next ch-sp, repeat from * across row, end ch 4, turn.

Repeat Rows 2 and 3 for Pattern Stitch. When repeat Row 2 work groups of trs over single trs, then reverse.

355. Multiple of 10 stitches plus 5.

Row 1: Ch 2, 1 tr in 3rd and 4th chs from hook, * sk 3 sts, (2 tr, ch 2, 2 tr) in next st, sk 3 sts, 1 tr in next 3 sts, repeat from * across row, end tr in last 3 sts, ch 2, turn.

Row 2: Sk first tr, 2 tr in next 2 tr, * (2 tr, ch 2, 2 tr) in next ch-2 sp of previous row, tr in each of next 3 tr, repeat from * across row, end ch 2, turn.

Repeat Row 2 for Pattern Stitch.

356. Multiple of 2 stitches plus 1.
Row 1: 1 tr in 5th ch from hook, * ch 1, sk 1, tr in next ch, repeat from * across row, ch 4, turn. Turning ch counts as 1 tr.
Row 2: 1 tr in first ch, * 2 tr in next sp, repeat from * across, ch 4, turn.
Row 3: 1 tr between first and second groups, * ch 1, tr between next 2 groups, repeat from * across row, end tr in turning ch, ch 4, turn.
Repeat Rows 2 and 3 for Pattern Stitch.

357. Multiple of 4 stitches plus 2.
Row 1: Hdc in 2nd ch from hook, hdc in next ch, * ch 2, sk 2, hdc in next 2 chs, repeat from * across, end ch 1, turn.
Row 2: Hdc in first 2 hdc, * ch 2, sk 2, hdc in next 2 hdc, ch 1, turn. repeat from * across row,
Repeat Row 2 for Pattern Stitch.

358. Multiple of 7 stitches plus 1.
Row 1: Dc in 4th ch from hook (counts as 2 dc) * sk 2 chs, V st in next ch (dc, ch 2, dc), sk 2 chs, dc in next 2 chs, ch 3, turn.
Row 2: Ch 3 (counts as first dc), dc in next dc, * V st under ch-2 of next V st, 1 dc in next 2 sts, repeat from * across, end 1 dc in each of last 2 sts, ch 3, turn.
Row 3: Repeat Row 2.
Row 4: Dc in next dc, * ch 4, sk V st, 1 dc in next 2 dcs, repeat from * across row, end 1 dc in each of next 2 dc, ch 3, turn.
Rows 5,6: Repeat Row 4.
Row 7: Dc in next dc, * go under all ch-4 lps of rows 4, 5, 6 work long V st in V st of Row 3 (tr, ch 2, tr in same sp), 1 dc in next 2 dcs; repeat from * across, end dc in last 2 dcs, ch 3, turn.
Row 8: Repeat Row 2.
Repeat Rows 2-8 for Pattern Stitch.

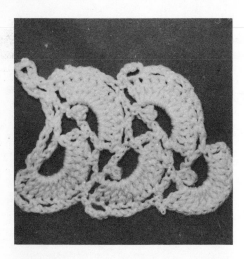

359. *Row 1:* Sc in 7th ch from hook, (ch 3, sk 2 chs, sc in next ch) twice, ch 5, sc in 4th ch from hook, ch 1, *picot-lp made,* sk 2 chs, sc in next ch; leave last 3 chs free, ch 7, turn.

Row 2: Sk p-lp, sc in center ch of next ch-3 lp, ch 3, turn.

Row 3: Make 13 dc in ch-7 lp (Shell), sk 2 chs of starting ch, sc in last ch, ch 4, turn.

Row 4: Sk first 2 sts, sc in next dc, (ch 3, sk 2 dc, sc in next dc) 3 times, ch 3, sk 2 dc, sc in top of ch-3, ch 5, sc in 4th ch from hook, ch 1 *(p-lp),* sc in center of next free ch-3 lp, do not work over remaining sts, ch 7, turn.

Row 5: Sk p-lp, sc in center of next ch-3 lp, ch 3, turn.

Row 6: 13 dc in ch-7 lp (shell made), sc in 2nd ch of next free ch-lp, ch 4, turn.

Repeat Rows 4-6 for Pattern Stitch.

360. Multiple of 6 stitches.

Row 1: Sk 5 ch, tr in next ch, sk 2, * 1 tr in next ch, ch 2, tr in same ch, sk 2 chs, repeat from * across, end ch 3, turn.

Row 2: Work groups of 4 tr in each ch-2 sp of previous row, ch 4, turn.

Row 3: 1 tr in base of 4th ch, * (tr, ch 2, tr) between each 4 tr group of previous row, repeat from * across row, end 1 tr in base of last group, ch 4, turn.

Row 4: Work groups of 4 tr in each ch-2sp, ch 4, turn.

Repeat Rows 3 and 4 for Pattern Stitch.

361. Multiple of 6 stitches plus 1.

Row 1: (Yo, pull up lp, draw thru 2 lps) 3 times, yo and thru all lps on hook for half cluster in 4th ch from hook, * ch 1, sk 5 chs, work half cluster, ch 3, sl st, half cluster all in next ch, repeat from * across, end ch 4, turn.

Row 2: Cluster in each ch-1 sp across row, dtr in the base of cluster of previous row, ch 1, turn.

Row 3: Sc in sp before cluster, * sc in top of next cluster, sc between clusters, sc in top of next cluster, ch 3, repeat from * across, end ch 1, turn.

Rows 4,5,6: 1 hdc in each st across row, end ch 1, turn.

Row 7: Ch 2, cluster in first hdc, * ch 1, sk 5 sps, cluster in hdc, repeat from * across row, end ch 6, turn.

Repeat Rows 2-7 for Pattern Stitch.

362. Even number of stitches.
Row 1: Hdc in 3rd ch from hook, hdc in each ch across, end ch 5, turn.
Row 2: Sl st in 2nd hdc, * ch 5, sk 1, sl st in next hdc, repeat from * across row, end hdc in top of turning ch, ch 3, turn.
Row 3: Sc in top of ch-5, * ch 2, sc in 3rd ch of ch-5 group, repeat from * across row, end sc in 3rd ch of turning ch-5.
Row 4: Ch 5, * sl st in next sc, ch 5, repeat from * across, end ch 3, hdc in last st, ch 4, turn.
Row 5: * sc in 3rd ch of ch-5, ch 2, repeat from * across, end ch 3, hdc in last st, ch 4, turn.
Row 5: * sc in 3rd ch of ch-5, ch 2, repeat from * across, end ch 1, turn.
Row 6: Hdc in first sc, * hdc in ch-2 sp, hdc in next sc, repeat from * across, end ch 1, turn.
Row 7-12: Sc in each st across row, end ch 1, turn.
Repeat Rows 1-12 for Pattern Stitch.

363. Multiple of 13 stitches.
Row 1: 1 dc in 2nd ch from hook, 1 dc in next st, * ch 3, sk 3, 1 dc in next 3 sts, repeat from * across, end ch 3, sk 3, 2 dc in next 2 sts, ch 1, turn.
Row 2: 1 dc in first st, * 5 dc in ch-3 sp, sk 1 dc, 1 dc in next st, repeat from * across row, end ch 2, turn.
Row 3: Dc in first 2 dc, * ch 3, dc in last dc of next dc group, dc in next 2 dc, repeat from * across row, end ch 3, turn.
Repeat Rows 2 and 3 for Pattern Stitch.

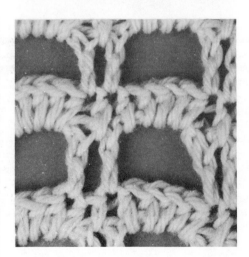

364. Multiple of 4 stitches plus 1.
Row 1: Dc in 3rd ch from hook, * ch 3, sk 2 sts, dc in next 2 chs, repeat from * across row, end ch 2, turn.
Row 2: Dc in 2nd dc, * 5 hdc in ch-3 sp, hdc between next 2 dc, repeat from * across row, end hdc in turning ch, ch 2, turn.
Row 3: Dc in base of turning ch, * ch 3, dc in last hdc of 5 hdc group, dc in next sp, repeat from * across, end dc in turning ch, ch 3, turn.
Repeat Rows 2 and 3 for Pattern Stitch.

365. Multiple of 6 stitches plus 5.

Row 1: Hold on hook last lp of each dc, dc in 7th ch from hook, (sk 1, dc in next ch) 2 times; * yo and thru all lps on hook (cluster); ch 3, sk 1 hdc in next ch, ch 3, (sk 1, work a cluster), repeat from * across, end with cluster, ch 3, sk 1, hdc in last ch, ch 1, turn.

Row 2: Sc in first hdc, * ch 7, sc in hdc, repeat from * across, end with ch 7, sk 3 sts of turning ch, sc in next ch, ch 1, turn.

Row 3,4: Sc in first sc, * ch 7, sc in next sc, repeat from * across row, ch 6, turn.

Row 5: * 3 dc with ch-1 between dcs in tip of cluster 4 rows down (working over the 3 ch-7s below), ch 1 hdc in next ch 1, repeat from * across, end hdc in last sc, ch 6, turn.

Row 6: * cluster in next 3 dc, ch 3, hdc in hdc, ch 3, repeat from * across, end cluster, ch 3, sk 3 chs of turning ch, hdc in next ch, ch 1, turn.

Repeat Rows 2-6 for Pattern Stitch.

366. Multiple of 6 stitches plus 1.

Row 1: In 5th ch from hook * (dc, ch 1, dc) V st made, ch 2, sk 2, dc in next, ch 2, sk 2, repeat from * across row, end dc in last st, ch 3, turn.

Row 2: Work dc in each ch sp and in each dc across row, ch 5, turn.

Row 3: * sk 2 dc, V st in next dc, ch 2, sk 2, dc in next dc, repeat from * across row, ch 3, turn.

Repeat Rows 2 and 3 for Pattern Stitch.

367. Multiple of 2 stitches plus 1.

Row 1: Dc in 6th ch from hook, * ch 1, sk 1, dc in next ch, repeat from * across, turn.

Row 2: Ch 4, dc in 2nd dc, * ch 3, dc in next 5 dc, ch 3, dc in next dc, ch 1, dc in next dc, repeat from * across 4 times more, ending last dc in 2nd ch of turning ch. Turn.

Row 3: Ch 4, dc in 2nd dc, * ch 4 loosely, sk 2 dc, sc in next dc, ch 4, sk next 2 dc, dc in next dc, ch 1, dc in next dc, repeat from * 4 times more, ending last dc in 2nd ch of turning ch. Turn.

Row 4: Ch 5, dc in 2nd dc, * ch 9, dc in next dc, ch 1, dc in next dc, repeat from * across, end dc in turning ch. Turn.

Row 5: Ch 5, dc in 2nd dc, * ch 5, sc in 5th ch of ch-9, sk rest of ch-9, dc in next 2 dc, repeat from * across, end dc in turning ch. Turn.

Row 6: Ch 4, dc in 2nd dc, * ch 3, sk 2 chs, dc in next ch, (ch 1, dc) in each of next 2 chs of same ch, ch 1, dc in next 2 dc, repeat from * across, end dc in turning ch, turn.

Row 7: Ch 4, dc in 2nd dc, * ch 1, dc in next dc, repeat from * across, end ch 1, dc in 2nd ch of turning ch.

Repeat Rows 2-7 for Pattern Stitch.

368. Even number of stitches.
Row 1: 1 sc in 9th ch from hook, * ch 6, sk 5 chs, sc in next ch, repeat from * across row, end ch 6, sk 5 sts, sc in last ch.
Row 2: Ch 6, turn, * 1 sc under next ch-6 lp, ch 6, repeat from * across row, ending sc in center of ch-8 lp.
Row 3: Ch 6, turn, sc under next ch-6 lp, ch 6, repeat from * across row.
Repeat Row 3 for Pattern Stitch.

369. Multiple of 13 stitches.
Row 1: 2 tr in 4th ch from hook (leaf made), * ch 1, sk 5 chs, in next ch work (2 tr, ch 3, sl st, ch 3, 2 tr) 2 leaves made, repeat from * across, ending ch 1, sk 5 chs, in next ch work (2 tr, ch 3, sl st) ch 6, turn.
Row 2: * in ch 1 between next 2 leaves, work 2 tr, ch 3, sl st, ch 3, 2 tr (clover) ch 1, repeat from * across, sk last ch, ending dtr in ch at base of last leaf, ch 1, turn.
Row 3: Work (sl st, ch 2, 2 tr) in dtr, * ch 1, sk 2 leaves, in ch-1 sp between clovers, work 2 tr, ch 3, sl st, ch 3, 2 tr, repeat from * across, end ch 1, work (2 tr, ch 3, sl st) in top of turning ch-6. Ch 6, turn.
Repeat Rows 2 and 3 for Pattern Stitch.

370. Multiple of 8 stitches plus 7.
Row 1: Sc in 2nd ch from hook, sc in next 3 chs, * ch 5, sk 3, sc in next 5 chs, repeat from * across, end with ch 3, sc in last 4 chs, ch 1, turn.
Row 2: Sc in first 3 sc, * ch 3, sc in next lp, ch 3, sk 1, sc in next 3 sc, repeat from * across, end with ch 3, sc in last 3 sc, ch 1, turn.
Row 3: Sc in first 2 sc, * ch 3, sc in next lp, sc in next sc, sc in next lp, ch 3, sk 1 sc, sc in sc, repeat from * across, end ch 3, sc in last 2 sc, ch 3, turn.
Row 4: Dc in next sc, ch 3, * sc in next lp, sc in next 3 sc, sc in next lp, ch 5, repeat from * across, end ch 3, dc in last 2 sc, ch 1, turn.
Row 5: Sc in 2 dc, * ch 3, sk 1 sc, sc in next 3 sc, ch 3, sc in next lp, repeat from * across, end ch 3, sc in dc, sc in top of turning ch, ch 1, turn.
Row 6: Sc in 2 sc, * sc in next lp, ch 3, sk 1 sc, sc in next sc, ch 3, sc in next lp, sc in sc, repeat from * across, end ch 3, sc in next lp, sc in last 2 sc, ch 1, turn.
Row 7: Sc in 3 sc, sc in next lp, * ch 5, sc in lp, sc in 3 sc, sc in lp, repeat from * across, end sc in last lp, sc in last 3 sc, ch 1, turn.
Repeat Rows 2-7 for Pattern Stitch.

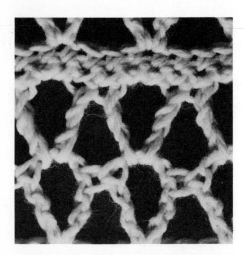

371. Multiple of 7 stitches plus 1.
Row 1: Sk 1, sc in each ch across.
Row 2: Sc in each sc, turn.
Row 3: Ch 6, sk 2 sc, in next sc (tr, ch 3, tr) shell, * sk 3 sc, shell in next sc, repeat from * across row, end sk 2, sc, tr in last sc.
Rows 4,5: Ch 6, * shell in center st of next shell, repeat from * across row, end ch 1, turn.
Row 6: Sc in turning ch, sc in tr, * 2 sc in ch 3 sp, sc in next 2 tr, repeat from * across row, end sc in turning ch, ch 1, turn.
Row 7: Repeat Row 2.
Repeat Rows 3-7 for Pattern Stitch.

372. Multiple of 6 stitches.
Row 1: Dc in 2nd ch from hook, in same ch make knot st * (insert hook into same ch and pull up a lp, yo and thru loop on hook, insert hook into same ch, draw up a lp, yo and thru all lps on hook) twice, sk 5 chs, dc in next ch, repeat from *, end completed knot st, ch 5, turn.
Row 2: * Dc in lp between knot st, chain 3, sl st in top of dc (picot), ch 5, repeat from * to end, ch 5, turn.
Row 3: * Knot st in 3rd ch of ch 5, ch 5, repeat from * end ch 5, turn.
Row 4: * Dc in 3rd ch of ch 5 lp, ch 3, sl st in top of dc, ch 5, repeat from *, end ch 5, turn.
Repeat Rows 2-4 for Pattern Stitch.

373. Multiple of 4 stitches plus 2.
Row 1: 1 tr in 5th ch from hook, * yo 2 times, insert hook into next ch and draw through, yo and thru 2 lps, yo, sk 2, insert hook into next ch and draw through, (yo and draw thru 2 lps) 4 times, ch 2, 1 tr into center of cross, repeat from * to within last 2 chs, 1 tr into next 2 chs, ch 4, turn.
Row 2: Sk 1 tr, 1 tr into next tr, * yo 2 times, insert hook into next st and draw thru, yo and thru 2 lps, yo, sk 2, hook into next st and draw thru (yo and thru 2 lps) 4 times, ch 2, 1 tr in center of cross, repeat from *, ending with 1 tr in next tr, 1 tr into top of ch 4, ch 4, turn.
Repeat Row 2 for Pattern Stitch.

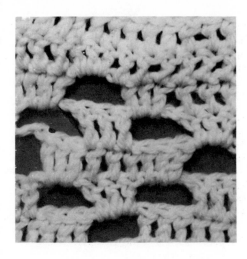

374. Multiple of 2 stitches plus 8.

Row 1: Dc in 4th ch from hook and in each ch across row, ch 3, turn.

Row 2: Sk first dc, dc in next 6 dc, * ch 3, sk 3 dc, dc in next 9 dc, repeat from * across row, end ch 3, sk 3 dc, dc in next 6 dc, dc in top of turning ch, ch 3, turn.

Row 3: Sk first dc, * dc in next 3 dc, ch 3, sk 3 dc, 3 dc in next ch-3 sp, ch 3, sk 3 dc, repeat from * across row. End with dc in last 3 dc, dc in top of turning ch, ch 7, turn.

Row 4: Sk first 4 dc, * 3 dc in next sp, dc in next 3 dc, 3 dc in next sp, ch 3, sk 3 dc, repeat from * across row. End dc in top of turning ch, ch 3, turn.

Row 5: * 3 dc in next sp, ch 3, sk 3 dc, dc in next 3 dc, ch 3, sk 3 dc, repeat from * across row. End with 3 dc in turning ch-sp, dc in 3rd ch of same turning ch, ch 3, turn.

Row 6: Sk first dc, * dc in next 3 dc, 3 dc in next sp, ch 3, sk next 3 dc, 3 dc in next sp, repeat from * across row. End with dc in last 3 dc, dc in top of turning ch, ch 3, turn.

Row 7: Sk first dc, dc in next 6 dc, 3 dc in next sp, * dc in next 9 dc, 3 dc in next sp, repeat from * across row, end with dc in last 6 dc, dc in top of turning ch, ch 3, turn.

Row 8: Sk first dc, dc in next dc and in each dc across row, dc in top of turning ch, ch 3, turn.

Repeat Rows 2-8 for Pattern Stitch.

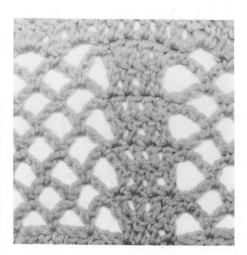

375. Multiple of 11 stitches plus 7.

Note: Be sure to count turning ch as first dc throughout pattern.

Row 1: 1 sc in 2nd ch from hook and in each ch across, ch 2, turn.

Row 2: Sk first sc, dc in each sc across row, end ch 2, turn.

Row 3: Sk first dc, dc in each of next 3 dc, * (ch 4, sk 2 dc, 1 sc in next dc) 3 times, ch 4, sk 2 dc, dc in each of next 4 dc, repeat from * across row, ending dc in each of last 3 dc, dc in top of turning ch, ch 2, turn.

Row 4: Sk first dc, dc in each of next 3 dc, * (sc under next ch-4 sp, ch 4) 3 times, dc under next ch-4 sp, dc in each of next 4 dc, repeat from * across, ending dc in each of last 3 dc, dc in top of turning ch, ch 2, turn.

Row 5: Sk first dc, dc in each of next 3 dc, sk next sc, * (ch 4, sc under next ch-4 sp) 3 times, ch 4, sk next sc, dc in each of next 4 dc, repeat from * across, ending dc in last 3 dc, dc in turning ch, ch 2, turn.

Row 6: Repeat Row 4.

Row 7: Repeat Row 5.

Row 8: Repeat Row 4.

Row 9: Repeat Row 5.

Row 10: Repeat Row 4.

Row 11: Sk first dc, dc in next 3 dc, * dc in next sc, 2 dc under ch-4 sp, dc in next 3 dc under ch-4 sp, dc in next sc, 2 dc under ch-4 sp, dc in next sc, dc in next 4 dc, repeat from * across, ending dc in last 3 dc, dc in turning ch, ch 2, turn.

Repeat Rows 3-11 for Pattern Stitch.

376. Multiple of 13 stitches.

Row 1: Dc in 4th ch from hook, sl st in next 3 chs, sk 1 ch, (dc, ch 1, tr, ch 1, dc) in next ch, * sk 1 ch, sl st in next 3 chs, sk 1 ch, (dc, ch 1, tr, ch 1, dc) in next ch, repeat from * across, ending sk 1 ch, sl st in next 3 chs, sk 1 ch, dc in next 2 chs, ch 1, turn.

Row 2: Dc in first st, * ch 5, dc in ch before tr of next pattern, sc in tr, dc in next ch after tr, repeat from * across, ending ch 5, dc in last st, ch 3, turn.

Row 3: Dc in first st, * sk 1, sl st in next 3 chs, sk 1 ch, dc in next st, tr in next, dc in next, repeat from * across, ending sk 1 ch, sl st in next 3 chs, dc in last st, ch 1, turn.

Row 4: Sl st in first st, * (dc, ch 1, tr, ch 1, dc) in 2nd sl st of group of 3 sl sts of previous row, sk 1 sl st in each of next 3 sts (dc, tr, dc of previous row), repeat from *, ending sl st in last st, ch 8, turn.

Row 5: * dc in ch before tr of previous row, sc in next tr, dc in next ch following tr, ch 5, repeat from * across, ending ch 2, tr in last st, ch 1, turn.

Row 6: Sl st in 2nd and 3rd sts from hook, * dc in next dc, tr in next sc, dc in next dc, sk 1 ch, sl st in next 3 sts, sk 1 ch, repeat from * across, ending dc in next dc, tr in next sc, dc in next dc, sk 1 ch, sl st in next 3 ch sts, ch 2, turn.

Row 7: Dc in first st, * sl st in the dc, tr and dc of previous row, sk 1 st, (dc, ch 1, tr, ch 1, dc) in 2nd sl st of 3 sl st group of previous row, sk 1 st, repeat from * across, ending sl st in dc, tr and dc of previous row, dc in last st, ch 2, turn.

Repeat Rows 2-7 for Pattern Stitch.

377. Multiple of 11 stitches plus 9.

Row 1: Sc in 2nd ch from hook and in each ch across, turn.

Row 2: Ch 4 (counts as 1 dc), sk first sc, dc in next sc, sk next 2 sc, * shell of 2 dc, ch 1, 2 dc in next sc, ch 3, sk next 4 sc, dc, ch 5, dc all in next sc (V) st made, ch 3, sk next 4 sc, repeat from * across, ending shell in next sc, sk 2 sc, dc in each of last 2 sc, turn.

Row 3: Ch 4 (dc), sk first dc, dc in next dc, * shell of 2 dc, ch 1, 2 dc in ch-1 sp of next shell, ch 3, cluster st in ch-5 sp (to make cluster, yo over hook twice, pull up lp in ch-5 sp, yo and thru 1 lp, yo and thru 2 lps, yo and pull up lp in same ch-5 sp, yo and thru 1 lp, (yo and thru 2 lps) twice, yo and thru 3 lps; (work cluster in same ch-5 sp) 4 times, ch 4, repeat from * across, end shell in ch-1 sp of last shell, dc in last dc, dc in turning ch.

Row 4: Ch 4 (dc), sk first dc, dc in next dc, * shell in ch-1 sp of next shell, ch 3, sk next ch-3, cluster in top of each cluster, ch 3, repeat from * across, end shell in ch-1 sp of last shell, dc in last dc and in top of turning ch.

Row 5: Ch 4 (dc), sk first dc, dc in next dc, * shell in ch-1 sp of next shell, (ch 3, dc, ch 1, dc) in center of cluster st, ch 3, repeat from * across, end shell in ch-1 sp of last shell, dc in last dc and dc in turning ch.

Row 6: Ch 4 (dc), sk first dc, dc in next, * shell in ch-1 sp of next shell, (sk next ch-3 sp, shell in next ch-3 sp) twice, sk next ch-3 sp, repeat from * across, end shell in ch-1 sp of last shell, dc in last dc and dc in turning ch.

Row 7: Ch 4 (dc), sk first dc, dc in next dc, * shell in ch-1 sp of next shell, repeat from * across, end dc in last dc and dc in turning ch.

Row 8: Ch 4 (dc), sk first dc, dc in next dc, * shell in ch-1 sp of next shell, ch 3, V st of dc, ch 5, dc in sp of next 2 shells, ch 3, repeat from * across, end shell in ch-1 sp of last shell, dc in last dc and dc in turning ch.

Repeat Rows 2-8 for Pattern Stitch.

378. Multiple of 4 stitches.

Row 1: In 4th ch from hook make picot (sc, ch 3, sc), * sk 3 chs, picot in next ch, repeat from *, end sk 3 chs, sc in last ch, ch-5 turn.

Row 2: Picot in 3rd ch of first ch 5 lp, ch 5, * picot in 3rd ch of next ch 5 lp, ch 5, repeat from *, ending sc in 3rd ch of turning ch, ch 5, turn.

Repeat Row 2 for Pattern Stitch.

379. Multiple of 7 stitches plus 1.

Row 1: Dc in 4th ch from hook, * (ch 2, sk 1, sc in next ch) twice, ch 2, sk 1 ch, dc in next 2 chs, repeat from * across row, turn.

Row 2: Ch 3, dc in 2nd dc, * ch 3, sc in 2nd ch 2 sp, ch 3, dc in next 2 dc, repeat from * across row, turn.

Row 3: Ch 3, dc in 2nd dc, * ch 2, sc in next ch-3 sp, ch 2, sc in next ch 3 sp, ch 2, dc in next 2 dc, repeat from * across row, turn.

Repeat Rows 2 and 3 for Pattern Stitch.

380. Multiple of 6 stitches plus 1.

Row 1: In the 6th chain from hook * holding back 1st lp of each dc, work 3 dc, yo and through all 4 lps (cluster) ch 3, sk 2, sc in next ch, ch 2, sk 2, repeat from * across, ending ch 3, sc in last ch, ch 3, turn.

Row 2: * work cluster in cluster, ch 3, sc in sc, ch 3, repeat from * across row, end ch 3, turn.

Rows 3,4: * Sc in cluster, ch 3, sc in sc, ch 3, repeat from *, end ch 3, turn.

Row 5: Work cluster in first sc, * ch 3, sc in sc, ch 3, cluster in next sc, repeat from * across, end ch 3, turn.

Repeat Rows 2-5 for Pattern Stitch.

381. Multiple of 4 stitches.

Row 1: Hdc in 2nd ch from hook and in each ch across, ch 2, turn.

Row 2: * Sk 1, (hdc, ch 2, hdc) shell in next st, sk 1, hdc in next st, repeat from * across, ch 2, turn.

Row 3: Work shell in each ch 2 sp, and hdc in each single hdc across row, ch 2, turn.

Repeat Row 3 for Pattern Stitch.

Flower Motif
Stitch Patterns

It's fun to create these whimsical, imaginary flowers because you can work with several different colors of yarn. Make a number of flower patterns and then sew or crochet the motifs together for the desired article.

Flower motifs are perfect for making vests, tableclothes and baby blankets. They also make terrific appliqués. Crochet an afghan and sprinkle it with colorful flowers. Or create an out-of-the-ordinary cloche hat by sewing on various spring flowers.

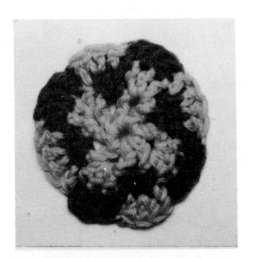

382. Ch 6, join with sl st to first ch to form ring, ch 5.

Rnd 1: * dc in ring, ch 2, repeat from * around 6 times. Join with sl st to first dc, ch 3.

Rnd 2: Work 2 dc in same sp as ch-3, * join B in last lp of last dc and work 3 dc in next ch-2 sp. *Note:* Twist yarn on wrong side only; with A work 3 dc in next ch-2 sp, repeat from * around, ending with a sl st in top of ch-3.

Rnd 3: Ch 3, 2 dc in next dc, dc in next dc, * with B, dc in next dc, 2 dc in next dc, dc in next dc, with A dc in next dc, 2 dc in next dc, dc in next dc, repeat from * around, join with sl st in ch-3. End off.

383. Ch 4, join with sl st to first ch to form ring, * ch 3, 2 dc in ring, ch 3, sl st in top of last dc for picot, dc in ring, ch 3, sl st in ring (petal made), ch 3, 3 dc in ring, ch 3, sl st in ring, repeat from * once more. End off.

384. Ch 6, join to first ch with sl st to form ring.
Rnd 1: Work 15 sc in ring, join with sl st to first sc.
Rnd 2: Sc in next sc, * 2 dc, tr, 2 dc in next sc, sc in next 2 sc, repeat from * around, join with sl st to first sc. End off.

385. *Rnd 1:* Ch 6, join with sl st to first ch to form ring, ch 5, * (dc, ch 2) 5 times in ring, sl st in top of ch-5. End off.
Rnd 2: Petal: With B, join in any ch-2 sp, ch 2, work (3 dc, hold back last lp of each dc, yo and thru all lps on hook), end off.
Repeat a Petal in each ch-2 sp around.

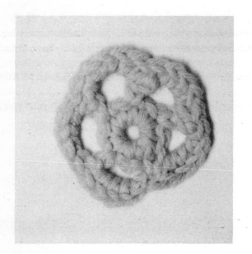

386. Ch 4, join to first ch with sl st to form ring.
Rnd 1: Ch 1, 10 sc in ring, join with sl st to first sc.
Rnd 2: * ch 4, sk 1 sc, sc in next sc, repeat from * around ending with ch 4, sk 1 sc, join with sl st to first sc.
Rnd 3: In each lp work sl st and 5 sc, in next lp sl st. End off.

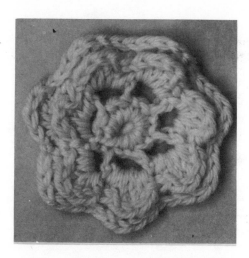

387. Ch 5, join to first ch with sl st to form ring.
Rnd 1: Ch 1, work 12 sc in ring, join with sl st to first sc.
Rnd 2: * ch 3, sk 1, sc in next sc, repeat from * around, join with sl st.
Rnd 3: In each lp work sc, hdc, 2 dc, hdc, sc. Join with sl st.
Rnd 4: * ch 3, sc around bar of next sc, repeat from * around. Join with sl st.
Rnd 5: Repeat Rnd 3. End off.

388. Ch 6, join to first ch with sl st to form ring.
Petal: * ch 6, work sc in 2nd ch from hook, hdc in next ch, dc in next ch, hdc in next ch, sc in next ch. Join with sl st in ring, repeat from * around until 8 petals are made. Join with sl st. End off.

389. Ch 5, join to first ch with sl st to form ring.
Rnd 1: Ch 6, (dc, ch 3 in ring) 5 times. Join with sl st in 3rd ch of ch-6, ch 1.
Rnd 2: Sc in sl st, * in next sp dc (ch 1, dc) 2 times, sc in next dc, repeat from * around. Join with sl st.
Rnd 3: * sc in sc, ch 1, sk 1 dc, in center of next dc (dc, ch 1) 5 times, sk 1, repeat from * around. Join with sl st to first sc. End off.

390. Ch 6, join to first ch with sl st to form ring. Ch 3.

Rnd 1: Work 13 dc in ring. Join with sl st to top of ch-3, ch 3.

Rnd 2: 2 dc in bottom of ch-3, * join Color B in last lp of last dc, 3 dc in next dc. *Note:* Twist yarn on wrong side and with A work 3 dc in next dc, repeat from * around. End with sl st to join. End off.

391. *Rnd 1:* Ch 8. Join with sl st to first ch to form ring.

Rnd 2: Ch 3, work 2 dc, ch 1, sc, ch 1, * 3 dc, ch 1, sc, ch 1 in ring, repeat from * around 4 times. Join with sl st. End off.

Center: Wrap yarn around a 3 inch cardboard 10 times. Remove from cardboard, tie yarn in center, knot and sl hanging thread thru center of flower, sew together on wrong side.

392. *Rnd 1:* Ch 3, join with sl st in first ch to form ring. Work 23 dc in ring. Join with sl st in top of ch-3.

Rnd 2: Ch 3, in same place as sl st make dc, ch 2, 2 dc (petal made), * sk 3 dc, in next dc (2 dc, ch 2, 2 dc). Repeat from * around (6 petals), ending with sk 3 dc, join with sl st in top of ch-3. End off.

393. Ch 6, join with sl st to first ch to form ring.

Rnd 1: Work 12 sc in ring.

Rnd 2: * sc in next sc, 2 sc in next sc, repeat from * around.

Rnd 3: * sc in next sc, ch 3, sk 2 sc, repeat from * around, end ch 3, join with sl st to first sc, ch 6.

Rnd 4: * In next ch-3 lp, work (sc, hdc, dc, tr, dc, hdc, sc) (petal), repeat from * around. Join with sl st in first sc. Fasten off.

394. With A, ch 5, join to form ring, work 8 sc in ring. Do not join or turn this or the following rnds. Place a marker at beg of each rnd.

Rnd 2: 3 sc in each st.

Rnds 3,4: Sc in each st.

Rnd 5: * Sc in next sc, 2 sc in next sc, repeat from * around.

Rnd 6: Work even (48) sts around. Fasten off.

Rnd 7: Join B in any st, * ch 9, sl st in 2nd ch from hook, sc in next ch, dc in next 3 chs, tr in next 3 chs, sk next 3 sts, sl st in next st, repeat from * around. Join and fasten off.

395. Ch 2, work 8 sc in first ch, join with sl st and turn.

Petal: Ch 3, 4 dc in same sp, turn.

Rnd 1: Ch 3 (counts as first dc), dc in same sp, 1 dc in each of next 3 dc, 2 dc in last dc, ch 2, turn.

Rnd 2: Dc in first st, hdc in next st, sl st in next 3 sts, dc, sc in last st, cut yarn.

2nd Petal: Skip 1 sc of first row, join yarn in next st, work same as first petal. Work 2 more petals in same manner.

396. *Rnd 1:* Ch 3, join with sl st to first ch to form ring. Ch 3, 23 dc in ring. Join with sl st in top of ch 3.

Rnd 2: Ch 3, in same place as sl st work dc, ch 2 and 2 dc (petal) * sk 3 dc, in next dc work 2 dc, ch 2, 2 dc. Repeat from * around (6 petals), ending with sk 3 dc, join to top of ch-3 with sl st.

Rnd 3: Sl st to next ch-2 sp, ch 3, 7 dc in same sp, * sk dc, sc between petals, 8 dc in next ch-2 sp, repeat from * around, ending with sc between petals, join to ch-3.

Stem: Join 2nd color in last st worked, ch 30, work sc in 2nd ch from hook and in each ch. Join with sl st in top of stem. End off.

397. With A, ch 4, join to first ch with sl st to form ring.

Rnd 1: Ch 4, * dc in ring, ch 1, repeat from * around 6 times, join with sl st in top of ch-4. End off.

Rnd 2: Join B in ch-1 sp, ch 2, dc, tr, dc, hdc in same sp, * in next sp (hdc, dc, tr, dc, hdc), repeat from * around, join with sl st. End off.

398. Ch 4.

Rnd 1: 3 dc in 4th ch from hook, work last 2 lps of 3rd dc with B, ch 4, turn.

Rnd 2: 3 dc in 4th ch from hook, sc in ch-3 sp of first rnd, ch 3, 3 dc in same sp, sc in center of ring, ch 3, 3 dc in same sp, sc, ch 3, 3 dc in same sp, join with sl st to first sc. End off.

Rnd 3: With C, join in any ch-3 sp, * sc, ch-3, 3 dc in same sp, sc, ch 3, 3 dc in center of next group, repeat from * around. Join with sl st to first sc. End off.

Rnd 4: With D, join in any ch-3 sp, (sc, ch 3, 3 dc) in same sp, * sk dc, sc, ch 3, dc in next dc, in next ch-3 sp (sc, ch 3, 3 dc), repeat from * around, end sl st in first sc. End off.

399. Ch 6, join to first ch with sl st to form ring.
Rnd 1: Ch 5, * dc in ring, ch 2, repeat from * around 4 times more, sl st in 3rd st of ch-5.
Rnd 2: Ch 4, 2 tr in same sp as sl st, * ch 2, tr in next sp, ch 3, sl st in last tr, ch 2, 3 tr in next tr, repeat from * around, join with sl st in 4th st of ch-4.
Work in *back loop only* of each tr from now on.
Rnd 3: Ch 4, tr in same place as sl st, * tr in next tr, 2 tr in next tr, ch 7, 2 tr in next tr of 3-tr group, repeat from * around. Join with sl st in top of ch-4.
Rnd 4: Ch 4, tr in same place as sl st, * tr in next 3 tr, 2 tr in next tr, ch 4, sk 3rd ch of ch-7, sc in next ch, ch 3, sc in same sp, ch 4, 2 tr in next tr. Repeat from * around. Join with sl st in top of turning ch. End off.

400. Ch 12, sc in 2nd ch from hook, hdc in next 3 chs, dc in next 3 chs, tr in next 3 chs, 10 tr in last ch—work along opposite side of ch, tr in next 3 chs, dc in next 3 chs, hdc in next 3 chs, sc in next ch. Fasten off. Make 5 more petals. After 6th petal do not fasten off work 2 sc across base of petal, * ch 1, 2 sc across next petal, repeat from * around, ch 1, join with sl st to sc of first petal. Fasten off.
Center Motif: Ch 4, join with sl st to form ring, ch 3, work 17 dc in ring, join in top of ch-3. Fasten off. Sew together on wrong side.

401. * Ch 20, sk 2 chs, sc in next 2 chs, hdc in next ch, dc in next 2 chs, tr in next 2 chs (hold back last lp of each tr, work tr in next 2 chs, yo and thru all 3 lps on hook) twice, dc in next 3 chs, hdc in next ch, sl st in each of last 5 chs, repeat from * 5 times more—6 petals made. Ch 1, work sc in base of each of 6 petals, ch 5, turn. Hold back last lp of each tr, work tr in each of 5 sc, 2 tr in last sc, yo and thru all lps on hook.
Stem: Ch 30, work hdc in each ch to base of flower. End off.

402. Ch 8, join with sl st to form ring.
Rnd 1: Ch 1, work 16 sc in ring, join in first sc.
Rnd 2: Ch 6, sk next sc, * dc in next sc, ch 3, sk 1 sc, repeat from * around.
Join with sl st in 3rd ch of ch-6.
Rnd 3: * 4 dc in next ch-3 sp, sc in next dc, repeat from * around, end sl st
in first sc—8 shells made. Fasten off.

403. Ch 6, join with sl st to form ring.
Rnd 1: 12 sc in ring, join with sl st to first sc. Ch 1.
Rnd 2: Sc in same sc, * ch 3, sk 1, sc in next sc, repeat from * around, end ch
3, sk 1 sc and join in first sc.
Rnd 3: * in next ch-lp work (sc, hdc, 3 dc, hdc, sc), repeat from * around,
end sl st in first sc. End off.
Rnd 4: Work in back of petals, join yarn in back lp of sc on 2nd rnd below
last and first petals, * ch 5, sc in back lp of next sc on 2nd rnd below
next 2 petals, repeat from * around, end ch 5, sc in joining st.
Rnd 5: * in next ch-lp work (sc, hdc, 5 dc, hdc, sc), repeat from * around,
end sl st in first sc. End off.
Rnd 6: Repeat Rnd 4 with ch 7 instead of ch 5 for each ch-lp.
Rnd 7: In each ch-lp work 11 sc. Join rnd. Fasten off.

404. Ch 9, join with sl st to form ring.
Rnd 1: Ch 3, work 23 dc in ring, join with sl st in top of ch-3.
Rnd 2: Ch 10, sc in 4th ch from hook, dc in next 4 chs, sk 1 dc in ring, dc in
next dc, * ch 8, sc in 4th ch from hook, dc in next 4 chs, sk 1 dc, dc in
next dc, repeat from * around, end ch 8, sc in 4th ch from hook, dc
in next 4 chs, sl st in 3rd ch of ch-10. End off.

405. Flower inside of square motif.
Small Motif: Ch 4, join with sl st to form ring.
Rnd 1: In ring work (sc, ch 2, dc, ch 2) 4 times. Join with sl st in ring. End off.
Rnd 2: With B in back lp of any sc, ch 3, in same st work dc and hdc; work in back lp of each st, sc in dc, * in next sc work hdc, 3 dc and hdc, sc in next dc, repeat from * around, end hdc and dc in same sc worked at beg of rnd. Join in back lp at top of ch-3. Fasten off.

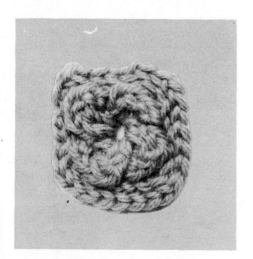

406. *Medium Motif:* Work Rnd 1 and 2 of small motif (Pattern 405). Do not end off.
Rnd 3: Work in back lp of each st on right side, * sl st loosely in each of 5 sts, sl st twice in corner st, repeat from * around. End off.

407. *Large Motif:* Work Rnds 1 and 2 of small motif (Pattern 405). Do not end off.
Rnd 3: Work in back lp of each st on right side, * sc in each of 5 sts, 3 sc in next st, repeat from * around, end last repeat with 1 sc in same st worked at beg of rnd. Join in first sc and fasten off.

408. *Rnd 1:* Ch 17, sl st in 2nd ch from hook, sc in next st, hdc in next st, dc in next 4 sts, tr in next 5 sts, dc in next 2 sts, hdc in next st, sc in next st, sl st in next st. End off. Do not turn.

Rnd 2: Join yarn in first sc, sc in next st, hdc in next st, dc in next 5 sts, hdc in next 3 sts, sc in next 2 sts, sl st in next 3 sts. Fasten off.

409. Ch 4.

Row 1: 3 dc in 4th ch from hook, work last 2 loops of 3 dc with color B, ch 4, turn.

Row 2: 3 dc in 4th ch from hook, sc in ch 3 space of first row, ch 3, 3 dc in same sp, sc in center of ring, ch 3, 3 dc in same sp, sc, ch 3, 3 dc in same sp, join with sl st to first sc. End off.

Row 3: With color C, join in any ch 3 space, *sc, ch 3, 3 dc in same space, sc, ch 3, 3 dc in center dc of next group. Repeat from * around, join with sl st to first sc. End off.

Row 4: With Color D, join in any ch 3 sp *(sc, ch 3, 3 dc), (sc, ch 3, dc) in center of next dc, in next ch 3 space repeat from * around and sl st in first sc. End off.

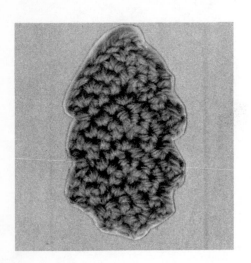

410. Ch 2.

Row 1: 3 sc in 2nd ch from hook, ch 2, turn.

Row 2: Sc in first sc, 3 sc in next sc, sc in last sc, ch 1, turn.

Row 3: Sc in 2nd sc, 3 sc in next sc, sc in 3 sc, ch 1, turn.

Row 4: Sc in 3 sc, 3 sc in next sc, sc in 3 sc, ch 1, turn.

Rows 5-8: Sc in 4th sc, 3 sc in next sc, sc in 3 sc, ch 1, turn.

Row 9: Sc in 4 sc, in next sc work sc, ch 3, sl st in last sc made, sc in next 3 sc. Fasten off.

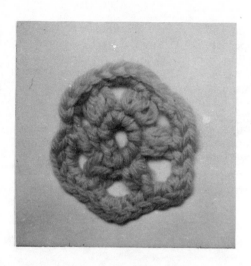

411. *Rnd 1:* Ch 6, join with sl st to form ring. Work 10 sc in ring. End off.
Rnd 2: With B join in any sc and * pull up lp, in next sc pull up lp, yo and thru all lps, ch 3, repeat from * around, join with sl st and work 4 sc in each ch-3 sp, sc in center of each petal around, join with sl st. End off.

412. With A ch 4, join with sl st to form ring.
Rnd 1: * sc in ring, ch 3, repeat from * 7 times more. Join with a sl st to first sc.
Rnd 2: Sl st in ch-3 sp, * ch 2, in same ch-3 sp (yo draw up a lp, yo and thru 2 lps) 4 times, yo and thru 5 lps on hook, ch 2, draw up a lp in same ch-3 sp, draw up a lp in next ch-3 sp, yo and thru 3 lps on hook, repeat from * around in each ch-3 lp, end sc in last lp worked, sl st in first sc.
Rnd 3: * ch 4, sc in st between clusters, repeat from * around, end sc in sl st. End off.
Rnd 4: Join B in st between clusters, ch 1, turn. Sl st in sc, * under ch-4 work (sc, hdc, 3 dc, hdc, sc) repeat from * around in each ch-4 sp. Join with a sl st and end off.

413. Ch 4, sl st to form ring.
Rnd 1: 12 sc in ring, sl st to first sc.
Rnd 2: * ch 3, sk 1 sc, sc in next sc, repeat from * around, sl st to first ch-3 lp.
Rnd 3: In each ch-3 lp (sc, hdc, dc, hdc, sc), end sl st in first sc.
Rnd 4: Join B in any sc of petals, * ch 4, sc in back lp of last sc of petal, repeat from * around, sl st in back of first ch-4.
Rnd 5: In each ch-4 lp work (sc, hdc, dc, tr, dc, hdc, sc). Sl st to first sc. End off.

414. *Paisley:* Ch 65, 2 dc in 4th ch from hook, * sk 2 chs, sl st in next ch, ch 3, 2 dc in same sp (shell), repeat from * 15 times, sk next 2 sts, hook in next st and in base of first shell, yo and draw thru all lps, ch 3, 2 dc in same sp, sk 2 sts, sl st in next, ** ch 3, 2 dc in same sp, sk 2 sts, sl st in next st, repeat from ** 4 times. End off.

Flower: Ch 8, join with sl st to form ring. *Rnd 1:* Ch 3, dc in ring, * ch 4, sl st in first ch for picot, 2 dc in ring, repeat from * 7 times. Ch 4, picot, join. Attach another strand of yarn and ch 5, * with single strand ch 5 and join with sl st in base of 4th shell from bottom, ch 2, dc in 2nd ch, tr in next 2 chs, dc in next ch, sl st in stem, repeat from * 1 time. End with sl st in base of paisley. End off. Sew 7 picots to paisley on wrong side leaving bottom 2 picots free.

415. Ch 10, sc in 2nd ch from hook and in each of next 7 chs, 3 sc in last ch; work on opposite side of ch, make sc in each of next 6 chs, * ch 3, turn; work in back lps of sts, make sc in each of next 6 sc, 3 sc in next sc, sc in each of next 6 sc, repeat from * around 4 times. Fasten off.

416. With A ch 5, join with a sl st to form a ring.

Rnd 1: Ch 1, * (yo, draw up a lp in center and retain on hook) twice, yo and draw thru all lps on hook, ch 1, (bean st) repeat from * 7 times more. Join with a sl st.

Rnd 2: Ch 1, bean st in first sp under ch-1, * 2 bean sts in next sp under ch-1, repeat from *, end bean st in same sp as first bean st. Join with a sl st. Fasten off.

Rnd 3: Join B in center between 2 bean sts, ch 3, 4 dc in same sp, * 5 dc under ch-1 between next 2 bean sts worked in one sp (shell), repeat from * around, end with a sl st. 8 shells around. End off.

417. With A ch 4, join with sl st to form ring.
Rnd 1: Work 8 sc in ring, join with sl st to first sc.
Rnd 2: Ch 5, hdc in first sc, * ch 3, hdc in next sc, repeat from * around 6 times more, ch 3, sl st to 2nd ch of ch-5. End off.
Rnd 3: Join B in any hdc, work sc in each spoke and 4 sc in each sp around. Join with sl st and end off.

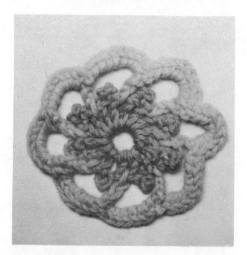

418. *Rnd 1:* Work same as for Paisley flower No. 414.
Rnd 2: Join B in same sp, ch 9, * dc in next 2 dc, ch 6, repeat from * around. Join in 3rd ch of ch-9.
Rnd 3: Ch 1, 8 sc over each lp around. Join and end off.

419. Ch 10, join with a sl st to first ch.
Rnd 1: Ch 4, hold last lp of each on hook, work 2 tr into ring, yo, draw thru all lps on hook (a 2 tr cluster made), * ch 6, 3 tr cluster into ring, repeat from * 6 times more, ch 6, sl st into first cluster.
Rnd 2: Sl st into each of first 3 chs, 1 dc into same lp, * ch 7, into next lp work (3 tr cluster, ch 5) twice, and a 3 tr cluster, ch 7, 1 dc into next lp, repeat from * omitting 1 dc at end of last repeat, sl st into first dc.

420. *Flower:* Ch 5, join with sl st to form ring.
Rnd 1: Work 9 dc in ring, ch 4.
Rnd 2: (1 tr, ch 1) in each st to end, join with sl st in 3rd ch of ch 4 (10 spaces).
Rnd 3: Sl st in 1st sp, ch 8, * dc in same sp, 2 dc in next sp, dc in next sp, ch 8, repeat from *, ending with 2 dc in last sp.
Rnd 4: * 12 dc in 1st lp, sk 1 dc, dc in each of next 2 dc, sk 1 dc, repeat from *, ending with sk 1 dc, sl st in next 2 dc.
Rnd 5: * Ch 3, sl st in next 2 dc, repeat from *, sl st across dcs between petals. End off.

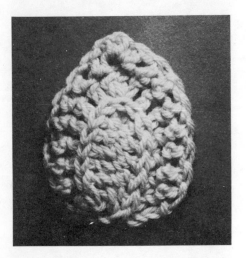

421. *Leaf:* Ch 8.
Row 1: Dc in 2nd ch from hook, dc in each of next 5 chs, 3 dc in next ch, dc in other half of next 6 chs, ch 1, turn.
Row 2: Dc in back lp of next 7 chs, 3 dc in back lp of next dc, 1 dc in back lp of next 7 dc, ch 1, turn.
Row 3: Sk first dc, dc in back lp of next 7 dc, 3 dc in back lp of next dc, dc in back lp of next 7 dc, ch 1, turn.
Repeat Row 3 10 times more (or desired length). End off.

422. Color A, ch 7, join with a sl st to form ring, ch 3, Do not turn.
Rnd 1: 3 tr in ring, remove hook and insert through top of ch 3, and into lp. Bring yarn through from back to front (cluster made), ch 3, * 4 tr in ring. Remove hook and make cluster by inserting hook through 1st of 4 trs and bringing lps through, ch 3, repeat from * 4 times, ending with sl st in top of 1st cluster. Join color B. Do not break off color A.
Rnd 2: Ch 3, 2 tr in same place as sl st, * 5 tr in sp, 3 tr in top of cluster. Repeat from *, ending with a sl st in ch 3.
Rnd 3: With Color A, ch 3, make cluster in same place as sl st, ch 3, * sk 1 tr. In next tr, work 1 cluster, ch 3, repeat from * ending with sl st in top of first cluster. End off.

Shell
Stitch Patterns

Similar to Lace patterns. Shells are delicate and "open" in character. They actually resemble little fan-shaped sea shells, and after working a few rows you'll begin seeing waves of water!

These patterns have excellent body, and the overall designs bespeak elegance. They create lovely sweaters, dresses and shawls as well as baby garments. Combine two or three shades of blue to make the prettiest baby carriage cover on the block.

423. Multiple of 4 stitches.
Make very loose chain.
Row 1: 4 dc in 4th ch from hook, ch 1, 4 dc in same st, * sk 1, sl st in next ch, sk 1, 4 dc in next ch, ch 1, 4 dc in same st, repeat from * across row, end with half shell, ch 1, turn.
Row 2: * shell in back lp of sl st, sl st in ch-1 of next shell, repeat from * across row, end row with half shell, ch 1, turn.
Repeat Row 2 for Pattern Stitch.

424. Multiple of 3 stitches.
Row 1: Sc in 2nd ch from hook, * ch 3, sk next 2 chs, sc in next ch, repeat from * across row, turn.
Row 2: Ch 3 (counts as 1 dc), dc in first sc (half shell made), * sc in next ch-3 lp, 3 dc in next sc (shell), repeat from * across row, end last repeat half shell of 2 dc in last sc, ch 1, turn.
Row 3: Sc in first dc, * ch 3, sc in center dc of next shell, repeat from * across row, end ch 3, sc in top of turning ch. Turn.
Repeat Rows 2 and 3 for Pattern Stitch.

425. Multiple of 6 stitches plus 4.

Row 1: Sc in 2nd ch from hook and in each ch across, end ch 1, turn.

Row 2: Sc in first sc, * sk 2 sc, in next sc (5 dc) shell, sk 2 sc, sc in next sc, repeat from * across row, end sk 2 sc, 3 dc in last sc (half shell), ch 1, turn.

Row 3: Sc in first dc of half shell, * shell in next sc, sc in center dc of next shell, repeat from * across row, end half shell in last sc, ch 1, turn.

Repeat Row 3 for Pattern Stitch.

426. Multiple of 6 stitches plus 3.

Row 1: Sk first ch, sc in next 2 chs, ch 2, 2 dc in the 2nd sc, * sk 2, sc in next 2 chs, ch 2, 2 dc in 2nd sc, repeat from * across row, ending 2 sc, ch 1, turn.

Row 2: Sc in each of 2 sc, * ch 2, 2 dc in last sc, 2 sc in 2 sc, repeat from * across row, ending 2 sc, ch 1, turn.

Repeat Row 2 for Pattern Stitch.

427. Multiple of 4 stitches plus 1.

Row 1: Sc in 2nd ch from hook, * ch 1, sk 1, dc in next st, ch 1, sk 1, sc in next st, repeat from * across row, ch 1, turn.

Row 2: * Sc in next sc, 3 dc (shell) in next dc, repeat from * across row, ending sc in last sc, ch 4, turn.

Row 3: * Sc in center dc of next shell, ch 1, dc in next sc, ch 1, repeat from * across row, ending dc in last sc, ch 3, turn.

Row 4: Dc in same st as turning ch (half shell), * ch 1, sc in next sc, shell in next dc, repeat from * across row, ending 2 dc in 3rd st of turning ch (half shell), ch 1, turn.

Row 5: Sc in first dc, * ch 1, dc in next sc, ch 1, sc in center dc of next shell, repeat from * across row, ending sc in top of turning ch, ch 1, turn.

Repeat Rows 2-5 for Pattern Stitch.

428. Multiple of 9 stitches.

Row 1: Dc in 4th ch from hook, * sk 3 chs, hold back last lp of each dc, work 2 dc in next ch, yo and thru all 3 lps (cluster), ch 3, cluster in same ch for cluster shell, repeat from * across row to last 4 chs, sk 3, cluster in last ch, ch 4, turn.

Row 2: Dc between cluster and next shell, ch 3, cluster in same sp, * cluster shell between next 2 cluster shells, repeat from * across row, end 2 dc in last shell in turning ch, ch 3, turn.

Row 3: Dc in dc, * cluster shell between 2 shells, repeat from * across row, end cluster in turning ch, ch 3, turn.

Repeat Rows 2 and 3 for Pattern Stitch.

429. *Row 1:* In 5th ch from hook work * 2 dc, ch 2, 2 dc (shell), ch 3 (for point) work 1 shell in same st as for first shell, repeat from *, end ch 4, turn.

Row 2: Shell in ch-2 sp of shell, shell in ch-3 point, shell in ch-2 sp of next shell, shell in turning ch, ch 4, turn.

Row 3: Work shell in each shell to point, in point work 1 shell ch 3, 1 shell, 1 shell in each shell to end, shell in turning ch, ch 4, turn.

Row 4: 1 shell in each shell to point, 1 shell in point, 1 shell in each shell to end, 1 shell in turning ch, ch 4, turn.

Repeat Rows 3 and 4 for Pattern Stitch.

430. Multiple of 6 stitches plus 1.

Row 1: Dc in 3rd ch from hook, * (2 dc, ch 1, 2 dc) all in next ch, (dc in next ch, hold back last lp), sk 3, dc in next ch, yo and thru all 3 lps on hook, repeat from * across row, end ch 3, turn.

Row 2: Dc in 3rd dc, * (2 dc, ch 1, 2 dc) in ch-1 sp, (dc in next st, hold back last lp on hook), sk 3, (dc in next st, hold back last lp on hook), yo and thru all 3 lps, repeat from * across row, end ch 3, turn.

Repeat Row 2 for Pattern Stitch.

431. Multiple of 6 stitches plus 2.

Row 1: Sc in 2nd ch from hook, * sk 1, 3 dc in next ch (shell made), sk 1, sc in next st, repeat from * across row, end sc in last st, ch 2, turn.

Row 2: Dc in first st (insert hook in both lps), * sk 1, sc in next st (center of shell of previous row), sk 1, 3 dc in next st, repeat from * across, end 2 dc in last st, ch 1, turn.

Row 3: Sc in first st, * sk 1, 3 dc in next st, sk 1, sc in next st, repeat from * across row, end sc in last st, ch 2, turn.

Repeat Rows 2 and 3 for Pattern Stitch.

432. Multiple of 6 stitches plus 1.

Row 1: Sc in 2nd ch from hook, * sk next 2 chs, ch 1, work shell of (dc, ch 1) 3 times in next ch, sk next 2 chs, sc in next ch, repeat from * across row, end ch 6, turn.

Row 2: Sc in center dc of first shell, * ch 3, dc in next sc, ch 3, sc in center dc of next shell, repeat from * across, end ch 3, dc in last sc, ch 1, turn.

Row 3: Sc in first dc, * ch 1, shell of (dc, ch 1) 3 times in next sc, sc in next dc, repeat from * across row, end last repeat sc in 3rd ch of turning ch, ch 6, turn.

Repeat Rows 2 and 3 for Pattern Stitch.

433. Multiple of 8 stitches.

Row 1: Hdc in 2nd ch from hook, hdc in next 2 chs, * 3 dc in next ch (shell), hdc in next 3 chs, repeat from * across row, end hdc in last st, ch 2, turn.

Row 2: Hdc in first 3 hdc, * 3 dc in center dc of shell, 3 hdc in next 3 hdc, repeat from * across row, end ch 2, turn.

Repeat Row 2 for Pattern Stitch.

434. Multiple of 5 stitches plus 2.

Note: Work pattern on right side only.

Row 1: Sc in first ch, * sk next ch, work 1 shell (dc, ch 1, dc) twice in next ch, sk 2 chs, sc in next ch, repeat from * across, end shell in last ch. Do not turn.

Row 2: *Sc in 2nd dc of first shell, shell of dc (ch 1, dc) 3 times in next sc, repeat from * across, end sc in 2nd dc of last shell. Do not turn.

Row 3: * Shell of dc (ch 1, dc) 3 times in next sc, repeat from * across row, ending dc, ch 1, dc in last sc. Do not turn.

Repeat Row 3 for Pattern Stitch.

435. Multiple of 4 stitches plus 2.

Row 1: Sc in 2nd ch from hook, * sk 1, 3 dc in next st (shell), sk 1, sc in next st, repeat from * across row, end sc in last st, ch 2, turn.

Row 2: Dc in first st, * sk 1, sc in next st, sk 1, 3 dc in next st, repeat from * across row, end 2 dc in last st, ch 1, turn.

Row 3: Sc in first st, * sk 1, 3 dc in next st, sk 1, sc in next st, repeat from * across row, end sc in last st, ch 2, turn.

Repeat Rows 2 and 3 for Pattern Stitch.

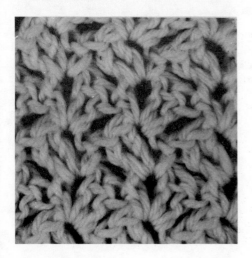

436. Multiple of 3 stitches.

Row 1: *Sk 2 chs, work (2 dc, ch 2, sc) shell, repeat from * across row, end ch 2, turn.

Row 2: Work shell in ch-2 sp of each shell across row, end ch 2, turn.

Repeat Row 2 for Pattern Stitch.

437. Multiple of 16 stitches.

Row 1: Dc in 3rd ch from hook, dc in each of next 2 chs, sk 2 chs, sl st in next ch, * ch 2, dc in each of next 3 chs, sk 2, sl st in next ch, repeat from * across row, end last shell with dc in last 4 chs, turn.

Row 2: Sl st across top of 4 dc, sl st under ch-2 lp of shell, * ch 2, 3 dc under same ch-2 lp, sl st under ch-2 lp of next shell, repeat from * across to last shell, make shell in ch-2 lp of last shell, turn.

Repeat Row 2 for Pattern Stitch.

438. Multiple of 4 stitches plus 2.

Row 1: Dc in 2nd ch from hook, * sk 1, 3 dc in next ch, sk 1, dc in next ch, repeat from * across row, end dc in last st, ch 2, turn.

Row 2: 2 dc in first st, sk 1, * dc in center of next shell, sk 1, 3 dc in next dc, repeat from * across row, end ch 2, turn.

Row 3: Dc in center of first shell, * sk 1, 3 dc in next dc, sk 1, dc in center of next shell, repeat from * across row, end ch 2, turn.

Repeat Rows 2 and 3 for Pattern Stitch.

439. Multiple of 3 stitches plus 2.

Row 1: 3 dc in 6th ch from hook, * sk 2 chs, 3 dc in next ch, repeat from * across row, end dc in last ch, ch 3, turn.

Row 2: 3 dc in center of each shell, end dc in turning ch, ch 3, turn.

Repeat Row 2 for Pattern Stitch.

440. Multiple of 3 stitches plus 2.
Row 1: 5 dc (shell) in 3rd ch from hook, * sk 2 chs, 5 dc in next ch, repeat from * across row, end dc in last ch, ch 3, turn.
Row 2: Dc, ch 3, dc (open shell) in 3rd dc of each shell, ending dc in top of turning ch, ch 3, turn.
Repeat Rows 1 and 2 for Pattern Stitch.

441. Multiple of 4 stitches plus 3.
Row 1: 3 dc in 4th ch from hook, * sk 1, dc in next ch, sk 1, 3 dc in next ch (shell), repeat from * across row, end sk 1, dc in last ch, turn.
Row 2: Ch 2, sc in 2nd dc, * ch 1, sk 1, sc in next dc, repeat from * across row, end sc in last dc, turn.
Row 3: Ch 3, sk 1 sc, * 3 dc in ch-1 sp, sk sc, dc in next ch-1 sp, sk sc, repeat from * across row, end dc in last ch-1 sp. Turn.
Repeat Rows 2 and 3 for Pattern Stitch.

442. Multiple of 3 stitches plus 1.
Row 1: Dc in 6th ch from hook, * ch 2, sk 2, dc in next ch, repeat from * across row, end ch 3, turn.
Row 2: Dc in first dc, * 2 dc, ch 1, 2 dc in next dc, repeat from * across row, end dc in turning ch, ch 4, turn.
Row 3: * Dc in ch-1 sp, ch 2, repeat from * across row, end ch 4, turn.
Repeat Rows 2 and 3 for Pattern Stitch.

443. Multiple of 4 stitches plus 2.

Row 1: Dc in 3rd ch from hook, dc in each ch across row, end ch 5, turn.

Row 2: Work 6 dc in 3rd ch from hook (fan made), * sk 2 dc, dc in next dc, ch 3, 6 dc in top of last dc, repeat from * across row, end dc in turning ch, ch 1, turn.

Row 3: Sc in each dc across first fan, * sk 2 dc of next fan and work sc in next 5 dc, repeat from * across, end sc in last 4 dc, ch 5, turn.

Repeat Rows 2 and 3 for Pattern Stitch.

444. Multiple of 9 stitches.

Row 1: 3 dc in 4th ch from hook, * sk 3 chs, work sc, ch 3, and 3 dc in next ch, repeat from * across row, end sk 3 chs, sc in last ch, ch 3, turn.

Row 2: 3 dc in first sc, * (sc, ch 3, 3 dc) under next ch-3 lp, repeat from * across row, end sc under turning ch, ch 3, turn.

Repeat Row 2 for Pattern Stitch.

445. Multiple of 5 stitches plus 4.

Row 1: Sk 2 chs, 6 dc in next ch, * sk 2 chs, sc, sk 2, 6 dc in next ch, repeat from * across row, end sc in last ch, ch 2, turn.

Row 2: 1 dc in back lp of each dc of previous row across row, ch 2, turn.

Row 3: Sc in first dc, sk 2 dc, 6 dc in sp between 3rd and 4th dc of previous row, * sk 3 dc, sc, sk 3 dc, 6 dc in next sp, repeat from * across row, ending sc in turning ch, ch 2, turn.

Repeat Rows 2 and 3 for Pattern Stitch.

446. Multiple of 6 stitches plus 3.

Row 1: 4 tr into 6th ch from hook, * ch 4, skip 5 ch, 5 tr into next ch, repeat from * to within last 9 ch, ch 4, sk 5 chs, 4 tr into next ch, sk 2, 1 tr into next ch, ch 3, turn.

Row 2: 2 tr into first tr, * in next sp work (3 tr, ch 3, 3 tr) repeat from *, ending sk 4 tr, 3 tr in next ch, ch 6, turn.

Row 3: * 5 tr into next ch 3 sp, ch 4, repeat from * to within last sp, 5 tr in next ch sp, ch 3, 1 tr in 3rd ch of ch 3, ch 6, turn.

Row 4: 3 tr into first sp, * in next sp work (3 tr, ch 3, 3 tr) repeat from * to within last sp, 3 tr in next sp, ch 3, 1 tr in 3rd ch of ch 6, ch 3, turn.

Row 5: 4 tr into first ch 3 sp, * ch 4, 5 tr in next sp, repeat from * to within last sp, ch 4, 4 tr in next sp, 1 tr into 3rd ch of ch 6, ch 3, turn.

Repeat Rows 2-5 for Pattern Stitch.

Color
Stitch Patterns

The newest crochet designs mix and match colors and patterns. Try creating a variety of textures by crocheting two or more differing yarn qualities into one article. Thick and thin. Wooly and shiny. Or crochet with two colors for a tweed effect.

Experiment with the woven stitch Pattern 448, which is crocheted with two colors, using a third color for weaving. How about alternating colors every row or two?

These designs consist of a succession of strong patterns of bright colors—the decorative effects are due to the relations between colors. The color combinations transform the various patterns into contrasts that cooperate with each other for an overall design—sometimes color is emphasized, sometimes pattern.

447. Multiple of 3 stitches plus 2.

Row 1: With A hdc in first 2 chs, * with B 1 hdc in next ch, with A hdc in next 2 chs, repeat from * across row, end ch 1, turn.

Row 2: With A hdc in each st across row, turn.

Row 3: With B ch 1, hdc in first 2 sts, * with A hdc in next st, with B hdc in next 2 sts, repeat from * across row. End ch 1, turn.

Row 4: With B hdc in each st across row, turn.

Repeat Rows 1-4 for Pattern Stitch.

448. Multiple of 2 stitches plus 1.

Mesh: Row 1: Dc in 6th ch from hook, * ch 1, sk next ch, dc in next ch, repeat from * across row. End ch 4, turn.

Row 2: Sk first dc, * dc in next dc, ch 1, repeat from * across row. End dc in 3rd ch of turning ch, ch 4, turn.

Repeat Row 2 for Pattern Stitch, alternating colors every 4, then 2 rows for striped pattern or alternate colors as you wish.

Weaving: Cut 3 strands of yarn about one foot longer than twice the length of the garment. Thread yarn into tapestry needle or tie yarn to safety pin. Starting at lower edge (leave 3 inches of yarn hanging) draw yarn * over first bar then under second bar, repeat from * across length of garment to top, go over top edge and continue alternating weave in same manner as first woven row to lower edge. Alternate colors every 2 rows or as desired.

Finishing: Work back stitch across all woven ends and tack to wrong side; hem in place.

449. Work with double strand of yarn using 2 different colors.
Row 1: Hdc in 3rd ch from hook, hdc in each ch across, ch 2, turn.
Row 2: Hdc in each st across, ch 2, turn.
Repeat Row 2 for Pattern Stitch.

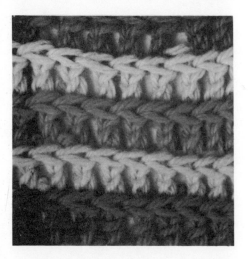

450. *Row 1:* Work dc in each ch across row. End off.
Row 2: On right side; join B with sl st in sp just below first st, ch 1, 1 dc under the 2 horizontal lps of each st across row, end off.
Repeat Row 2 for Pattern Stitch. Be sure to begin each row on the right side.

451. Multiple of 7 stitches plus 5.
Row 1: With B hdc in 4th ch from hook (counts as 2 hdc), hdc in each ch across, ch 1, turn.
Row 2: With B hdc in each st across, work last 3 lps off with A, turn.
Row 3: With A ch 1, * hdc in next 5 sts, hdc around bar of next hdc on Row 1 (yo and insert hook from right to left under next hdc on Row 1), pull up lp, yo and thru 3 lps, sk st behind this hdc, and repeat from * across row. End hdc in last 5 sts, ch 1, turn.
Row 4: With B, hdc in each st across row, work off last 3 lps of last hdc with A, turn.
Row 5: With A, ch 1, hdc in next 2 sts, * long hdc around next 2 sts on last A row, hdc in next 5 sts, repeat from * across row. End hdc in last 2 sts, ch 1, turn.
Row 6: With B hdc in each st across row, work off last 3 lps of last hdc with A, turn.
Row 7: With A ch 1, * hdc in next 5 sts, 1 hdc around next 2 sts on last B row, sk st behind 1 hdc, repeat from * across row. End hdc in last 5 sts, ch 1, turn.
Row 8: With B, hdc in each st, work off last 3 lps of last hdc with A, turn.
Repeat Rows 2-8 for Pattern Stitch.

452. Multiple of 2 stitches plus 1.

Row 1: With A dc in 4th ch from hook, * sc in next ch, dc in next ch, repeat from * across row. Do not turn.

Row 2: Join B in top of ch on right side, work sc in each dc and dc in each sc. End off.

Row 3: Pick up A ch 3, turn and work in established pattern.

Row 4: Join B, ch 1, and work in established pattern.

Repeat Rows 3 and 4 for Pattern Stitch.

453. Multiple of 6 stitches.

Work on Right Side only. End off colors at end of every row.

Row 1: Pull up lp in 4th ch from hook, sk 1, pull up lp in next ch, yo and thru all lps, * ch 1, pull up lp in same st, sk 1, pull up lp in next ch, yo and thru all lps on hook, repeat from * across row. End off.

Row 2: Join yarn in 2nd ch from end, ch 4, pull up lp in first sp, * lp in next sp, yo and thru all lps, ch 1, pull up lp thru last sp worked, lp in next sp, yo and thru all 3 lps, ch 1, repeat from * across row. End off.

Repeat Row 2 for Pattern Stitch.

454. Multiple of 4 stitches plus 2.

Row 1: With A 1 dc in 2nd ch from hook, * sk 1 ch, with B (3 dc in next ch) shell made, sk 1, with A 1 dc in next ch, repeat from * across row. End with A 1 dc in last ch, ch 2, turn.

Row 2: With A dc in first dc, * with B 3 dc in center dc of shell, with A dc in dc, repeat from * across row. End dc in dc, ch 2, turn.

Repeat Row 2 for Pattern Stitch.

455. Multiple of 2 stitches plus 1.

Note: Every other shell is worked with B. All chains at end of rows and all single crochets are worked with Color A. Be sure to twist yarn on wrong side.

Row 1: 3 dc (shell) in 3rd ch from hook, * sk 1, shell in next ch, repeat from * across row, end ch 3, turn.

Row 2: Shell in center of first shell, * sc in sc, shell in center of next shell, repeat from * across row. End ch 3, turn.

Repeat Row 2 for Pattern Stitch.

456. *Row 1:* With A dc in each st across row, join B, ch 1, turn.

Row 2: Sc in top lp only of each st across row, join A, ch 2, turn.

Repeat Rows 1 and 2 for Pattern Stitch.

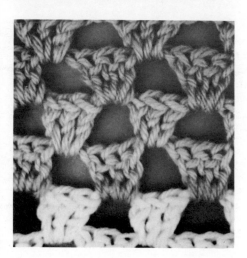

457. Multiple of 6 stitches plus 1.

Row 1: 3 dc in 6th ch from hook (shell), * ch 2, sk 5 chs, 3 dc in next ch, repeat from * across row. End ch 5, turn.

Row 2: * 1 shell in ch-2 sp, ch 2, repeat from * across row, end 1 shell in turning ch, join B, ch 5, turn.

Repeat Row 2 for Pattern Stitch. Alternate colors every 2 rows.

458. Multiple of 5 stitches.

Row 1: With A dc in 3rd ch from hook, dc in each ch across row, work off last 2 lps of last dc with B, ch 1, turn.

Row 2: 2 sc in each st across row. End sc in turning ch, work off last 2 lps of sc with A, ch 2, turn.

Row 3: Sk 2, * dc in next st, sk 1, repeat from * across row. End dc in turning ch and work last 2 lps off with Color B, ch 1, turn.

Repeat Rows 2 and 3 for Pattern Stitch.

459. Multiple of 9 stitches plus 6.

Row 1: With A work 1 sc in each ch across row.

Row 2: Join B in first sc, pull up lp, ch 1 in same lp, pull up lp in next 2 sc, yo and thru 1 lp, yo and thru 2 lps 2 times. Drop B, draw A thru lp on hook, ch 2, pull up lp in next 3 chs (sk first ch), pull up lp in back of 3 B lps, yo and thru all 7 lps, ch 1. Drop A, * with B ch 1, thru A lp, draw lp thru eye, yo and pull up lp and pull up lp thru next 3 sc, ending lp thru first lp on hook, and then thru 2 lps (6 times). Drop B, pull lp thru lp on hook and thru back of 6 B sts, draw thru all lps, ch 1. Repeat from * across row. End with eye, ch 1, turn.

Row 3: Work 1 row sc with A, (sc in eye, sc in first A sts and sc in B sts), work 3 sc in each eye of each flower across row.

Repeat Rows 2 and 3 for Pattern Stitch.

460. Multiple of 4 stitches plus 1.

Row 1: Dc in 4th ch from hook, * sc in next 2 chs, dc in next 2 chs, repeat from * across row. End by joining B, turn.

Row 2: With B sc in each dc, dc in each sc across row. Join Color A.

Row 3: Ch 3, turn, dc in each sc, sc in each dc across row.

Row 4: Pick up B on right side. Do Not Turn and work in established pattern.

Repeat Rows 3 and 4 for Pattern Stitch.

461. Multiple of 6 stitches plus 4.
Row 1: 1 hdc in 3rd ch from hook, hdc in each ch across row, end ch 1, turn.
Row 2: Repeat Row 1.
Row 3: Note: Each flower is worked on a separate bobbin. 1 hdc in first 2 sts, * popcorn in next st (yo, pull up lp 3 times and thru all lps on hook for popcorn), hdc in next 5 sts, repeat from * across row, end hdc in last 2 sts, ch 1, turn.
Row 4: Hdc in first st, * popcorn in next 3 hdc, hdc in next 3 sts, repeat from * across row, end hdc in last st, ch 1, turn.
Row 5: Repeat Row 3.
Rows 6,7: Hdc in each st across row, ch 1, turn.
Repeat Rows 3-7 for Pattern Stitch.

462. *Row 1:* With A hdc in 3rd ch from hook, hdc in each ch across row, turn.
Row 2: With B ch 1, sc in each st across row, ch 1, turn.
Row 3: With B 1 hdc in each st across row, turn.
Row 4: With A repeat Row 2.
Row 5: With B repeat Row 3.
Repeat Rows 2-5 for Pattern Stitch.

463. Multiple of 2 stitches plus 1.
Row 1: With A hdc in 2nd ch from hook, * with Color B hdc in next ch, with A hdc in next ch, repeat from * across row, end ch 1, turn.
Row 2: With A hdc in each st across row, ch 1, turn.
Row 3: With A hdc in first st, with * B hdc in next st, with A hdc in next st, repeat from * across row. End ch 1, turn. End off B.
Repeat Rows 2 and 3 for Pattern Stitch.
Note: Color B is worked on wrong side only. Be sure to twist yarn on wrong side when changing colors.

464. Multiple of 4 stitches plus 1.
Row 1: With B hdc in 2nd ch from hook,* hdc in next ch, with B hdc in next ch, with A hdc in next 2 chs, repeat from * end ch 1, turn.
Row 2: With A hdc in each st across row, ch 1, turn.
Row 3: Repeat Row 2.
Row 4: With B hdc in each st across row, ch 1, turn.
Row 5: With B hdc in first 2 sts,* with A hdc in next st, with B hdc in next 2 sts, repeat from * across row. End ch 1, turn.
Row 6: With B hdc in each st across row, end ch 1, turn.
Row 7: With A hdc in each st across row, end ch 1, turn.
Row 8: With A hdc in first 2 sts,* with B hdc in next st, with A hdc in next 2 sts, repeat from * across row, end ch 1, turn.
Repeat Rows 2-8 for Pattern Stitch.
Note: Be sure to twist yarn on wrong side only.

465. Multiple of 22 stitches.
Row 1: Sc in 2nd ch from hook, 1 sc in next 6 chs, * 3 sc in next ch, sc in next 7 chs, skip 2 chs, 1 sc in next 7 chs, repeat from *, end 3 sc in next ch, sc in next 7 chs, ch 1, turn.
Row 2: Skip 1 sc, sc in back lp of each of next 7 sc, * 3 sc in back lp of next sc, sc in back lp of next 7 sc, sk 2, sc in back lp of next 7 sc, repeat from *, 3 sc in back lp of next sc, sc in back lp of next 7 sc, *do not work last st*, ch 1, turn.
Repeat Row 2 for Pattern Stitch.
Note: Work last 2 lps of last sc with next color. Alternate colors on even rows only.

466. Multiple of 8 stitches plus 4.
Note: Always keep yarn to wrong side of work.
Row 1: With A, dc in 4th ch from hook (counts as 2 dc), dc in next 2 chs, work off last 2 lps with B, * with B dc in next 4 chs and work off last 2 lps with A, with A dc in next 4 chs, work off last 2 lps with B, repeat from * across row, change colors in last st as before, ch 3, turn.
Row 2: Ch (counts as 1 dc), sk first dc, dc in next 3 dc, change colors in last st, * dc in next 4 dc, change colors in last st, repeat from * across, ch 3, turn.
Repeat Row 2 for Pattern Stitch. Be sure to reverse colors on each row for checked pattern.

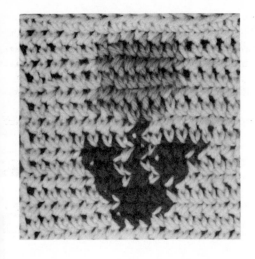

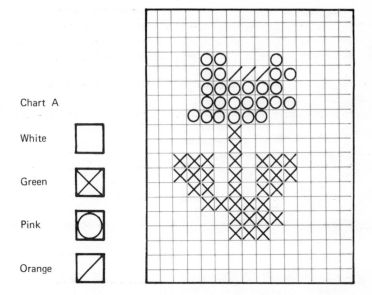

Chart A

White

Green

Pink

Orange

467. *Picture Motifs:* General Directions: Pattern Stitch.
Row 1: Sc in 2nd ch from hook, and in each ch across, ch 1, turn.
Row 2: Work in reverse sc; * hold yarn in front of work, insert hook under yarn from back to front in next sc, pull lp thru and finish sc, repeat from * across. ch 1, turn.
Row 3: Sc in each sc across row, ch 1, turn.
Repeat Rows 2 and 3 for Pattern Stitch.
Note: When changing colors, work last sc or reverse sc of one color until there are 2 lps on hook, drop strand to wrong side of work, pick up new color and finish sc.
Design: Follow General Directions and see chart for desired design.
Chart A. Flower Motif
Chart B. Heart Motif

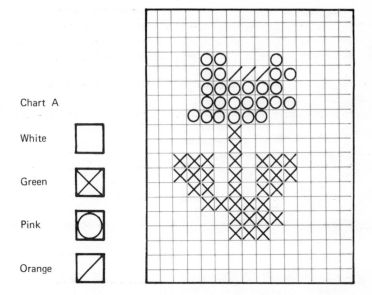

Chart B

Pink

Green

468. Multiple of 4 stitches.

Row 1: Sk 2 chs, dc in each ch across row, end ch 3, turn.

Row 2: Dc in each dc across row, end ch 3, turn.

Row 3: Sk 1 dc, dc in next dc, ch 1, * sk 1, dc in next dc, repeat from * across row, end ch 3, turn.

Row 4: Dc in first dc, * ch 1, dc in next dc, repeat from * across row, end ch 3, turn.

Row 5: Dc in each dc and dc in each ch-1 sp across, end ch 3, turn.

Row 6: Repeat Row 2.

Repeat Rows 2-6 for Pattern Stitch.

Weaving: Thread tapestry needle with 3 strands of yarn and working from side to side, weave under then over each mesh across each mesh row.

469. Multiple of 7 stitches.

Row 1: With A, sk 5 chs, in next ch (2 dc, ch 2, 2 dc) shell, * sk 2 chs, dc in next ch, sk 2, shell in next ch, repeat from * across row, end draw Color B through last 2 lps of last dc, ch 3, turn.

Row 2: Work shell in each ch-2 sp, dc in each dc, ch 3, turn.

Repeat Row 2 for Pattern Stitch, alternating colors every 2 rows.

Popcorn and Cluster
Stitch Patterns

These stitches combine texture and design—they have a three-dimensional quality which most of the other patterns do not. Popcorns and Clusters are ideal for bulky sweaters, hats and jackets, coats and ponchos—not only for their textural effect, but for their warmth.

A hint: these patterns require more yarn per stitch than others, so make sure you estimate adequate yarn requirements.

470. Multiple of 3 stitches plus 1.
Row 1: 1 dc in each st across row, ch 1, turn.
Row 2: 1 dc in first st *, in next st (yo, draw up lp and pull thru 2 lps) 5 times, 1 dc in next 2 sts, repeat from * across row. End ch 1, turn.
Row 3: 1 dc in each st across row, ch 1, turn.
Row 4: Repeat Row 2, beginning in 2nd dc.
Row 5: Repeat Row 3.
Repeat Rows 2 and 3 for Pattern Stitch.

471. Multiple of 2 stitches plus 1.
Row 1: 1 dc in 2nd ch from hook, 1 dc in each ch across row, end ch 2, turn.
Row 2: Dc in 2nd dc, * ch 1, sk 1, dc in dc, repeat from * across row, end dc in turning ch, ch 3, turn.
Row 3: 3 dc (shell) ch 1, in each dc across row, end dc in turning ch, ch 4, turn.
Row 4: Popcorn (yo, pull up lp) 3 times and thru all lps on hook, ch 2, in center dc of each shell across row, end dc in turning ch, ch 3, turn.
Row 5: 1 shell, ch 1, in center of each popcorn across row, end ch 2, turn.
Repeat Rows 2-5 for Pattern Stitch.

472. Multiple of 4 stitches.

Row 1: (1 sc, 1 tr, 1 sc) all in 3rd ch from hook, * ch 1, sk 1 ch, sc in next ch, repeat from * across row, end sc in last ch, ch 3, turn.

Row 2: * sc in top of tr, ch 3, sc in sc, repeat from * across row, end ch 3, turn.

Row 3: Repeat Row 1.

Row 4: Repeat Row 2.

Row 5: 3 sc in each ch-3 sp across row, end sc in turning ch, ch 3, turn.

Repeat Rows 1-5 for Pattern Stitch.

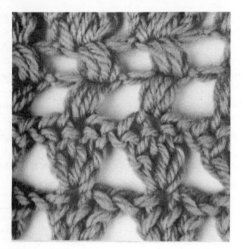

473. Multiple of 5 stitches plus 1.

Row 1: 1 dc, 1 popcorn (yo, draw up lp) 3 times, yo and thru all lps on hook, 1 dc all in 3rd ch from hook, * ch 1, sk 2 sts, 1 dc, 1 popcorn, 1 dc in next ch, repeat from * across row, end ch 2, turn.

Row 2: (1 dc, 1 popcorn, 1 dc) group st in center of each shell across row, end dc in turning ch, ch 2, turn.

Rows 3,4: 3 dc, ch 1, in center of each shell across row, end dc in turning ch, ch 2, turn.

Rows 5,6: 1 popcorn, ch 1, in center of each shell across row, end dc in turning ch, ch 2, turn.

Repeat Rows 2-6 for Pattern Stitch.

474. Multiple of 4 stitches.

Row 1: Dc in 4th ch from hook and in each ch across row, ch 3, turn.

Row 2: Yo hook, pull up lp in first dc, yo pull up lp in next dc, yo and pull up lp in same dc, yo and thru all 7 lps, ch 1, * yo hook and pull up lp in next dc 2 times, yo and pull up lp in dc just worked, yo and thru 7 lps, ch 1, repeat from * across row, end yo, pull up lp in last dc, yo and pull up lp in top of turning ch, yo and pull up lp in same ch, yo and thru all 7 lps, ch 3, turn.

Row 3: Dc in top of first st, * 1 dc in top of next st, repeat from * across row, end dc in top of last st, dc in top of turning ch, ch 3, turn.

Repeat Rows 2 and 3 for Pattern Stitch.

475. Multiple of 3 stitches plus 1.

To Make Popcorn: * Yo and draw up lp in st, repeat from * twice more in same st, yo and thru all 7 lps on hook.

Row 1: In 4th ch from hook, * popcorn, ch 2, popcorn in same st as previous popcorn, ch 1, sk 2 sts, repeat from * across row, end dc in last st, ch 1, turn.

Row 2: * 3 sc in ch-2 sp between popcorns, 1 sc in ch-1 sp, repeat from * across row, end sc in top of turning ch, ch 3, turn.

Row 3: * Popcorn in center of 3 sc group of previous row, ch 2, popcorn in same st as previous popcorn, ch 1, sk 3 sc, repeat from * across row, end dc in last st, ch 1, turn.

Repeat Rows 2 and 3 for Pattern Stitch.

476. Multiple of 3 stitches.

Row 1: Sk 2 chs, * yo and draw up lp 4 times in same ch, yo and draw thru 8 lps, yo and draw thru 2 lps, ch 1, sk 1, yo and draw up lp in next ch, repeat from * across row, ch 2, turn.

Repeat Row 1 for Pattern Stitch placing the group st in the ch-sp between groups.

477. Multiple of 6 stitches.

Row 1: Dc in 4th ch from hook, * ch 1, sk next st, dc in next ch, repeat from * across row, end ch 1, sk next ch, dc in last 2 chs, ch 3, turn.

Row 2: Sk first dc, dc in next dc, (ch 1, dc in next dc) 4 times, * dc in next ch, dc in next dc for a block, (ch 1, dc in next dc) 7 times, repeat from * across row, end last repeat with (ch 1, dc in next dc) 4 times, dc in top of turning ch, ch 3, turn.

Row 3: Dc in 2nd dc, (ch 1, dc in next dc) 3 times, * dc in next ch, dc in next dc, ch 1, sk 1 dc, dc in next dc, dc in next ch, dc in next dc (ch 1, 1 dc) 5 times, repeat from * across row, end last repeat with (ch 1, dc in next dc) 3 times, dc in top of turning ch, ch 3, turn.

Row 4: Dc in 2nd dc and continue working a sp over each sp as before and dc in each dc across row, end dc in top of turning ch, ch 3, turn.

Rows 5,6: Repeat Row 4.

Repeat Rows 2-6 for Pattern Stitch.

478. Multiple of 2 stitches plus 1.

Row 1: Hold back last lp of each dc; work 4 dc in 4th ch from hook, yo and thru 5 lps, ch 1 (puff st made), * sk next ch, puff st in next ch, repeat from * across row. End ch 1, turn.

Row 2: Sc in top of 2 lps of first puff st, * sc in each ch-1 sp and top 2 lps of next puff st, repeat from * across row. End ch 1, turn.

Row 3: Pull up lp the size of puff st, puff st in next sc, * sk 1 sc, puff st in next sc, repeat from * across row. End ch 1, turn.

Repeat Rows 2 and 3 for Pattern Stitch.

479. Multiple of 5 stitches.

Row 1: Dc in 4th ch from hook, hdc in each ch across, ch 5, turn.

Row 2: Work 4 dc in 3rd ch from hook, holding back last lp of each dc, yo and thru all lps on hook (popcorn made), sk 2 dc, * tr in next dc, ch 2, work popcorn in center of same popcorn, repeat from * across row. End tr in last dc, ch 5, turn.

Row 3: Work 4 dc in 3rd ch from hook (hold back last lp of each dc), yo and thru all lps on hook, * tr in center of next popcorn, ch 2, work popcorn in center of *previous popcorn*, repeat from * across row. End tr in center of popcorn of *previous row*, ch 5, turn.

Repeat Row 3 for Pattern Stitch.

480. Multiple of 3 stitches plus 2.

Row 1: 1 hdc in 2nd ch from hook, hdc in each ch across row, end ch 4, turn.

Row 2: Sk 2 sts, (yo, pull up lp, yo and thru 1 lp, yo and thru 2 lps, yo and pull up lp, yo and thru 1 lp, yo and pull up lp and draw thru 2 lps, yo and thru 2 lps, yo and thru last 4 lps on hook) leaf made, * ch 2, sk 2 sts, leaf in next hdc, repeat from * across row, end hdc in turning ch, ch 1, turn.

Row 3: Hdc *under* first 2 sts, * hdc in center of leaf, 2 hdc *under* ch-2 sp, repeat from * across row. End ch 4, turn.

Repeat Rows 2 and 3 for Pattern Stitch.

481. Multiple of 6 stitches.

Row 1: Yo, hook in 2nd ch from hook, pull lp thru 2 times, yo, sk 1 ch, hook in next ch and pull lp thru. Yo and thru all lps on hook, ch 1, * yo, hook in same ch, pull lp thru 2 times, yo, sk 1, hook in next ch and pull lp thru, yo and thru all lps on hook, ch 1, repeat from * across, end ch 1, turn.

Row 2: Yo, hook in first ch, draw lp thru 2 times, yo, hook in st at top of next group, draw lp thru, yo and thru all lps on hook, ch 1, * yo, hook in top of same st, draw lp thru 2 times, yo, hook in next group and draw lp thru, yo and thru all lps on hook, ch 1, repeat from * across, end yo, hook in top of same group 2 times, yo and hook in turning ch, draw lp thru, yo and thru all lps on hook, ch 1, turn.

Repeat Row 2 for Pattern Stitch.

482. Multiple of 3 stitches plus 1.

Row 1: 3 dc (shell) in 2nd ch from hook, * sk 2 chs, 3 dc in next ch, repeat from * across row. End ch 3, turn.

Row 2: * popcorn (yo, pull up lp) 4 times and thru all lps on hook in center of next shell, ch 1, repeat from * across row. End dc in turning ch, ch 2, turn.

Row 3: Shell in center of each popcorn, dc in turning ch, ch 3, turn.

Repeat Rows 2 and 3 for Pattern Stitch.

483. Multiple of 6 stitches plus 2.

Row 1: Dc in 4th ch from hook, dc in 3rd ch, * ch 1, sk 1, popcorn in next st (yo, draw up lp) 3 times and thru all lps on hook (popcorn made), ch 1, sk 2, dc in next st, dc in ch before last dc worked (cross st made), repeat from * across row. End ch 3, turn.

Row 2: * popcorn in each popcorn, ch 1, cross st in cross st, ch 1, repeat from * across row. End ch 3, turn.

Repeat Row 2 for Pattern Stitch.

484. Multiple of 21 stitches.

Row 1: 1 hdc in 2nd ch from hook, hdc in next 9 chs, * in next st (yo, pull up lp) 4 times and thru all lps on hook for popcorn, 1 hdc in next 10 chs, repeat from *, ch 2, turn.

Row 2: Hdc in next 9 hdc, * popcorn, hdc in hdc, popcorn, hdc in next 9 hdc, repeat from * across row. End ch 2, turn.

Row 3: * Hdc in 8 hdc, popcorn, hdc in 5 hdc, popcorn, repeat from * across row. End ch 2, turn.

Row 4: * Hdc in 7 hdc, popcorn, repeat from * across row. End ch 2, turn.

Row 5: * Hdc in 6 hdc, popcorn, hdc in next 7 hdc, popcorn, repeat from * across row. End ch 2, turn.

Row 6: Repeat Row 4.

Row 7: Repeat Row 3.

Row 8: Repeat Row 2.

Row 9: * Hdc in 10 hdc, popcorn, repeat from * across row. End ch 2, turn.

Repeat Rows 2-9 for Pattern Stitch.

485. Multiple of 2 stitches.

Row 1: In 3rd ch from hook, * yo, draw up lp, yo and thru 1 lp, yo and thru 2 lps, yo, draw up lp, thru 1 lp, yo and draw thru 2 lps, draw thru 3 lps, (cluster stitch) ch 1, sk 1, repeat from * across row, end ch 2, turn.

Row 2: Work cluster st in each ch-sp between clusters of previous row, ch 2, turn.

Repeat Row 2 for Pattern Stitch.

486. Multiple of 5 stitches.

Row 1: Hold back last lp of each dc, work 2 dc in 3rd ch from hook, yo and thru 3 lps on hook (cluster made), * ch 1, sk 1 ch, cluster of 2 dc in next ch, repeat from * across row to last 2 chs, end ch 1, sk next ch, dc in last ch, ch 3, turn.

Row 2: * cluster in next ch-1 sp, ch 1, repeat from * across row, work last cluster in last ch-1 sp, ch 1, dc in top of turning ch, ch 3, turn.

Repeat Row 2 for Pattern Stitch.

487. Multiple of 3 stitches plus 1.

Row 1: Sc in 2nd ch from hook, dc in same ch, * sk 1 ch, work sc, dc in next ch (cluster), repeat from * across, end ch 2, turn.

Row 2: * sk next dc, work sc, dc in next sc, repeat from * across row, end ch 2, turn.

Repeat Row 2 for Pattern Stitch.

488. Multiple of 2 stitches plus 1.

Row 1: Sk 2 chs, yo and draw up lp 3 times in same ch, yo and thru all lps, * ch 1, sk 1 ch, yo and draw up lp 3 times in next ch, yo and thru all lps, repeat from * across, ch 2, turn.

Row 2: Yo and draw up lp 3 times in center of popcorn of previous row, yo and thru all lps, * ch 1, yo and draw up lp 3 times in center of next popcorn, yo and thru all lps, repeat from * across row, ch 2, turn.

Repeat Row 2 for Pattern Stitch.

489. Multiple of 6 stitches plus 3.

Row 1: 1 tr in 4th ch from hook, 1 tr in each ch, ch 5, turn.

Row 2: Sk 3 tr, * 4 tr in next tr, remove loop from hook, insert hook into first tr of treble group, then into dropped lp and draw it through (popcorn), ch 2, sk 2 tr, 1 tr into next tr, ch 2, sk 2, repeat from * omitting ch 2 at end of last repeat and working last tr into 3rd tr of ch 3, ch 3, turn.

Row 3: * tr 2 into next sp, 1 tr in next popcorn, 2 tr in next sp, 1 tr in next tr, repeat from * working last tr into 3rd ch of ch 5, ch 5, turn.

Repeat Rows 2 and 3 for Pattern Stitch.

490. Worked on odd or even number of stitches.

Row 1: Dc in 3rd ch from hook, dc in each ch to end, ch 3, turn.

Row 2: * yo, hook into next st, draw 1 lp thru (yo, hook into same sp, draw lp through) twice, (7 lps on hook), yo and draw thru 7 lps, dc in next st, repeat from * across row, ch 2, turn.

Row 3: Work 1 dc in back lp of each st to end, ch 3, turn.

Repeat Rows 2 and 3 for Pattern Stitch.

491. Multiple of 3 stitches plus 1.

Row 1: In 4th ch from hook (yo, draw up lp, draw thru 2 lps) twice, yo draw thru last 3 lps (bean st), ch 1, sk 1, * in next ch (yo draw up a lp, yo, draw thru 2 lps) 3 times, yo draw thru last 4 lps (bean st), ch 1, sk 1, repeat from * across, end dc in last st, ch 3, turn.

Row 2: In top lp of each ch-1 sp, work bean st, ch 1 across row, end dc in turning ch, ch 1, turn.

Repeat Row 2 for Pattern Stitch.

492. Multiple of 4 stitches.

Row 1: Puff st (yo, draw up lp) 3 times in 2nd ch from hook, * sc in next ch, sk 2 chs, puff st in next ch, repeat from *, end sc in last ch, ch 1, turn.

Row 2: * Sc in sc, sc in top of puff st, 2 sc in (sk 2 ch) sp, repeat from *, end ch 1, turn.

Row 3: Puff st in first sc, ch 1, * sc in next sc, sk 2 sc, puff st in sc, end sc in turning ch, ch 1, turn.

Repeat Rows 2 and 3 for Pattern Stitch.

Varietal
Stitch Patterns

Among all the types of pattern designs, these are the most successful. They are both practical and versatile; and you'll find them ideal for just about anything you wish to make. The designs are closely crocheted, so the patterns tend to be flat rather than having a raised surface, and they will have a uniform quality, no matter how inexperienced or sloppy your hooking becomes.

Many of these designs are the result of experimenting with basic crochet stitches and then improvising with different needle techniques to create new patterns.

493. Multiple of 2 stitches.
Row 1: Sc in each ch across row, end ch 1, turn.
Row 2: Yo, pull up lp in last horizontal lp of first st and thru 2 lps, * yo, pull up lp in last horizontal lp of next st and thru 2 lps, repeat from * across, end ch 1, turn.
Repeat Rows 1 and 2 for Pattern Stitch.

494. *Row 1:* Sc in 2nd ch from hook, sc in each ch across, end ch 1, turn.
Row 2: Sc in each st across, ch 1, turn.
Row 3: Sc in top lp only of each st across row, end ch 1, turn.
Row 4: Repeat Row 3.
Row 5: Repeat Row 2.
Repeat Rows 2-5 for Pattern Stitch.

495. *Row 1:* Sc in each ch across row, end ch 1, turn.
Row 2: Sc under lower horizontal bar in each st across row, end ch 1, turn.
Repeat Row 2 for Pattern Stitch.

496. Multiple of 3 stitches plus 1.
Row 1: Sc in 2nd ch from hook, sc in next ch, * ch 1, sk 1, sc in next 2 chs, repeat from * across row, end ch 1, turn.
Row 2: 2 sc, ch 1, in each ch-1 sp across row, end ch 1, turn.
Repeat Row 2 for Pattern Stitch.

497. *Row 1:* Sc in each ch across row, end ch 1, turn.
Row 2: Sc in top lp only of each st across row, end ch 1, turn.
Repeat Row 2 for Pattern Stitch.

498. *Row 1:* Dc in each ch across row, end ch 1, turn.
Row 2: Dc under the lowest horizontal bar in each st across row, end ch 1, turn.
Repeat Row 2 for Pattern Stitch.

499. Multiple of 2 stitches plus 1.
Row 1: Sc in 3rd ch from hook, * ch 1, sk 1, sc in next st, repeat from * across row, end ch 1, turn.
Row 2: * sc in next ch-1 sp, ch 1, repeat from * across row, end sc in turning ch, ch 1, turn.
Repeat Row 2 for Pattern Stitch.

500. Multiple of 4 stitches.
Work pattern on right side only. End off at end of each row.
Row 1: Work 1 dc in each st across row, end off.
Row 2: Join yarn with sl st in chain, ch 3, dc in next st, * dc in front of next post, dc in next st, repeat from * across row. End off.
Row 3: Join yarn with sl st in chain, ch 3, * dc in next st, dc in back of next post, repeat from * across row. End off.
Repeat Rows 2 and 3 for Pattern Stitch.

501. Multiple of 2 stitches plus 1.
Row 1: Hdc in 3rd ch from hook, * ch 1, sk 1, hdc in next ch, repeat from * across row, end ch 3, turn.
Row 2: Hdc, ch 1, in each hdc across row, end hdc in 2nd ch of turning ch, ch 3, turn.
Repeat Row 2 for Pattern Stitch.

502. Multiple of 3 stitches plus 2.
Row 1: Pull up lp in 3rd ch from hook, pull up lp in next 2 chs, yo and thru all lps (puff st made), * ch 1, (pull up lp, yo and pull up lp) in top of puff st, ch 1, pull up lp in next 3 chs, yo and thru all lps, repeat from * across row, end ch 1, turn.
Row 2: Pull up lp in top of first puff st, pull up lp in last lp of puff st, pull up lp under ch-1 sp, yo and thru all lps, * ch 1, (pull up lp, yo, pull up lp) in top of puff st, ch 1, pull up lp in top of next puff st, pull up lp in last lp of puff st, pull up lp under ch-1 sp, yo and thru all lps on hook, repeat from * across, end ch 1, turn.
Repeat Row 2 for Pattern Stitch.

503. Multiple of 2 stitches plus 1.
Row 1: Hdc in 3rd ch from hook, * ch 1, sk 1, hdc in next ch, repeat from * across row, end ch 1, turn.
Row 2: Sc, ch 1, in each ch-1 sp across row, end sc in turning ch, ch 1, turn.
Row 3: Hdc in each ch-1 sp across row, end hdc in turning ch, ch 1, turn.
Repeat Rows 2 and 3 for Pattern Stitch.

504. Multiple of 3 stitches plus 1.
Row 1: Sk 2 chs, * pull up lp in next 3 chs, yo and thru 1 lp, yo and thru 2 lps, yo and thru 2 lps, yo and thru 2 lps, pull up lp in back of each of 3 sts just made, yo and thru all 4 lps, ch 1, repeat from * across, end ch 1, turn.
Row 2: Pull up lp in first 2 sts, * pull up lp in next sp, yo and thru 1 lp, yo and thru 2 lps, yo and thru 2 lps, yo and thru 2 lps, pull up lp in back of each of 3 sts just made, yo and thru all 4 lps, ch 1, pull up lp in next 2 sts, repeat from * across row, end ch 1, turn.
Repeat Row 2 for Pattern Stitch.

505. *Row 1:* Hdc in each ch across row, end ch 1, turn.
Row 2: Hdc in bottom lp only in each hdc across row, end ch 1, turn.
Row 3: Hdc in top lp only in each hdc across row, ch 1, turn.
Repeat Rows 2 and 3 for Pattern Stitch.

506. *Row 1:* Hdc in 2nd ch from hook and in each ch across, end ch 1, turn.
Row 2: Hdc in vertical lp between each 2 horizontal bars across row, end ch 1, turn.
Repeat Row 2 for Pattern Stitch.

507. Multiple of 2 stitches plus 1.
Row 1: Sc in 2nd ch from hook, * ch 1, sk next ch, sc in next ch, repeat from * across, end ch 1, turn.
Row 2: Sc in first sc, ch 1, sc in next sc, repeat from * across row, end ch 1, turn.
Repeat Row 2 for Pattern Stitch.

508. *Row 1:* Hdc in 2nd ch from hook, hdc in each ch across, end ch 1, turn.
Row 2: Hdc under the 2 horizontal bars in each st across, ch 1, turn.
Repeat Row 2 for Pattern Stitch.

509. *Row 1:* Hdc in each ch across, ch 2, turn.
Row 2: Hdc under the 2 horizontal lps in each hdc across row, end ch 2, turn.
Repeat Row 2 for Pattern Stitch.

510. Multiple of 8 stitches.
Row 1: Hdc in each ch across, ch 2, turn.
Row 2: Hdc in front horizontal lp only of first 3 sts, * hdc in back lp of next hdc, hdc in horizontal lp in next 3 sts, repeat from * across, end hdc in back lp of turning ch, ch 2, turn.
Repeat Row 2 for Pattern Stitch.

511. Multiple of 2 stitches plus 1.
Row 1: Hdc in 2nd ch from hook, * ch 1, sk 1, hdc in next ch, repeat from * across row, end ch 2, turn.
Row 2: Hdc, ch 1 in each ch-1 sp across row, end ch 2, turn.
Repeat Row 2 for Pattern Stitch.

512. Multiple of 4 stitches.
Row 1: Sc in 2nd ch from hook, draw up lp in same ch, * sk 1, draw up lp in next ch, yo and thru all 3 lps on hook, ch 1, draw up lp in same ch as last st, repeat from * across row, end ch 1, sc in last ch of last pattern, ch 1, turn.
Row 2: Sc in first sc, draw up lp between first sc and first pat of last row, * draw up lp between next 2 pats, yo and thru all lps on hook, ch 1, draw up lp in same sp as last st, repeat from * across row to within last pat, work pat over last pat, ch 1, sc in sc of previous row, ch 1, turn.
Repeat Row 2 for Pattern Stitch.

513. *Row 1:* Dc in 2nd ch from hook, dc in each ch across, end ch 1, turn.
Row 2: Sk 1, hdc in each st across row, ending ch 1, turn.
Row 3: Sk 1, sc in each st across row, ending ch 1, turn.
Repeat Rows 1-3 for Pattern Stitch.

514. *Row 1:* Hdc in each ch across row, end ch 2, turn.
Row 2: Go in top lp of each hdc from back to front, work hdc in each st across row, end ch 2, turn.
Repeat Row 2 for Pattern Stitch.

515. Multiple of 2 stitches plus 1.
Row 1: Dc in 3rd ch from hook, * ch 1, sk 1, dc in next ch, repeat from * across row, end ch 2, turn.
Row 2: * hook under ch-1 sp, yo and thru 1 lp, hook under same ch-1 sp, yo and draw thru lp, yo and draw thru 3 lps, repeat from * across row, end ch 2, turn.
Row 3: * hook in sp between next 2 sts, pull up lp, yo and thru 1 lp, pull up lp yo and thru lp, yo and thru 3 lps, repeat from * across row, end sc in top ch, ch 2, turn.
Repeat Rows 2 and 3 for Pattern Stitch.

516. *Row 1:* Sc in 2nd ch from hook and in each ch across, end ch 1, turn.
Row 2: Sc under the lower horizontal bar in each st across row, end ch 1, turn.
Repeat Row 2 for Pattern Stitch.

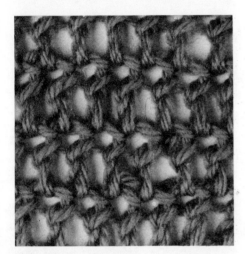

517. *Row 1:* Sk 2 chs, dc in each ch across row. End off.
Row 2: Join yarn in ch, ch 1, work dc under the 2 horizontal lps of each st across row. End off.
Repeat Row 2 for Pattern Stitch. Be sure to end off at end of each row. Work Pattern on right side only.

518. Multiple of 8 stitches.
Row 1: Hdc in 2nd ch from hook, hdc in each ch across, end ch 1, turn.
Row 2: Hdc in back lp of first 2 sts, * hdc in front lp of next 2 sts, hdc in back lps of next 2 sts, repeat from * across row, end hdc in front lps of last 2 sts, ch 1, turn.
Row 3: Hdc in front lps of first 2 sts, * hdc in back lps of next 2 sts, hdc in front lps of next 2 sts, repeat from * across row, end ch 1, turn.
Repeat Rows 2 and 3 for Pattern Stitch.

519. *Row 1:* Hdc in each ch across row, ch 2, turn.
Row 2: Hdc in first st, * working in top lp only, hdc in next st, hdc in next st, repeat from * across, end ch 2, turn.
Note: If you end row 2 in top lp of hdc, begin next row, hdc in whole st and vice versa.
Repeat Row 2 for Pattern Stitch.

520. Multiple of 2 stitches plus 1.
Row 1: Hdc in 2nd ch from hook, hdc in each ch across, end ch 1, turn.
Row 2: 2 sc in first hdc, * ch 1, sk 1, 2 sc in next hdc, repeat from * across row, end ch 1, turn.
Row 3: Dc in 2nd sc, hdc in each sc across row, end ch 1, turn.
Repeat Rows 2 and 3 for Pattern Stitch.

521. Multiple of 4 stitches.
Row 1: Hdc in each ch, ch 2, turn.
Row 2: Hdc in top lp of first hdc, * hdc in bottom lp of next hdc, hdc in top lp of next hdc, repeat from * across, end hdc in top lp, ch 2, turn.
Repeat Row 2 for Pattern Stitch.

522. Multiple of 2 stitches plus 1.
Row 1: Sc in 2nd ch from hook, sc in each ch across, end ch 1, turn.
Row 2: Hdc in first st, * sk 1, 2 hdc in next st, repeat from * across row, end ch 1, turn.
Row 3: Sc in each st across row, end ch 1, turn.
Repeat Rows 2 and 3 for Pattern Stitch.

523. Multiple of 8 stitches plus 5.
Row 1: Sc in 2nd ch from hook, sc in next 4 chs, * dc in next 3 chs, sc in next 5 chs, repeat from * across row, end ch 1, turn.
Row 2: Sc in each sc, dc in each dc, end ch 1, turn.
Row 3: Repeat Row 2.
Row 4: Dc in each sc, sc in each dc across row, end ch 1, turn.
Rows 5,6: Repeat Row 4.
Row 7: Repeat Row 2.
Repeat Rows 2-7 for Pattern Stitch.

524. Multiple of 4 stitches.
Row 1: Sc in 2nd ch from hook, * dc in next ch, sc in next ch, repeat from * across row, end sc in last ch, ch 1, turn.
Row 2: Dc in first st, * sc in next st, dc in next st, repeat from * across row, end dc in last st, ch 1, turn.
Row 3: Sc in each dc, dc in each sc across row, end ch 1, turn.
Repeat Rows 2 and 3 for Pattern Stitch.

525. Multiple of 2 stitches plus 1.
Row 1: In 3rd ch from hook sc, hdc, * sk 1, in next ch sc, hdc, repeat from * across row, end ch 2, turn.
Row 2: In first st, sc, hdc, * sk 1, sc, hdc in next st, repeat from * across row, end ch 2, turn.
Repeat Row 2 for Pattern Stitch.

526. Multiple of 8 stitches.
Row 1: Dc in 3rd ch from hook, dc in next 2 chs, * sc in next ch, 3 dc in next 3 chs, repeat from * across row, end sc in last ch, ch 1, turn.
Row 2: Sc in first sc, * dc in next 3 dc, sc in sc, repeat from * across, end sc in last sc, ch 1, turn.
Repeat Row 2 for Pattern Stitch.

527. Multiple of 5 stitches.
Row 1: * sk 1 ch, pull up lp in next 4 chs, yo and thru all 5 lps on hook, ch 1, repeat from * across row, end ch 3, turn.
Row 2: Work dc in each st across row, end dc in turning ch, ch 1, turn.
Row 3: * pull up lp in each of next 4 chs, yo and thru all 5 lps on hook, ch 3, repeat from * across, end ch 3, turn.
Repeat Rows 2 and 3 for Pattern Stitch.

528. *Row 1:* Hdc in 3rd ch from hook, hdc in each ch across row, end ch 1, turn.
Row 2: Sk first st, sc in each st across row, end sc in turning ch, ch 1, turn.
Row 3: Repeat Row 2.
Row 4: Sk first st, hdc in each st across row, end hdc in turning ch, ch 1, turn.
Row 5: Repeat Row 4.
Repeat Rows 2-5 for Pattern Stitch.

529. Multiple of 2 stitches.
Row 1: Sk 4 chs, * yo, pull up lp in next 2 chs, yo and thru 2 lps, yo and thru 2 lps, yo and thru 2 lps, sl st in bottom of same st, repeat from * across row, end ch 3, turn.
Repeat Row 2 for Pattern Stitch.

530. Multiple of 4 stitches plus 2.
Row 1: Sk 2 chs, hdc in each ch across, end ch 2, turn.
Row 2: Hdc in first st, * hdc under horizontal lp in next st, hdc in top lp in next st, hdc in back lp in next st, hdc in next st, repeat from * across row, end hdc in back lp of last hdc, ch 2, turn.
Repeat Row 2 for Pattern Stitch.

531. Multiple of 2 stitches plus 1.
Row 1: Sk 2 chs, * sc, hdc, sc in next ch, sk 1, repeat from * across row, end ch 1, turn.
Row 2: (Sc, hdc, sc) in each hdc across row, end ch 1, turn.
Repeat Row 2 for Pattern Stitch.

532. Multiple of 2 stitches.
Row 1: Sk 4 chs, * pull up lp in each of next 2 chs, yo and thru 2 lps, yo and thru 2 lps, pull up lp in top of same st, yo and thru all lps (chain st made), repeat from * across row, end ch 3, turn.
Row 2: Sk 2 sts, * pull up lp in top of next 2 sts, yo and thru 2 lps, yo and thru 2 lps, pull up lp in top of same st, yo and thru 2 lps, repeat from * across. Work 1 chain st in first 2 sts of turning ch, ch 3, turn.
Repeat Row 2 for Pattern Stitch.

533. Multiple of 2 stitches.
Row 1: Sk 3 chs, * sc, ch 1, sc in next ch, ch 1, sk 1, repeat from * across row, end ch 1, turn.
Row 2: (Sc, ch 1, sc) in ch-1 sp between first 2 sc, * sc, ch 1, sc in next ch-1 sp between next 2 sc, repeat from * across row, end ch 1, turn.
Repeat Row 2 for Pattern Stitch.

534. *Row 1:* Sk first 2 chs, dc in each ch across, ch 1, turn.
Row 2: * dc in back lp at top of each dc of previous row, repeat from * across, ch 1, turn.
Repeat Row 2 for Pattern Stitch.

535. *Row 1:* Sc in 2nd ch from hook, sc in each ch across, ch 1, turn.
Row 2: Yo over left index finger, insert hook in first sc, * draw 2 strands (strand on top of finger and strand under index finger) thru st to a 1 inch lp on index finger; remove finger, hold lp in back, yo and thru 3 lps on hook (lp st made), repeat from * across, ch 1, turn.
Row 3: Sc in each lp st across row, ch 1, turn.
Repeat Rows 2 and 3 for Pattern Stitch.

536. Multiple of 5 stitches.
Row 1: Hdc in 3rd ch from hook, hdc in each ch across row, end ch 1, turn.
Row 2: 2 sc in each st across row, end ch 1, turn.
Row 3: Sk 2, * hdc in next st, sk 1, repeat from * across row, end hdc in turning ch, ch 1, turn.
Repeat Rows 2 and 3 for Pattern Stitch.

537. *Row 1:* Sc in 2nd ch from hook, sc in each ch across row, ch 3, turn.
Row 2: Dc in 2nd sc, dc in each sc across row, ch 1, turn.
Row 3: Sc in each dc, ch 4, turn.
Row 4: Tr in 2nd sc, tr in each sc across row, ch 3, turn.
Repeat Rows 2-4 for Pattern Stitch.

538. Multiple of 2 stitches.
Row 1: Sk 3 chs, dc in each ch across, end ch 1, turn.
Row 2: Sk 1 st, * pull up lp in back of dc, pull up lp in front of same dc, yo and thru all lps, repeat from * across, repeat same st in turning ch, ch 2, turn.
Row 3: Dc in each st across row, end ch 1, turn.
Repeat Rows 2 and 3 for Pattern Stitch.

539. Multiple of 2 stitches.
Row 1: Sk 2 chs, hdc in each ch across, end ch 1, turn.
Row 2: Sk 1 st, * pull up lp in back of next st, pull up lp in front of same st, yo and thru all 3 lps, repeat from * across row, end ch 1, turn.
Row 3: Hdc in each st across row, end hdc in turning ch, ch 1, turn.
Repeat Rows 2 and 3 for Pattern Stitch.

540. Work same as for Pattern Number 515. Work on right side only. End off at end of each row.

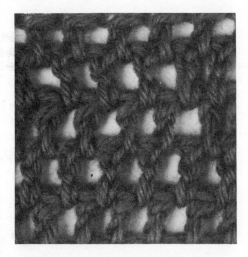

541. *Row 1:* Sk 2 chs, dc in each ch across row, end ch 1, turn.
Row 2: dc under both horizontal lps of each st of previous row across row, end ch 1, turn.
Repeat Row 2 for Pattern Stitch.

542. *Row 1:* Hdc in 3rd ch from hook, hdc in each ch across, ch 1, turn.
Row 2: Hdc under first 2 vertical bars and work the same in all vertical bars across row, end ch 1, turn.
Repeat Row 2 for Pattern Stitch.

543. *Row 1:* Sk 2 chs, dc in each ch across, end ch 2, turn.
Row 2: Dc in the bottom horizontal lp in each dc across row, end ch 2, turn.
Repeat Row 2 for Pattern Stitch.

544. Multiple of 6 stitches.
Row 1: Sk 2 chs, hdc in each ch across row, end ch 2, turn.
Row 2: Hdc in bottom lp only of first 2 sts, * hdc in next st, work in bottom lp only hdc in next 2 sts, repeat from * across row, end hdc in whole st. Ch 2, turn.
Repeat Row 2 for Pattern Stitch.

545. Multiple of 4 stitches.
Row 1: Sk first 2 chs, * draw up lp thru next 2 chs, yo and draw thru 2 lps, yo and thru last 2 lps, ch 1, repeat from * across row, end ch 1, turn.
Row 2: Work 1 dc in each group, 1 dc in each ch between groups, ch 1, turn.
Row 3: Repeat Row 1, working first 2 lps in 2nd and 3rd dc of previous row. End ch 1, turn.
Repeat Rows 2 and 3 for Pattern Stitch.

546. Multiple of 16 stitches.

Row 1: Sk 2 chs, dc in next 4 chs, tr in next 5 chs, * 5 dc in next 5 chs, repeat from * across row, end ch 3, turn.

Row 2: * 5 dc in 5 tr, 5 tr in next 5 dc, repeat from * across row, end ch 3, turn.

Repeat Row 2 for Pattern Stitch.

547. Multiple of 3 stitches plus 1.

Row 1: In 3rd ch from hook 2 dc, * sk 1, 2 dc in next st, repeat from * across row, end ch 2, turn.

Row 2: Sk 1, dc in back lp of next dc, * sk 1, 2 dc in back lp of next dc, repeat from * across row, end 2 dc in turning ch, ch 2, turn.

Repeat Row 2 for Pattern Stitch.

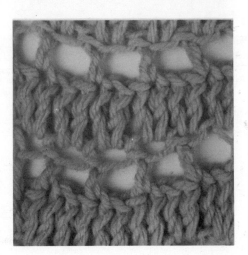

548. Multiple of 3 stitches.

Row 1: Dc in each ch across, end ch 3, turn.

Row 2: * sk 2 sts, dc in next st, repeat from * across row, end ch 2, turn.

Row 3: 2 dc in each dc across row, end 3 dc in turning ch, ch 3, turn.

Repeat Rows 2 and 3 for Pattern Stitch.

549. Multiple of 4 stitches plus 1.
Row 1: 1 tr in 4th ch from hook, * dc, sk 3 chs, (tr, ch 1, tr) in next ch, repeat from * across row, end ch 3, turn.
Row 2 and Following Rows: Tr in first dc, * dc in ch-sp (tr, ch 1, tr in next dc), repeat from * across row, end dc in last sp, ch 3, turn.

550. Multiple of 4 stitches.
Row 1: Sk 2 chs, * sc, hdc in next ch, sk 1, repeat from * across row, end ch 1, turn.
Row 2: Sc, hdc in each sc across row, end ch 1, turn.
Repeat Row 2 for Pattern Stitch.

551. Multiple of 7 stitches.
Row 1: (dc, ch 1, dc) in 6th ch from hook (V) made, * sk 2 chs, V st in dc, ch 1, dc in next ch, repeat from * across row to last 3 chs, end sk 2 chs, dc in last ch, turn.
Row 2: Ch 3 (counts as dc), * V st in ch-1 sp, repeat from * across row, end dc in turning ch.
Repeat Row 2 for Pattern Stitch.

552. Multiple of 3 stitches plus 2.
Row 1: Hdc in each st across, end ch 2, turn.
Row 2: Sk 1, hdc in next st, * sk 1, hdc in next 2 sts, repeat from * across row, end ch 2, turn.
Row 3: Hdc in first st, * 2 hdc in next st, hdc in next st, repeat from * across row, end ch 2, turn.
Repeat Rows 2 and 3 for Pattern Stitch.

553. Multiple of 2 stitches.
Row 1: Sc in 2nd ch from hook and in each ch across row, end ch 2, turn.
Row 2: * sk 1, dc in next sc, dc in skipped sc, repeat from * across row, end dc in last sc, ch 1, turn.
Row 3: Sc in each st across row, end ch 2, turn.
Repeat Rows 2 and 3 for Pattern Stitch.

554. Multiple of 2 stitches plus 1.
Row 1: Hdc in 3rd ch from hook, * sk 1, hdc in next ch, repeat from * across row, end ch 1, turn.
Row 2: Hdc in turning ch, 2 hdc in each st across row, end ch 1, turn.
Row 3: * sk 1, hdc in next st, repeat from * across row, end ch 1, turn.
Repeat Rows 2 and 3 for Pattern Stitch.

555. Multiple of 2 stitches.
Row 1: Hdc in 2nd ch from hook and in each ch across, end ch 2, turn.
Row 2: * sk 1, hdc in next st, repeat from * across row, end ch 1, turn.
Row 3: 2 hdc in each st across row, end ch 1, turn.
Repeat Rows 2 and 3 for Pattern Stitch.

556. Multiple of 3 stitches plus 1.
Row 1: 2 dc in 2nd ch from hook, * sk 1 ch, 2 dc in next ch, repeat from * across, end ch 2, turn.
Row 2: * sk 1 dc, 2 dc in next dc (go under 2 horizontal threads), repeat from * across row, end ch 2, turn.
Repeat Row 2 for Pattern Stitch.

557. Multiple of 3 stitches plus 2.
Row 1: Sc in 2nd ch from hook and in each ch across, turn.
Row 2: Ch 3, sk first sc, dc in next sc, * ch 1, sk next sc, dc in next sc, repeat from * across row, end ch 1, turn.
Row 3: Sc in first dc, * sc in next ch-1 sp, sc in next dc, repeat from * across row, end sc in last ch-3 sp, turn.
Repeat Rows 2 and 3 for Pattern Stitch.

558. Multiple of 4 stitches.
Row 1: Sk 3 chs, * hook in next ch and pull up lp, yo and thru 1 lp, yo and thru 1 lp, yo and thru 2 lps, repeat from * across row, end ch 2, turn.
Row 2: Sk first st, * in next st, pull up lp yo and thru 1 lp, yo and thru 1 lp yo and thru 2 lps, repeat from * across row, end ch 2, turn.
Repeat Rows 1 and 2 for Pattern Stitch.

559. Multiple of 14 stitches plus 7.
Row 1: Sc in 2nd ch from hook, sc in next 5 chs, * ch 3, sk 3, sc in next ch, ch 3, sk 3, sc in next ch, sc in next 6 chs, repeat from * across row, end ch 1, turn.
Row 2: * Sc in 6 sc, ch 3, sc in sc, ch 3, sc in next 6 sc, repeat from * across row, end ch 1, turn.
Rows 3,4,5: Repeat Row 2.
Row 6: Ch 3, sc in 3rd sc, ch 3, sk 2, * 3 sc in each ch-3 lp, ch 3, sk 2, sc in next sc, ch 3, repeat from * across row, end sc in turning ch, ch 1, turn.
Rows 7,8,9: Repeat Row 6.
Repeat Rows 2-9 for Pattern Stitch.

560. Multiple of 2 stitches plus 1.
Row 1: Dc in 2nd ch from hook, * tr in next ch, dc in next ch, repeat from * across row, end ch 1, turn.
Repeat Row 1 for Pattern Stitch working dc over tr and tr over each dc.

561. Multiple of 4 stitches.
Row 1: Dc in 3rd ch from hook and in each ch across, end ch 2, turn.
Row 2: Dc in back lp of first st, * dc in top horizontal lp in next dc, dc in back lp of next st, repeat from * across row, end dc in front lp of last dc, ch 2, turn.
Repeat Row 2 for Pattern Stitch.

562. Multiple of 2 stitches.
Row 1: Hdc in 3rd ch from hook and in each ch across, end ch 3, turn.
Row 2: * Sk 1, dc in next st, repeat from * across row, end ch 2, turn.
Row 3: 2 hdc in top lp only of each dc across row, end ch 2, turn.
Repeat Rows 2 and 3 for Pattern Stitch.

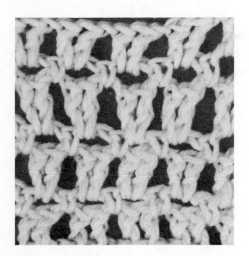

563. Multiple of 3 stitches plus 1.
Row 1: Dc in 4th ch from hook, * ch 1, sk 1, dc in each of next 2 chs, repeat from * across row, end ch 3, turn.
Row 2: Sc in ch-1 sp, * ch 2, sc in next sp, repeat from * across row, end sc in top of turning ch, ch 3, turn.
Row 3: Dc in first sp to complete first double st, * ch 1, 2 dc in next sp, repeat from * across row, end ch 3, turn.
Repeat Rows 2 and 3 for Pattern Stitch.

564. Multiple of 2 stitches plus 1.
Row 1: Sk first 3 chs, tr in next ch, tr in 3rd ch just skipped, * sk 1, tr in next ch, tr in skipped ch, repeat from * across row, end ch 2, turn.
Row 2: Work same as for Row 1—crossing trs across row, end ch 2, turn.
Repeat Row 2 for Pattern Stitch.

565. Multiple of 2 stitches.
Row 1: Sk 2 chs, * sc, dc in next ch, sk 1, repeat from * across row, end ch 1, turn.
Row 2: Dc, sc in each sc across row, end ch 1, turn.
Row 3: Sc, dc in each dc across row, end ch 1, turn.
Repeat Rows 2 and 3 for Pattern Stitch.

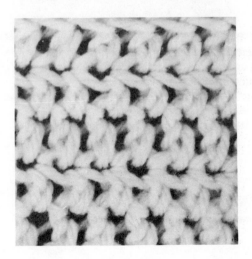

566. *Row 1:* Hdc in 2nd ch from hook and in each ch across, end ch 2, turn.
Row 2: Hdc in each hdc across row, end ch 2, turn.
Repeat Row 2 for Pattern Stitch.

567. Multiple of 2 stitches plus 1.

Row 1: Sc in 2nd ch from hook, * ch 1, sk 1, sc in next ch, repeat from * across row, end ch 1, turn.

Row 2: Sc in first sc, * ch 1, sc in next sc, repeat from * across row, end ch 1, turn.

Repeat Row 2 for Pattern Stitch.

Fringe: Wind yarn several times around a 4 inch cardboard, cut open at one end. Hold 8 strands together and fold in half to make a lp. Insert hook under ch-1 sp and draw lp thru and pull tight. Continue in this manner placing a fringe in each ch-1 sp. Trim fringe evenly.

568. Multiple of 2 stitches plus 1.

Row 1: Dc in 6th ch from hook, * ch 1, sk 1, dc in next ch, repeat from * across, end ch 4, turn.

Row 2: Dc in 2nd dc, * ch 1, dc in next dc, repeat from * across row, end dc in turning ch, ch 4, turn.

Repeat Row 2 for Pattern Stitch.

569. Multiple of 10 stitches.

Row 1: Sk 3 chs, dc in each ch across, ch 3, turn.

Row 2: 2 dc under and around 2nd and 3rd dc, * dc around next dc (in back of), 3 dc under and around next 3 dc, repeat from * across row, ending 3 dc under and around last 3 dc, ch 3, turn.

Row 3: Dc in each of 2 dc and * dc in front of next dc, dc in next 3 dc, repeat from * across row, end ch 3, turn.

Repeat Rows 2 and 3 for Pattern Stitch.

570. *Row 1:* Sc in 2nd ch from hook and in each ch across to end of row, turn.
Row 2: Ch 3, dc in each st across row, turn.
Row 3: Ch 1, sc in each st across row, turn.
Repeat Rows 2 and 3 for Pattern Stitch.

571. Multiple of 4 stitches.
Row 1: Sc in 2nd ch from hook, dc in next ch, * sc in next ch, dc in next ch, repeat from * across row, ch 1, turn.
Row 2: * Sc in dc, dc in sc, repeat from * across row, ch 1, turn.
Repeat Row 2 for Pattern Stitch.

572. Multiple of 2 stitches plus 1.
Row 1: Dc in 2nd ch from hook, * ch 1, sk 1, dc in next ch, repeat from * across row, end ch 2, turn.
Row 2: * Dc in ch-1 sp, ch 1, repeat from * across row, end dc in last sp, ch 2, turn.
Row 3: *Dc in ch-1 sp, ch 1, repeat from * across row, end ch 2, turn.
Repeat Row 3 for Pattern Stitch.

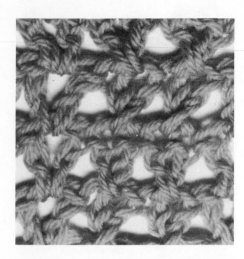

573. Multiple of 8 stitches plus 4.
Row 1: Dc in 6th ch from hook, sk 1 (dc, ch 1, dc), V st in next ch, * (sk 1, dc in next ch, dc in skipped ch), cross st in next 2 chs, sk 1, V st, sk 1, V st, repeat from * across row, ending with 2 V sts, ch 3, turn.
Row 2: Dc in first ch-1 sp, V st in V st, cross st in next 2 cross sts, V st in next 2 V sts, repeat from * across row, ending with 2 V sts, ch 3, turn.
Repeat Row 2 for Pattern Stitch.

574. *Row 1:* Hdc in 2nd ch from hook and in each ch across, end ch 1, turn.
Row 2: Sl st in top lp of each hdc across row, end ch 2, turn.
Repeat Rows 1 and 2 for Pattern Stitch.

575. Multiple of 2 stitches plus 1.
Row 1: Dc in 3rd ch from hook, * sc in next ch, dc in next ch, repeat from * across row, end ch 1, turn.
Row 2: Dc in each sc, sc in each dc to end, end ch 1, turn.
Repeat Row 2 for Pattern Stitch.

576. *Row 1:* Hdc in 2nd ch from hook, hdc in each ch across row, end ch 1, turn.
Row 2: Hdc in back lp of first st, * hdc in front lp of next st, hdc in back lp of next st, repeat from * across row, end hdc in back lp of last st, ch 1, turn.
Row 3: Hdc in front lp of first st, * hdc in back lp of next st, hdc in front lp of next st, repeat from * across row, end hdc in front lp of last st, end ch 1, turn.
Repeat Rows 2 and 3 for Pattern Stitch.

577. Multiple of 11 stitches.
Row 1: Dc in 7th ch from hook, ch 1, dc in back of 5th ch from hook for a cross st, * sk 2, dc in next ch, ch 1, dc in back of skipped ch, repeat from * across row, end dc in last ch, ch 4, turn.
Row 2: * sk first dc of cross st, dc in 2nd dc of cross st, ch 1, dc in skipped dc, repeat from * across row, end dc in turning ch, ch 4, turn.
Repeat Row 2 for Pattern Stitch.

578. Multiple of 11 stitches plus 1.
Row 1: Hdc in 3rd ch from hook, * hdc in next 3 chs, (sk 1, dc in next ch, dc in skipped ch), cross st made 2 times more, hdc in next 4 chs, ch 1, turn.
Row 2: * hdc in 4 hdc, work cross st 3 times, repeat from * across row, end hdc in last 4 hdc, ch 1, turn.
Repeat Row 2 for Pattern Stitch.

579. Multiple of 5 stitches.
Row 1: Dc in 4th ch from hook, dc in each ch across row, turn.
Row 2: Ch 4, sk 2 dc, dc in next dc, * ch 1, sk 1 dc, dc in next dc, repeat from * across row, turn.
Row 3: Ch 3, * dc in ch-1 sp, dc in dc, repeat from * across row, turn.
Repeat Rows 2 and 3 for Pattern Stitch.

580. Multiple of 5 stitches plus 4.
Row 1: Dc in 4th ch from hook, * sk 1, (dc, ch 1, dc) all in next ch (V st), sk 2 chs, (dc, ch 1, dc) in next ch, repeat from * across row, end sk 1 ch, dc in last 2 chs, ch 3, turn.
Row 2: Sk first dc, dc in each st across row and dc in each ch, ch 3, turn.
Row 3: Sk first st, dc in next st, sk 1, V st in next sp, * sk 2 sts, V st in next st, repeat from * across row, end sk 1 st, dc in last 2 sts, ch 3, turn.
Repeat Rows 2 and 3 for Pattern Stitch.

581. Multiple of 2 stitches.
Row 1: Sk 4 chs, * yo, pull up lp in next 2 chs, yo and thru 2 lps, yo and thru 2 lps, yo and thru last 2 lps (twist st), ch 1, repeat from * across row, end ch 3, turn.
Row 2: * Yo, pull up lp in ch-1 sp, pull up lp in next st, yo and thru 2 lps, yo and thru 2 lps, yo and thru last 2 lps, ch 1, repeat from * across row, end twist st in turning ch, ch 3, turn.
Repeat Row 2 for Pattern Stitch.

582. *Row 1:* Hdc in 3rd ch from hook and in each ch across, ch 1, turn.
Row 2: * Hdc in hdc, work next hdc under the 2 horizontal bars, repeat from * across row, end hdc under last 2 horizontal bars, ch 1, turn.
Repeat Row 2 for Pattern Stitch.

583. *Row 1:* Dc in 3rd ch from hook and in each ch across row, ch 1, turn.
Row 2: Hdc in back lp only of each dc across row, end ch 2, turn.
Repeat Rows 1 and 2 for Pattern Stitch.

584. *Row 1:* Tr in 3rd ch from hook, tr in each ch across, ch 1, turn.
Row 2: Dc in each tr across row, ch 2, turn.
Row 3: Tr in each dc across row, ch 1, turn.
Repeat Rows 2 and 3 for Pattern Stitch.

Geometric
Stitch Patterns

These compositions are symmetrical and balanced. Shapes and relationships are established by linear boundaries and flat masses of color. The patterns seem controlled, but the spontaneity is up to you. Let your color palette go wild. Use tangerine, pistachio, rose, hot pinks and deep purples. Cerulean blue! Gather together all the colors in the rainbow.

These patterns are fun to make. As with Flower motifs and Appliques, make them separately and join them together. They make snappy handbags and a multitude of novelty items. Whip up an art-deco pillow in no time at all. Or, in less than an afternoon, create a colorful vest out of two large shapes.

585. *Ecology Symbol: Rnd 1:* Ch 18, join with sl st to form ring. Turn and ch 7, join with sl st to opposite side of circle.
Rnd 2: Work a sl st in next ch and work sc in each ch around. End off.

586. Ch 6, join with sl st to form ring.
Rnd 1: Ch 6, * tr in ring, ch 2, repeat from * around 6 times more, join with sl st to top of ch-6.
Rnd 2: Sl st in next sp, ch 4, 4 tr in same sp, * ch 2, 5 tr in next sp, repeat from * around. Join with sl st to top of ch-4.
Rnd 3: Ch 4, tr in same place as sl st, tr in next 4 tr, * tr in first ch of ch-2, ch 3, tr in next ch of same ch-2, tr in next 5 tr, repeat from * around. Join with sl st in top of ch-4. Fasten off.

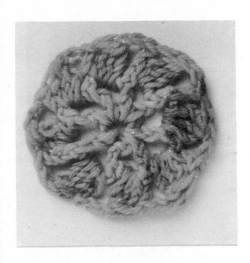

587. *Rnd 1:* Ch 6, join with sl st to form ring.
Rnd 2: Ch 6, * (dc, ch 2) 5 times in ring, sl st to join.
Rnd 3: Ch 2, hold back last lp of each dc, work (3 dc, yo and thru all lps on hook) in each ch-2 sp around. Join with sl st and fasten off.

588. Ch 4, join with sl st to form ring.
Rnd 1: Ch 5, in ring work (dc, ch 2) 5 times, join with sl st to 3rd ch of ch-5.
Rnd 2: Sl in next sp, ch 4, hold back last lp of each tr, work 4 tr in same sp, yo and draw thru all 5 lps on hook, * ch 9, work 5 tr in next sp, yo and draw thru all 6 lps on hook (cluster made), repeat from * around, end with ch 9, join with sl st at start of cluster.
Rnd 3: Ch 1, sc in same place of join, * ch 9, sk 4 chs, work cluster in next ch of ch-9, sc in top of next cluster, repeat from * around, end last repeat with ch 9, join to first sc. End off.

589. With A, ch 6, join with sl st to form ring, ch 2, work 15 dc in ring. End off.
Rnd 1: With B, join in any dc, ch 2, in same sp work 2 dc, hold back last lp of each dc on hook, yo and thru all lps, * ch 2, sk 1, sc in next dc, ch 2, sk 1, 3 dc in next dc (hold back last lp of each dc, yo and thru all lps) popcorn made, repeat from * around. Join with sl st to top of ch-2. End off.
Rnd 2: Join C in any sc, ch 2, work 2 dc in same sp, * 2 dc in next sp, dc in popcorn, 2 dc in next ch-2 sp, 3 dc in sc, repeat from * around. Join with sl st to top of ch-2. End off.

590. Ch 8, join with sl st to form ring.

Rnd 1: Ch 1, 16 sc in ring. Join with sl st to first sc.

Rnd 2: Ch 4, dc in next st, (ch 1 dc in next st) 14 times, ch 1, join with sl st to 3rd st of ch-4.

Rnd 3: Ch 1, 2 sc in turning ch-sp, 2 sc in each ch-1 sp, join with sl st to first sc.

Rnd 4: Ch 3, dc in same st 3 times, * ch 3, sk 2 sts, (draw up lp in next st, yo and thru 1 lp, yo and thru 2 lps, yo and thru all 3 lps) twice, (cluster made), repeat from * around. End ch 3 and join with sl st in top of ch-3. End off.

591. With A, ch 6, join with sl st to form ring, ch 2, work 16 dc in ring. Join with sl st to top of ch-2. End off.

Rnd 1: Join B in any dc, * ch 3, sk 1, sc in next dc, repeat from * around. Join with sl st in top of ch-3. End off.

Rnd 2: Join C in any ch-3 sp, ch 2, 2 dc, ch 2, 3 dc in same sp, * 2 dc in next sp, (3 dc, ch 2, 3 dc) in next sp, repeat from * around. Join with sl st to top of ch-2. End off.

Rnd 3: On wrong side join D in any dc, ch 1, sc in each dc around. Join with sl st to ch-1. End off.

592. Ch 4, join with sl st to form ring.

Rnd 1: Ch 3, * dc in ring, ch 1, repeat from * 6 times more, join with sl st in top of ch-3. End off.

Rnd 2: Join 2nd color in any ch-1 sp, ch 2, 2 dc in same sp, * ch 1, 3 dc in next ch-1 sp, repeat from * around, join with sl st in top of ch-2. End off.

593. Ch 3.

Rnd 1: 5 sc in 2nd ch from hook.

Rnd 2: 3 sc in each sc around—15 sc. Join with sl st to 1st sc.

Rnd 3: *Sc in next sc, ch 6, sl st in 2nd ch from hook, sc in next ch, hdc in next st, dc in next st, tr in next st, tr in base of sc in circle, sk 2 sc, repeat from * 4 times. Join with sl st to 1st ray of star and fasten off.

594. With A ch 4, join with sl st to form ring.

Rnd 1: Ch 4, * dc in ring, ch 1, repeat from * around 6 times more. Join with sl st in top of ch-4. End off.

Rnd 2: Join B in ch-1 sp, ch 3, 2 dc in same sp, ch 1, * 3 dc in next sp, ch 1, repeat from * around. Join with sl st in top of ch-3. End off.

Rnd 3: Join C in ch-1 sp, ch 3, 2 dc in same sp, ch 1, * in next sp 3 dc, ch 3, 3 dc (corner), ch 1, 3 dc in next sp, ch 1, repeat from * around 2 times more, ch 1. Join with sl st to top of ch-3. End off.

595. Ch 8, join with sl st to form ring.

Rnd 1: Ch 3, work 20 dc in ring, join with sl st to top of ch-3. Fasten off.

596. Ch 5, join with sl st to form ring.

Rnd 1: Ch 2, work 11 dc in ring, join with sl st. End off.

Rnd 2: Join B in any dc, ch 2, * 2 dc in next dc, dc in next dc, repeat from * around. Join with sl st to top of ch-2. End off.

Rnd 3: Join C in any dc, ch 2, work (2 dc, ch 1, 3 dc) in same sp, * dc in next 3 dc, (3 dc, ch 1, 3 dc) in next dc for corner, dc in next 4 dc, (3 dc, ch 1, 3 dc) in next dc and dc in next 3 dc, (3 dc, ch 1, 3 dc) in next dc and dc in last 4 dc. Fasten off.

597. With A, ch 4, join with sl st to form ring.

Rnd 1: Ch 3, work 11 dc in ring. Join with sl st to top of ch-3. End off.

Rnd 2: With B, join in top of any dc, ch 2, work dc in back lp of same st, * dc in front lp, dc in back lp of next st, repeat from * around—24 dc. Join with sl st to top of ch-2. End off.

Rnd 3: With C, join in any dc, ch 2, work (dc, ch 2, 2 dc) in same sp, * dc in next 5 dc, (2 dc, ch 2, 2 dc) for a corner in next dc, repeat from * around. Join with sl st. End off.

Rnd 4: With D, join in any ch-2 sp, work dc, ch 2, 2 dc in same sp, * dc in next 9 dc, (2 dc, ch 2, 2 dc) for a corner in next st, repeat from * around. Join with sl st. End off.

598. Ch 8, join with sl st to form ring. * ch 4, 4 dc in ring. (Hold back last lp of each dc, yo and thru all lps on hook), repeat from * 3 times more. End off.

Rnd 2: With B join in any ch-4 lp, ch 3, 2 dc, ch 3, 3 dc in same sp, dc in center of popcorn, * 3 dc, ch 3, 3 dc in next lp, dc in center of next popcorn, repeat from * 2 times more. Join with sl st to top of ch-3. End off.

Rnd 3: With C join in any corner, ch 3, dc, ch 3, 2 dc in same sp, dc in next 7 dc, * 2 dc, ch 3, 2 dc in next lp, dc in popcorn, repeat from * 2 times more. Join with sl st to top of ch-3. End off.

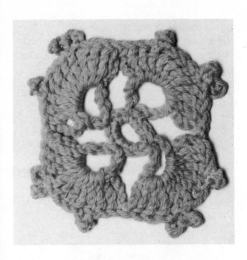

599. Ch 8, join with sl st to form ring.

Rnd 1: Ch 1, work 12 sc in ring. Join with sl st in first sc.

Rnd 2: Ch 8, tr in same sc as sl st, * ch 10, sk 2 sc, (tr, ch 3, tr) in next sc, repeat from * around twice, ch 5, join with tr in 5th ch of ch-8.

Rnd 3: * 3 tr in next ch-3 sp, ch 4, sl st in last tr (picot) in ch-3 sp last worked, make (4 tr, picot) twice and 3 tr, sc in next ch-10 lp, repeat from * around. Join with sl st in first tr of rnd. End off.

600. Ch 2.

Row 1: 3 sc in 2nd ch from hook, ch 1, turn.

Row 2: 2 sc in first sc (inc. made), sc in each sc, 2 sc in last sc (inc. made), ch 1, turn.

Row 3: Work 2 sc in first sc, sc in each sc, work 2 sc in last sc, ch 1, turn.

Repeat Rows 2 and 3 until desired width.

Row 4: Join 2nd color in last lp of last sc, ch 1, turn. Decrease 1 sc at both ends of each row until 1 sc remains. End off.

601. Ch 2.

Row 1: Work same as for Pat. No. 600.

Row 2: Work same as for Pat. No. 600.

Row 3: Pick up front lp only of each sc, work 2 sc in first sc, sc in each sc, 2 sc in last sc, ch 1, turn.

Repeat Rows 2 and 3 for Pattern Stitch working until desired width.

Row 4: Work same as for Pat. No. 600.

602. Work Pattern Number 600 through to end of square.
Triangle: Row 1: Join yarn on right side, work 10 sc across row, ch 1, turn.
Row 2: Decrease (pull up lp in first and 2nd sc, yo and thru all lps), sc in each sc across to within last 2 sts, dec, ch 1, turn.
Repeat Row 2 until 1 sc remains. End off.
Repeat triangle in edge of each square.

603. *Rnd 1:* Ch 3, join with sl st to form ring. Work 2 dc in ring, * ch 2, 3 dc, repeat from * around twice, ch 2, join with sl st to top of ch-3.
Rnd 2: Ch 3, dc in ch-2 sp, sk first dc, dc in next 2 dc, * (2 dc, ch 2, 2 dc) in next ch-2 sp, sk next dc, dc in next 2 dc, repeat from * twice, 2 dc in last ch-2 sp, ch 2, join with sl st to top of ch-3.
Rnd 3: Sl st to ch-2 sp and ch 3, dc, ch 2, 2 dc in same sp, * dc in next 5 dc, in next corner (2 dc, ch 2, 2 dc), repeat from * around. Join with sl st in top of ch 3.
Rnd 4: Sl st to ch-2 sp and ch 3, dc, ch 2, 2 dc, * dc in next 8 dc, in next corner 2 dc, ch 2, 2 dc, repeat from * around. Join with sl st, end off.

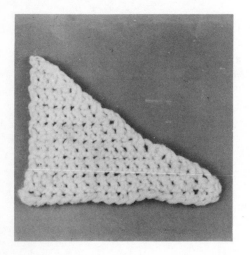

604. Ch 19 loosely.
Row 1: Sc in 2nd ch from hook and in each ch across, ch 1, turn.
Row 2: Pull up lp in each of first 2 sc, yo and thru all 3 lps on hook (dec made), sc in each sc across, ch 1, turn.
Row 3: Sc in each sc to last 2 sc, dec 1 sc, ch 1, turn.
Repeat Rows 2 and 3 for Pattern Stitch until 1 sc remains. Fasten off.

605. *Small Medallion:* With A ch 4, join with sl st to form ring.
Rnd 1: With A ch 1, work 12 hdc in ring. Drop A.
Rnd 2: With B sl st to first hdc, ch 1, hdc in same st, * 2 hdc in each of 2 hdc, hdc in next hdc, repeat from * around, end 2 hdc in last 2 hdc—20 hdc. Join with sl st in first hdc. Fasten off.

606. *Large Medallion:* Work same as for Pattern Number 605 through Rnd 1.
Rnd 2: With B sl st in first hdc, ch 1, hdc in same st as sl st, * 2 hdc in next hdc, hdc in next hdc, repeat from * around—18 hdc. Drop B to wrong side.
Rnd 3: With A sl st in first hdc, ch 1, hdc in same st, * 2 hdc in next hdc, hdc in next hdc, repeat from * around. 27 hdc. Drop A to wrong side.
Rnd 4: With B sl st in first hdc, ch 1, hdc in same st, * 2 hdc in each of next 2 hdc, hdc in next hdc, repeat from * around to last 2 hdc, end 2 hdc in next hdc, hdc in last hdc—44 hdc. Drop B to wrong side.
Rnd 5: With a sl st in first hdc, ch 1, hdc in same st, hdc in each hdc around; join with sl st in first hdc. End off.

607. With first color, ch 4, join with sl st to first ch to form ring.
Rnd 1: Ch 3, 2 dc in ring, * ch 2, 3 dc in ring, repeat from * twice more, ch 2, join with sl st to top of ch-3. End off.
Rnd 2: Join 2nd color in any ch-2 sp, ch 3, 2 dc, ch 2, 3 dc in same sp, * sk 3 dc, 3 dc, ch 2, 3 dc in next sp, repeat from * twice more, join with sl st to top of ch-3. End off.
Rnd 3: Join 3rd color in any ch-2 corner sp, ch 3, 2 dc, ch 2, 3 dc in same sp, * sk 3 dc, 3 dc in next sp, sk 3 dc, 3 dc, ch 2, 3 dc in next corner sp, repeat from * around, ending sk 3 dc, 3 dc in next sp, sk 3 dc, join with sl st to top of ch-3.
Rnd 4: Join 4th color and work as for Rnd 3, having 2 groups of 3 dc between corners. Fasten off.

608. With A ch 6, join with sl st to form ring.

Rnd 1: Work 14 dc in ring. Join with sl st. End off.

Rnd 2: Join B in any dc, ch 2, 2 dc, ch 1 in same sp, * sk 1, in next dc (3 dc, ch 1), repeat from * around. Join with sl st in top of ch 2, end off.

Rnd 3: Join C in any ch-1 sp, ch 2, work dc, ch 1, in same sp, * work 2 dc in center of 3-dc group, ch 1, 2 dc, ch 1, in next ch-1 sp, repeat from * around. Join with sl st. End off.

Rnd 4: Join D in any ch-1 sp, * ch 4, sc in next ch-1 sp, repeat from * around. Join with sl st. End off.

Rnd 5: Join B in any ch-1 of ch-4 loop, sl st in next st, * ch 4, sc in center of next lp, repeat from * around. Join with sl st. End off.

Rnd 6: Sl st to next lp, ch 2, work 3 dc in same sp, 4 dc in next lp and in each lp around. Join with sl st. End off.

Rnd 7: Join D in center of any 4 dc group, * ch 6, sc in center of next group, repeat from * around. Join with sl st. End off.

609. *Note:* Join colors in last lp of last dc on each row.

Row 1: Dc in 2nd ch from hook, * sk 1, 2 dc in next ch, repeat from * across.

Row 2: Join B, ch 3, turn, * 2 dc in sp before next group, repeat from * across, end 1 dc in turning ch.

Row 3: Join C, ch 3, turn. 1 dc in sp before next group, * 2 dc in next sp, repeat from * across.

Row 4: Repeat Row 2 with Color D.

Row 5: Repeat Row 3 with Color C.

Row 6: Repeat Row 2 with Color B.

Row 7: Repeat Row 3 with Color A, ch 1, turn. * Work 1 sc in each st to corner, 3 sc in corner, repeat from * around. Join with sl st. Fasten off.

610. Ch 4, join with sl st to form ring.

Rnd 1: Ch 2, in ring work dc, * ch 1, 2 dc, repeat from * 3 times more, end ch 1, join with sl st in top of ch-2. End off.

Rnd 2: Join 2nd color in any ch-1 sp, * yo and pull up lp 3 times, yo and draw thru all lps on hook (popcorn), ch 4, repeat from * 4 times more, join with sl st.

Rnd 3: Work 5 sc in each ch-4 sp and 1 sc in top of each popcorn around, join with sl st in first sc. End off.

611. With A ch 5, join with sl st to form ring.

Rnd 1: Ch 3 (counts as 1 dc), in ring 2 dc, (ch 1, 3 dc) 3 times, ch 1. Join with sl st to top of ch-3.

Rnd 2: Sl st in next 2 dc, * in next sp work 1 sc, ch 3, 1 sc for a corner, ch 3, repeat from * till there are 4 corners, ch 3. Join with sl st to first sc.

Rnd 3: Sl st in next sp, ch 3, 2 dc, ch 1, 3 dc in same sp, * ch 1, 3 dc in next sp, ch 1, in next sp (3 dc, ch 1, 3 dc) for a corner, repeat from * around. Join with sl st and end off.

Rnd 4: With B join in any ch-1 sp of corner, 1 sc in same sp, * ch 3, sc in next sp, repeat from * around working sc, ch 3, sc in each of the corners. Join with sl st.

Rnd 5: With B work 3 dc, ch 1 in each ch-3 lp, increase at corners.

Repeat Rnds 4 and 5 for Pattern Stitch increasing each row in corner spaces.

612. *Granny Square*

Rnd 1: Ch 4, join with sl st to 1st Ch to form a ring.

Rnd 2: Ch 2 (counts as 1 dc), 2 dc in ring, * ch 1, 3 dc in ring, repeat from * twice more, ch 1, join with sl st in top of ch-2. End off.

Rnd 3: Join 2nd color in any ch-1 sp, * 5 dc in sp for a corner, 1 dc in center of next 3 dc group, repeat from * 3 times more, join to first st. End off.

Rnd 4: Join 3rd color between 3rd and 4th sts of any corner group and work 6 dc for corner, * 3 dc in next single dc, 6 dc in center of next corner group, repeat from * twice, 3 dc in next single dc, join to first st. End off.

Rnd 5: Join 4th color and * work 6 dc in center of a corner group, sk next 2 dc of same group and work 3 dc in next dc, 1 dc in center of next 3 dc group, 3 dc in first st of next corner, repeat from * 3 times more, join to first st. End off.

Weave in ends on wrong side.

613. With A ch 5, join to first ch with sl st to form ring.

Rnd 1: Ch 3 (counts as 1 dc), in ring work 2 dc, ch 1, (3 dc, ch 1) 5 times. Join with sl st in top of ch-3.

Rnd 2: Sl st in next 2 dc, * sc in ch-1 sp, ch 3, repeat from * around. Join with sl st to first sc.

Rnd 3: Sl st in lp, ch 3, 2 dc, ch 1, 3 dc in same lp, ch 1, in each remaining lp (3 dc, ch 1) 2 times. Join with sl st. End off.

Rnd 4: With B join in ch-1 sp, sc in same sp, * ch 3, sc in next sp, repeat from * around, end ch 3. Join with sl st and end off.

Rnd 5: Join C in any lp ch 3, 2 dc in same lp, ch 1, * in next lp (3 dc, ch 1) 2 times (increase made), 3 dc in next lp, ch 1, repeat from * around. Join with sl st.

Rnd 6: Repeat Row 2.

Rnd 7: Sl st to lp, work in group pattern with ch 1 between patterns. Increase 6 group patterns around. Be sure not to increase groups over previous increase groups. Join with sl st.

Rnd 8: Repeat Row 2.

Rnd 9: Repeat Row 7.

614. With A ch 6, join with sl st to first ch to form ring.

Rnd 1: Ch 2, work 2 dc, ch 1 in ring, 3 dc, ch 1 in ring, repeat from * around. Join with sl st. End off.

Rnd 2: Join B in any ch-1 sp, ch 2, 2 dc, ch 1, 3 dc in same sp, ch 1, in each ch-1 sp work (3 dc, ch 1, 3 dc, ch 1) for a cluster shell. Join with sl st, end off.

Rnd 3: Join A in ch-1 sp between cluster shells, ch 2, 2 dc in same sp, ch 1, * cluster-shell in next ch-1 sp, 3 dc in next ch-1 sp, repeat from * around. Join with sl st. End off.

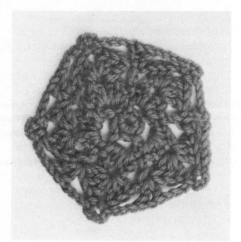

615. Ch 3, join with a sl st to form ring.

Rnd 1: Work 8 sc in ring. Join with a sl st to first sc.

Rnd 2: * ch 3, sk 1 sc, sc in next sc, repeat from * around, end with sc in base of first ch-3.

Rnd 3: * In ch-3 sp work (sc, hdc, dc, ch 2, dc, hdc, sc, ch 1), repeat from * around, end with sl st in first sc.

Rnd 4: Sl st in last ch-1 sp, ch 4, * in ch-2 sp work (3 dc, ch 2, 3 dc, ch 1), under next ch-1 sp work (dc, ch 1), repeat from * around, end with sl st in 3rd ch of ch-4.

Rnd 5: Ch 4, dc in same sp, ch 3, * in next ch-2 sp work (sc, ch 3, sc, ch 3), in next dc work (dc, ch 1, dc, ch 3), repeat from * around, end with ch 3, sl st in 3rd ch of ch-4. End off.

616. With A ch 7, join to first ch with sl st to form ring.

Rnd 1: Ch 3 (counts as dc), 13 dc in ring—14 dc. Join with sl st in top of ch-3.

Rnd 2: Ch 9, tr in next dc, * ch 5, tr in next dc, repeat from * around, ch 5, sl st in 4th ch of starting ch.

Rnd 3: With B join in any ch-lp, ch 3; hold back last lp of each tr, work 3 tr in first sp, yo and thru all 4 lps on hook, * ch 5; hold back last lp of each tr, work 4 tr in next ch-5 lp, yo and thru all 5 lps on hook, repeat from * around, end ch 5, sl st in top of ch-3.

Rnd 4: Join C in any ch-5 sp, ch 3, 2 dc in same sp, * ch 5, 3 dc in next ch-5 sp, repeat from * around, end sl st in top of ch-3. Fasten off.

Note: Twist yarn to wrong side when changing colors.

617. Ch 6, join with sl st to form ring.
Rnd 1: Work 12 sc in ring. Do not join; be sure to mark ends of rnds.
Rnd 2: * sc in next sc, 3 sc in next sc. Repeat from * around—24 sc.
Rnds 3,5,7,9: Sc in each sc around.
Rnd 4: * sc in each of 3 sc, 3 sc in next sc. Repeat from * around—36 sc.
Rnd 6: * sc in next 3 sc, 3 sc in next sc. Repeat from * around—48 sc.
Rnd 8: * sc in 7 sc, 3 sc in next sc, repeat from * around—60 sc. Join and fasten off.

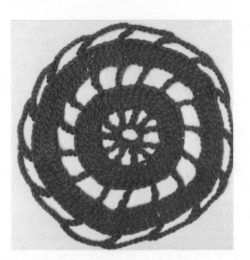

618. Ch 10, join with sl st to first ch to form ring.
Rnd 1: Ch 6, * tr in ring, ch 2, repeat from * around 10 times. Join with sl st to 4th ch of ch-6.
Rnd 2: Ch 4, 2 tr in same sp, * tr in tr, 3 tr in next sp, repeat from * around. Join with sl st to top of ch-4.
Rnd 3: Ch 9, sk 2 tr, * tr in next tr, ch 5, sk 2 tr, repeat from * around. Join with sl st to 4th ch of ch-9.
Rnd 4: Ch 4, tr in next 5 chs, * tr in tr, tr in next 5 chs, repeat from * around. Join with sl st to top of ch-4.
Rnd 5: Ch 12, * sk 5 tr, tr in next tr, ch 8, repeat from * around. Join with sl st to 4th ch of ch-12. End off.

619. With A ch 5, join to first ch with sl st to form ring, ch 3.
Rnd 1: In ring work 2 dc, (ch 1, 3 dc) 3 times, ch 1, join with sl st in top of ch-3.
Rnd 2: Sl st in next 2 dc, * in next sp (sc, ch 3, sc) for a corner, ch 3, repeat from * around till there are 4 corners, ch 3, join with sl st to first sc. End off.
Rnd 3: Join B in any ch-3 corner, ch 3, 2 dc, ch 1, 3 dc in same sp, join * A in last lp of last dc and work 3 dc in next ch-3 sp, with B work 3 dc, ch 1, 3 dc in next sp, repeat from * around, join with sl st to top of ch-3. End off.
Rnd 4: Join B in ch-3 lp, sc, ch 3, sc in same lp, work ch 3, sc between each block and sc, ch 3, sc in each corner, join with sl st in top of ch-3. End off.
Rnd 5: Join C in any corner-lp ch 3, 2 dc, ch 1, 3 dc in same lp, * with A, 3 dc in next 3 lps, with C, 3 dc, ch 1, 3 dc, in next corner lp, repeat from * around, join with sl st to top of ch-3. End off.
Rnd 6: With Color B repeat Rnd 4.
Rnd 7: Repeat Rnd 5. End off.

620. Ch 8, join with sl st to form ring.

Rnd 1: Ch 3, 15 tr in ring, join with sl st in 3rd ch.

Rnd 2: Ch 4, (1 tr, ch 1) in each tr, join with sl st in 3rd ch.

Rnd 3: Ch 5, (1 tr, ch 3) in each tr, join with sl st in 3rd ch.

Rnd 4: Sl st in first sp, ch 4, 1 cluster in first ch 3 sp, (make 3 dc and hold last lp of each dc on hook), yo and thru all 4 lps on hook, ch 3. Work a cluster in each ch 3 sp of previous round, join with sl st in top of ch 4. End off.

621. Ch 4. Join with sl st to form ring.

Rnd 1: Ch 3, work 3 dc in ring, (ch 3, 4 dc in ring) 3 times, ch 3, join with sl st to top of ch 3. Break off.

Rnd 2: Sc in any ch 3 sp, (ch 10, sc in next ch-3 sp) 3 times, ch 10, sl st in first sc.

Rnd 3: (Work 12 sc in next ch 10 lp, sc in next sc) 3 times, 12 sc in next ch-10 lp.

Rnd 4: Ch 5, * dec 1 sc as follows: draw up lp in each of next 2 sc, yo hook, draw through all 3 lps on hook (dec completed), sc in each of next 8 sc, dec 1 sc, (dec completed), sc in each of next 8 sc, dec 1 sc, ch 5, skip next sc between lps. Repeat from * twice more, dec 1 sc, sc in each of next 8 sc, dec 1 sc.

Rnd 5: * Ch 5, 4 dc in next ch 5 lp, ch 5, dec 1 sc, sc in each of next 6 sc, dec 1 sc. Repeat from * 3 times more.

622. Ch 4. Join with sl st to form ring.

Rnd 1: Ch 3, work 1 dc in ring, (ch 1, 2 dc in ring) 4 times, ch 1, join with sl st to top of ch 3. Break off.

Rnd 2: Sl st in any ch-1 sp, ch 3, in same sp work 1 dc, ch 1 and 2 dc (first corner), * ch 1, in next ch-1 sp work 2 dc, ch 1 and 2 dc (another corner). Repeat from * 3 times more (5 corners), ch 1, join. Break off.

Rnd 3: Sl st in any ch 1 corner sp, work first corner in same sp, * ch 1, 2 dc shell in next ch-1 sp, ch 1, corner in next corner sp. Repeat from * 3 times more, ch 1, shell in next sp, ch 1, join.

Rnd 4: Sl st in any ch-1 corner sp, work first corner in same sp, * (ch 1, shell in next ch-1 sp) twice, ch 1, corner in next corner sp. Repeat from * 3 times more, (ch 1, shell in next sp) twice, ch 1, join.

623. Ch 4. Join with sl st to form ring.

Rnd 1: Ch 3, work 11 dc in ring; join with sl st to top of ch 3.

Rnd 2: Work 2 sc in same place as sl st, (sc in each of next 2 dc, 3 sc in next dc) 3 times, sc in each of next 2 dc, work sc in same place as first 2 sc.

Rnd 3: * In next sc work sc, ch 2, and sc for corner, sc in each of next 4 sc. Repeat from * around, join to first sc.

Rnd 4: * In next corner sp work sc, ch 2 and sc, sc in each of next 6 sc. Repeat from * around, join.

Rnd 5: Repeat 4th round, but work 8 sc instead of sc, between corners.

Rnd 6: Repeat 4th round, join 2nd color in sc of corner, work 10 sc between corners.

Rnd 7: Repeat 4th round, work 12 sc between corners.

624. Ch 6. Join with sl st to form ring.

Rnd 1: Ch 8, (work tr in ring, ch 4) 7 times; sl st in 4th ch of ch 8 (8 spokes).

Rnd 2: Work 6 sc in each sp around.

Rnd 3: Sc in next sc, (hdc in next sc, dc in next 8 sc, hdc in next sc, sc in each of next 2 sc) 4 times, ending last repeat with 1 sc instead of 2 (4 petals made with 12 sts each).

Rnd 4: Sl st in next 6 sts, ch 8, sc in same st as last sl st, ch 5, sk next 3 sts, sc in next st, ch 5, sk next 4 sts, sc in next st, ch 5, sk next 2 sts, dc in next st, * ch 5, sc in same st, ch 5, sk 3 sts, sc in next st, ch 5, sk next 4 sts, sc in next st, ch 5, sk next 2 sts, dc in next st. Repeat from * twice more, ending last repeat by joining with sl st in 3rd ch of ch 8.

Rnd 5: * 11 sc in ch 5 corner lp, 4 sc in next 3 lps, repeat from *. Join with sl st in first sc of previous round.

625. Ch 6. Join with sl st to form ring.

Rnd 1: (Ch 6, sc in ring) 4 times. Break off.

Rnd 2: Sl st and sc in any ch 6 lp, ch 1, work sc in same lp, * ch 1, tr in ring (working over sc on first round), ch 1, work sc, ch 1 and sc in next ch-6 lp (corner). Repeat from * twice more, ch 1, tr in ring, ch 1, join with sl st to first sc. Break off.

Rnd 3: Sl st in any corner ch-1 sp, ch 3, in same sp work dc, ch 2 and 2 dc (first corner), * (ch 1, dc in next ch-1 sp) twice, ch 1, in next corner sp work 2 dc, ch 2 and 2 dc (another corner). Repeat from * twice more (ch 1, dc in next ch 1 sp) twice, ch 1, join with sl st to top of ch 3. Break off.

Rnd 4: Work first corner in any corner ch-2 sp, ch 1, skip next ch-1 sp, work 3 dc shell in next ch-1 sp, * ch 1, skp next ch-1 sp, work a corner in next corner sp, ch 1, sk ch-1 sp, shell in next ch-1 sp. Repeat from * twice more, ch 1, join. Break off.

Rnd 5: Work a first corner in any corner ch-2 sp, * (ch 1, shell in next sp) twice, ch 1, work a corner in next corner sp. Repeat from * twice more, (ch 1, shell in next sp) twice, ch 1, join.

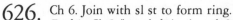

626. Ch 6. Join with sl st to form ring.

Rnd 1: Ch 5, * work dc in ring, ch 2, repeat from * 10 times more, join with sl st to 3rd ch of ch 5.

Rnd 2: Ch 3, * work 3 dc in each of next 2 ch-2 sps, in next sp work 2 dc, ch 3 and 2 dc (corner made). Repeat from * around, end last repeat with corner of 2 dc, ch 3 and 1 dc, join to top of ch 3.

Rnd 3: Sl st in corner sp, 4 sc in corner sp, ch 10, * 4 sc in next corner sp, ch 10. Repeat from * around join to first sc.

Rnd 4: Sc in same st as last sl st and in each of next 3 sc, 15 sc over ch-1 lp,* sc in each of next 4 sc, 15 sc over ch 10 lps, repeat from * around, join to first sc.

Rnd 5: * Ch 4, sk 2 sc, sc in next sc, ch 6, sk 7 sc, in next sc work 3 dc, ch 3 and 3 dc, ch 6, sk 7 sc, sc in next sc. Repeat from * around, end last repeat with sl st in base of ch 4. Fasten off.

627. Ch 6. Join with sl st to form ring.

Rnd 1: Ch 3, work 2 dc in ring, (ch 1, 3 dc in ring) 3 times, ch 1, join with sl st to top of ch 3.

Rnd 2: Sl st in next 2 dc, sl st in next ch-1 sp, ch 3, in same sp work 2 dc, ch 1 and 3 dc (first corner made), * ch 1, in next ch-1 sp work 3 dc, ch 1, and 3 dc (another corner). Repeat from * around, ch 1, join.

Rnd 3: Sl st in next 2 dc, sl st in next corner sp, ch 3, * work corner in corner sp, ch 2, in next sp work dc, ch 2 and dc (V st made), ch 2. Repeat from * around, join.

Rnd 4: Sl st in next 2 dc, sl st in next corner sp, * work corner in corner sp, ch 3, in ch-2 sp of V st work dc, ch 3 and dc, ch 3. Repeat from * around, join. End off.

628. Ch 6. Join with sl st to form ring.

Rnd 1: Ch 3, (yo, insert hook in ring and draw up lp, yo and draw through 2 lps on hook) twice; yo and draw through all 3 lps on hook (first cl made), * ch 5, (yo, insert hook in ring and draw up lp, yo and draw through 2 lps on hook) 3 times, yo and draw through all 4 lps on hook (another cl made), ch 1, work cl. Repeat from * twice more, ch 5, work cl, ch 1, join with sl st in top of first cl.

Rnd 2: Sl st in next ch-5 space, work first cl in same sp, ch 3, work another cl in same sp (first corner made), * ch 1, work 3 dc in next ch-1 sp, ch 1, in next ch-5 sp work cl, ch 3 and cl (another corner made). Repeat from * twice more, ch 1, work 3 dc in next sp, ch 1, join to first cl.

Rnd 3: Sl st in next ch-3 sp, work first corner in same sp, * ch 2, dc in next sp, dc in each of next 3 dc, dc in next sp, ch 2, work corner in next sp. Repeat from * twice more, ch 2, dc in next sp, dc in each of next 3 dc, dc in next sp, ch 2, join.

Rnd 4: Sl st in next ch-3 sp, work first corner in same sp, * ch 2, dc in next sp and in each dc to next sp, dc in sp, ch 2, work corner in next sp. Repeat from * twice more, ch 2, dc in next sp, dc in each dc to next sp, dc in sp, ch 2, join.

Rnd 5: Repeat Round 4. End off.

629. Color A, ch 7, join with a sl st to form a ring, ch 1, do not turn.

Rnd 1: 16 dc in ring, sl st, ch 1.

Rnd 2: *Sk 1 dc, 7 tr in next dc (shell), sk 1 dc, 1 dc in next dc, repeat from *, ending with sl st in ch 1. Join Color B.

Rnd 3: Ch 3, 7 tr in same place as sl st, * ch 1, 1 dc in center of shell, ch 1, 8 tr in next dc, repeat from * ending with ch 1, 1 dc in center of shell, ch 1, sl st in top of ch 3.

Rnd 4: Ch 3, 1 dc in next sp, * in dc work (1 tr, ch 1) 3 times, sk 3 tr in next tr, work (1 tr, ch 1) 4 times, in next tr work (1 tr, ch 1) 4 times, 1 dc in next space, repeat from *, ending with sl st in top of ch 3.

630. Square with corner clusters.

Ch 4. Join with sl st to form ring.

Rnd 1: 8 dc in ring, join with sl st in first dc.

Rnd 2: * 3 dc in same place as sl st, 1 dc in next dc, repeat from * ending with sl st in first dc, ch 3.

Rnd 3: 1 tr in next st, ch 1, * 4 tr in center of 3 dc group, remove hook, insert in top of first tr and pull loop through (cluster), ch 3, work another cluster in same place (corner), ch 1, 1 tr in each of next 3 dcs, ch 1, repeat from *, ending with sl st in top of ch 3, ch 3.

Rnd 4: 1 tr in next tr, * tr in next ch-1 sp, ch 1, in corner sp work cluster, ch 3, cluster, ch 1, tr in next 3 tr, repeat from * ending with sl st in top of ch 3.

Continue in this manner, having 2 or more tr in each panel between clusters in each row. Work until desired size, then work final row: 1 dc in each tr to corner, 1 dc in ch-1 sp, 1 dc in top of 1st corner cluster, (1 dc, 3 tr, 1 dc) in corner sp. Repeat in this manner to end of round, sl st in 1st dc. End off.

Group
Stitch Patterns

These designs have several stitches worked into them. The patterns are very easy to make; they hold their shape beautifully and work up quickly. They are more open than the Afghan patterns, but not as loose as Lace. Think of a Group stitch as a block of color; then make a checkerboard design by alternating colors for every other Group stitch. Create ribbons of color by changing colors on every row.

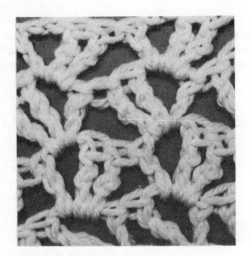

631. Multiple of 3 stitches plus 1.
Row 1: Tr in 3rd st from hook, ch 2, dc in same st, * sk 2 sts, (tr, ch 2, dc) in next st, repeat from * across, end ch 2, turn.
Row 2: * 2 tr, ch 2, dc in ch-2 sp of previous row, repeat from * across row, end tr in turning ch, ch 2, turn.
Repeat Row 2 for Pattern Stitch.

632. Multiple of 4 stitches plus 3.
Row 1: Dc in 2nd ch from hook, sk 1, 3 dc in next st, * sk 1, 1 dc in next st, sk 1, 3 dc in next st, repeat from * across row, end ch 1, turn.
Row 2: * dc in 2nd dc of last group, 3 dc in next dc, repeat from * across row, end ch 2, turn.
Row 3: Dc in 2nd dc of last group, * (2 dc, ch 2, dc) in next dc, repeat from * across row, end ch 2, turn.
Row 4: (1 dc, ch 1, dc) in ch-1 sp, * (2 dc, ch 1, dc) in ch-1 sp, repeat from * across row, end ch 1, turn.
Repeat Rows 2-4 for Pattern Stitch.

633. Multiple of 3 stitches plus 1.
Row 1: (hdc, tr, hdc) in 3rd ch from hook, * sk 2 chs, (hdc, tr, hdc) in next ch, repeat from * across row, end ch 2, turn.
Row 2: * (hdc, tr, hdc) in tr of previous row, repeat from * across row, end ch 2, turn.
Repeat Row 2 for Pattern Stitch.

634. Multiple of 2 stitches plus 1.
Row 1: Sc in 2nd ch from hook, and in each ch across, turn.
Row 2: Ch 3 (counts as dc), dc in first sc for group st, * sk 1 sc, 2 dc in next sc for group, repeat from * across row, end last group in last sc, turn.
Row 3: Ch 3 (dc), * 2 dc in sp before next group, repeat from * across row, end dc in turning ch, turn.
Row 4: Ch 3 (dc), dc in sp before next group, * group in sp before next group, repeat from * across row, end group in last sp.
Repeat Rows 3 and 4 for Pattern Stitch.

635. Even number of stitches.
Row 1: In 3rd ch from hook, * (yo, pull up lp and thru 2 lps, in next ch yo, pull up lp and thru all 4 lps) twist st, ch 1, repeat from * across row, end ch 2, turn.
Row 2: Twist st in each ch-1 sp across row, end ch 2, turn.
Repeat Row 2 for Pattern Stitch.

636. Even number of stitches.
Row 1: Dc in 2nd ch from hook, * ch 1, dc in next ch, repeat from * across row, end ch 2, turn.
Row 2: Work (yo, pull up lp and thru 2 lps, yo and pull up lp and thru 3 lps on hook), ch 1, in each ch-1 sp across row, end ch 2, turn.
Row 3: Dc, ch 1, in each ch-1 sp across row, end ch 2, turn.
Repeat Rows 2 and 3 for Pattern Stitch.

637. Multiple of 3 stitches plus 1.
Row 1: In 3rd ch from hook (sc, dc, hdc), * sk 2, in next st (sc, dc, hdc) repeat from * across row, end ch 2, turn.
Row 2: * sk 2, (sc, dc, hdc) in next st, repeat from * across row, end sc in top of turning ch, ch 2, turn.
Repeat Row 2 for Pattern Stitch.

638. Even number of stitches.
Row 1: In 3rd ch from hook * draw up lp and thru lp, in next ch draw up lp and draw thru 2 lps and draw thru last 2 lps on hook, ch 1, repeat from * across row, ch 2, turn.
Row 2: Work same as for Row 1 working group st in each ch-1 sp of previous row.
Repeat Row 2 for Pattern Stitch.

639. Multiple of 3 stitches plus 1.

Row 1: In 4th ch from hook * hold back last lp of each dc and work (4 dc in next ch, yo and thru all lps on hook) group st, ch 1, sk 2 chs, repeat from * across row, end ch 2, turn.

Row 2: Hold back last lp of each dc, work dc in 2nd and 3rd dcs of previous row, * ch 1, dc in next group, repeat from * across, end ch 2, turn.

Row 3: Work 2 dc, ch 1, in top of last dc of each group across row, end ch 2, turn.

Repeat Row 3 for Pattern Stitch.

640. Multiple of 6 stitches.

Row 1: Sk 2 chs, 2 tr in next ch, * sk 2 chs, dc, 2 tr in next ch, repeat from * across row, end 1 dc, ch 2, turn.

Row 2: 2 tr in first dc, * dc, 2 tr in next dc, repeat from * across row, end dc in turning ch, ch 2, turn.

Repeat Row 2 for Pattern Stitch.

641. Multiple of 3 stitches plus 1.

Row 1: 3 dc in 2nd ch from hook, * ch 1, sk 2 chs, 3 dc in next ch, repeat from * across row, end ch 1, turn.

Row 2: Sc in each st across row, end ch 3, turn.

Row 3: 3 dc in 2nd sc-sp, * ch 1, 3 dc in center of 3 dc-group, repeat from * across row, end ch 1, turn.

Repeat Rows 2 and 3 for Pattern Stitch.

642. Multiple of 2 stitches plus 1.

Row 1: 2 hdc in 4th ch from hook, * ch 1, sk 1, 2 hdc in next ch, repeat from * across row, end ch 2, turn.

Row 2: Hdc in center of first hdc group of previous row, * ch 1, 2 hdc in center of next group, repeat from * across row, end ch 2, turn.

Repeat Row 2 for Pattern Stitch.

643. Multiple of 2 stitches plus 1.

Row 1: Ch 1, * dc, tr in next st, sk 1, repeat from * across row, end dc in last st, ch 1, turn.

Repeat Row 1 working in the top of each dc of previous row.

644. Even number of stitches.

Row 1: Sk 3 chs, * in next ch work sc, yo and pull up lp, yo and thru all lps, ch 1, sk 1, repeat from * across row, end ch 1, turn.

Row 2: In each ch-1 sp (sc, yo, pull up lp, yo and thru all lps, ch 1) across row, end ch 1, turn.

Repeat Row 2 for Pattern Stitch.

645. Multiple of 4 stitches plus 1.
Row 1: Dc in 4th ch from hook, * sk 2, sc, 2 dc in next ch, repeat from * across row, ch 3, turn.
Row 2: Dc in first dc of first group, * sc, 2 dc in first dc of next group, repeat from * across row, end ch 3, turn.
Repeat Row 2 for Pattern Stitch.

646. Multiple of 4 stitches plus 2.
Row 1: Sc in 2nd ch from hook and in each ch across row, ch 1, turn.
Row 2: Sc in first sc, * sk 1, 3 sc in next sc, sk 1, sc in sc, repeat from * across row, end sc in last sc, ch 1, turn.
Row 3: * sc in sc, 3 sc in center sc of 3 sc group, repeat from * across row, end ch 1, turn.
Repeat Rows 2 and 3 for Pattern Stitch.

647. Multiple of 5 stitches plus 3.
Row 1: Sc in 2nd ch from hook, * ch 2, sk 2, sc in next 2 chs, repeat from * to within last 3 chs, ch 2, sk 2, sc in last ch, ch 1, turn.
Row 2: Sc in first sc, 2 sc in next sp, * ch 2, sk 2 sc, work 2 sc in next sp, repeat from * across, end with sc in last sc, ch 1, turn.
Row 3: Sc in first sc, ch 2, * sk 2, 2 sc in next sp, ch 2, repeat from * across row, end sc in last sc, ch 1, turn.
Repeat Rows 2 and 3 for Pattern Stitch.

Applique
Stitch Patterns

These decorative finishing touches can be used in many different ways. Colorful appliqués make children's outfits special and extra fun to wear. Make a smattering of large heart-shaped appliques, then decide whether to sew them on jackets or sweaters as pockets or elbow patches. Appliqué projects are good leftover yarn user-uppers. Brightly colored crayon stick shapes make exciting colored cutouts from a child's coloring book. These same stylized patterns are splendid on pillows, handbags, hats and mittens.

648. Ch 6, join with sl st to first ch to form ring, ch 2. Work 15 dc in ring. Join to top of ch-2 with sl st.

Rnd 1: * ch 6, sl st in 2nd ch from hook, ch 5, sk 1 dc in ring, join with sc, repeat from * around until 8 points have been made. Join with sl st to first ch of first point. End off.

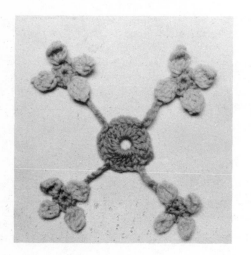

649. With A, ch 5, join with sl st to first ch to form ring, ch 2.

Rnd 1: Work 19 dc in ring, * ch 10, sl st in 3rd ch from hook, ch 1, turn.

Rnd 2: Work 7 sc in ring, join with sl st to top of ch-1. End off.

Rnd 3: Join B in any sc, ch 2, hold back last lp of each dc, work 3 dc in same sp, yo and thru all lps on hook. End off. Make Knot. Sk 1 sc, repeat Rnd 3 (3 times) more to complete flower.

Rnd 4: Sk 4 dc in ring, attach A in next dc, repeat from * until 4 flowers have been made.

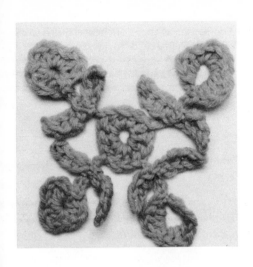

650. Ch 6, join with sl st to first ch to form ring, ch 2, work 12 dc in ring. End off.
Flowers: Join yarn in any dc, ch 8, (3 dc, sc, 3 dc, sc, 3 dc, sc) in 2nd ch from hook, sl st in next 3 chs, ch 5, * sc in 2nd ch from hook, hdc in next ch, dc in next ch, sc in last ch, sl st in center of stem, ch 5, repeat from * across. End off. ** Sk 2 dc and repeat flower in next dc, repeat from ** around. 4 flowers around.

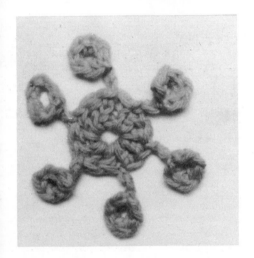

651. Ch 6, join with sl st to first ch, ch 2, work 12 dc in ring. End off.
Petal: Join yarn in any dc, ch 6, join with sl st in 4th ch from hook, work 6 sc in ring. Join with sl st to top of ch. End off. Skip 1 dc between petals. Work 5 more petals around.

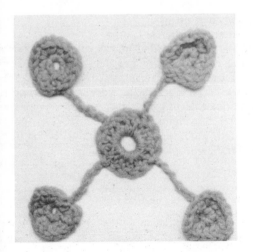

652. Ch 6, join with sl st to first ch to form ring, ch 2 and work 15 dc in ring. Join with sl st to top of ch-2.
Rnd 1: Ch 10, join with sl st to 3rd ch from hook, ch 1, turn. Work 5 sc in ring, join to first sc with sl st, ch 1, in same sp hdc, ch 1, 2 hdc, * hdc in next sc, (2 hdc, ch 1, 2 hdc) in next sc, repeat from * around once more and join with sl st in top of beg ch, ch 1. End off. ** Sk 3 dc, repeat Rnd 1. Repeat from ** 2 times more. 4 triangles around. End off.

653. Ch 5, in 3rd ch from hook work 3 dc, sc in next ch, 3 dc in next ch, turn work upside down, sl st in center sc, * ch 7, dc in 3rd ch, dc in next ch, tr in next 2 chs, dc in last ch, sl st in center, repeat from * once more, end sl st in center, ch 5 (feeler) end off. Join yarn in center top and work another feeler. End off. Work 2 feelers at base of butterfly.

654. Ch 3, sc in last 2 chs, ch 1, turn.
Row 1: Increase 1 st each end, ch 1, turn.
Work until there are 8 sc across row. Work even for 1 more row.
Row 2: Work sc in 3 sc, sl st in next 2 sc, sc in last 3 sc, ch 1, turn.
Row 3: Repeat Row 2.
Work 1 row sc around entire strawberry, end off.
Stem: Join green in center top and work 3 sc across, ch 1, turn. Sl st to center sc, ch 4, end off.
Texture: With Black work small back stitches on berry. End off.

655. Ch 3, sc in 2nd ch, sc in last ch, ch 1, turn.
Row 2: Increase 1 st in each st across row, ch 1, turn.
Row 3: Increase 1 st each end until there are 18 sc.
Rows 4-7: Work even on 18 sc.
Row 8: Sl st across 3 sts, work to last 3 sts, turn.
Dec 1 st at beg of next row, work 4 sc, sl st across 2 sc, work across row and work 1 row sc around outer edges.
Leaf and Stem: Ch 12, * dc in 2nd ch from hook, tr in next 2 chs, dc in next ch, sl st in center of stem, ch 5, repeat from *, end with sl st in center of stem. End off. Sew in place.

656. Heart Motif. Ch 3, work 3 tr in first ch, ch 3, sl st in same ch, ch 3, 6 tr in same ch, sl st in top of last tr, 2 tr in same ch, join with sl st to top of ch 3. Fasten off.

Edging & Border
Stitch Patterns

More decorative finishing touches make your crochet articles special. These patterns work well on dress hems and cuffs. Try using a pattern to border an afghan. Garments look "complete" when the edges or borders are crocheted in contrasting colors, for they tend to highlight the body of the article.

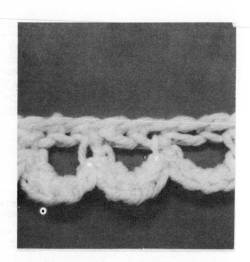

657. Even number of stitches.
Row 1: Sc in 2nd ch from hook and in each ch across, end ch 1, turn.
Row 2: * Ch 4, sk 1 ch, sc in next ch, repeat from * across, end ch 1, turn.
Row 3: * 5 sc in next lp, sl st in next sc, repeat from * across. Join with sl st and end off.

658. Multiple of 4 stitches plus 1.
Work pattern on right side of work.
Row 1: Make lp on hook, on right side of work begin at lower edge and sc in each st across. End off.
Row 2: Repeat Row 1.
Row 3: Begin as for Row 1; * dc in each of 3 sc, make popcorn (yo, pull up lp) 4 times in next sc, yo and thru all 9 lps on hook, ch 1, repeat from * across, end dc in last 3 sc. End off.
Row 4: Begin as for Row 1; sc in each dc and popcorn. End off.

659. Multiple of 6 stitches plus 2.
Make chain to desired length.
Row 1: Dc in 3rd ch from hook, dc in each ch across, ch 1, turn.
Row 2: Sc in same sp, * sk 2, 10 dc in next st, sk 2 sts, sc in next st, repeat from * across, end sc in last dc. End off.

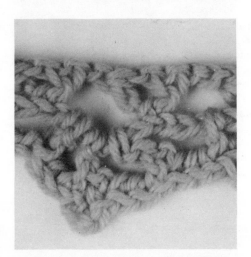

660. *Row 1:* *Ch 5, dc in 4th ch from hook, repeat from * for desired length (make an equal number of dc groups), ch 2, turn.
Row 2: Sc in 2nd st from hook, * ch 5, sc in each ch-lp, repeat from * across, end ch 2, dc in last st, turn.
Row 3: *Ch 3, 3 dc with ch-3 between each dc in center of next lp, ch 3, sc in next lp, repeat from * across, end ch 1, turn.
Row 4: * 3 sc in next 2 lps, sc in next dc, ch 3, sl st in sc, 3 sc in next 2 lps, repeat from * across, sl st in last st. End off.

661. *Row 1:* Ch 8, dc in 8th ch from hook, * ch 3, turn. 7 dc in top of dc last made, ch 7, turn. Dc in first dc, repeat from * for desired length.

662. Multiple of 3 stitches plus 2.
Make ch to desired length.
Row 1: Hdc in 2nd ch from hook, hdc in each ch across, ch 2, turn.
Row 2: (hold back last lp of each dc) work 3 dc in first hdc, yo and thru all lps, * ch 3, sk 2, ch 3, 4 dc in next hdc, yo and thru all lps, repeat from * across, end sc in last st. End off.

663. Multiple of 4 stitches plus 2.
Row 1: Dc in 2nd ch from hook, dc in each ch across row, ch 2, turn.
Row 2: (2 dc, ch 2, 3 dc) in 2nd dc, * sk 1, sc in next dc, sk 1, (3 dc, ch 2, 3 dc) in next dc, repeat from * across row. End sc in turning ch. End off.

664. Multiple of 4 stitches plus 1.
Row 1: Hdc in 2nd ch from hook, hdc in each ch across row, end ch 1, turn.
Row 2: In first hdc work (dc, ch 1, 2 dc), * sk 1, sc in next hdc, sk 1, (2 dc, ch 1, 2 dc) in next hdc, repeat from * across row, end ch 1, turn.
Row 3: * Sc in 2 dc, sc in ch-1 sp, 3 dc in center dc, sc in ch-1 sp, sc in next 2 dc, sc in sc, repeat from * across row. End off.

665. Even number of stitches.

Row 1: Sk first ch, sc in each st across, ch 1, turn.

Row 2: *Yo, draw up lp in next sc, yo draw up lp in next sc, yo and thru all lps (twist), ch 1, repeat from * across row, end with twist st, ch 1, turn.

Row 3: * Sc in center of twist st of previous row, sc in next sp, repeat from * across row, end sc in turning ch, ch 1, turn.

Repeat Rows 2 and 3 for Pattern Stitch.

666. Multiple of 12 stitches plus 5.

Rnd 1: 1 tr into 8th ch from hook, * ch 2, sk 2, tr into next ch, repeat from * to end, ch 5, turn.

Rnd 2: Sk first tr, tr into next tr, * ch 2, tr in next tr, repeat from *, end with sk 2 chs, tr in next ch, turn.

Rnd 3: Dc into first tr, ch 3, sk next tr, * hold last lp of each on hook, work 2 tr into next tr, yo and thru all lps on hook (cluster made), ch 4, (cluster into same tr) 3 times (4 cluster groups made), ch 3, sk next tr, dc into next tr, ch 3, sk next tr, repeat from *, work last dc into 3rd ch of ch 5. End off.

667. Ch 8, tr into 8th ch from hook, * ch 5, turn, sk 2, tr into next ch, repeat from * for required length, keeping a multiple of 2 sps, ch 8, turn.

Row 1: 3 tr into same place as last tr, * ch 3, tr in top to next tr, ch 3, 3 tr into base of same dc, repeat from * ending with ch 3, sk 2, tr in next ch, ch 1, turn.

Row 2: Sc in first tr, * ch 7, dc in next tr, repeat from *, end with ch 7, 1 dc into 5th ch of ch 8, ch 1, turn.

Row 3: Into each lp work 5 dc, ch 4, sl st in 4th ch from hook (picot) and 5 dc, sl st into first dc of previous row. End off.

668. *Row 1:* Sc in 2nd ch from hook, sc in each ch across row, end ch 1, turn.
Row 2: Sc in each sc across row, end ch 1, turn.
Row 3: Sc in first 5 sc, * ch 4, sl st in 4th ch from hook, ch 2, work hdc in ring, sl st in top of ch 2, sk 1 sc, sc in next 5 sc, repeat from * across row, end sc in last 5 sc. End off.

669. Ch 9, turn.
Row 1: 1 tr in 3rd ch from hook, tr in next ch, ch 2, sk 2 chs, 1 tr in next ch, ch 6, sk 1 ch, dc in last ch, ch 1, turn.
Row 2: * 1 dc in sp, ch 3, sl st in top of dc (picot), repeat from * 4 times, dc in tr, 2 dc in sp, dc in next 2 tr, dc in turning ch, ch 3, turn.
Row 3: (1 tr in next dc) twice, ch 2, sk 2 dc, 1 tr in next dc, ch 6, sk 2 picots, dc in next picot, ch 1, turn.
Repeat Rows 2 and 3 for Pattern Stitch.

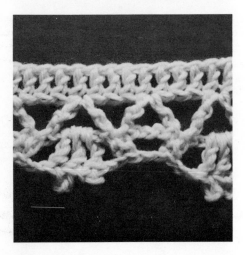

670. Work 1 row dc around edge of fabric. Join with a sl st.
Row 1: Ch 3, sk 3 dc, tr in next dc, * ch 3, tr in same dc as last tr, ch 3, sl st in top of last tr (picot), sk 3 dc, tr in next dc, repeat from *, ending with picot, sl st in top of starting chain, ch 1, turn.
Row 2: Sl st into picot just made, * ch 2, (tr, picot, tr, picot, tr) in sp, ch 2, sl st in next picot, ch 2, sl st in next picot, repeat from *. End off.

671. Ch 7.

Row 1: Sk 1 ch, dc in next 3 chs, ch 2, sk 2 chs, (tr, ch 2, 1 tr, ch 2, 1 tr) in last ch, ch 5, turn.

Row 2: Sk first sp, tr in center sp, (ch 2, tr) 3 times in same sp, ch 2, sk 2 dc, 1 tr in last dc, ch 7, turn.

Row 3: Tr in center sp of shell, (ch 2, tr) 3 times in same sp, ch 5, turn.

Row 4: 1 tr in center sp of shell, (ch 2, tr) 3 times in same sp, ch 2, tr in 3rd ch of ch 7, ch 7, turn.

Repeat Rows 3 and 4 for desired length, end with Row 3—omitting ch 5 at end of last row. Work along ch 5 lps as follows: 2 tr, 1 picot, (3 tr, 1 picot) twice, 2 tr in each ch-5 lp to end.

672. Ch 11.

Row 1: Tr in 11th ch from hook, ch 3, tr in same ch, ch 1, turn.

Row 2: Dc in first tr, 1 dc and 5 tr in ch-3 sp, tr in next tr, ch 3, tr in 3rd ch of ch-10, ch 7, turn.

Row 3: Sk ch-3 lp, (1 tr, ch 3, 1 tr) into next tr, ch 6, sk next 6 sts, sl st into next dc, ch 1, turn.

Row 4: 3 dc, picot, (dc, ch 3, sl st in top of dc) twice, 3 dc all in ch-6 lp, * 1 dc in next tr, 1 dc and 5 tr in ch-3 sp, 1 tr in next tr, ch 3, tr in 3rd ch of ch 7, repeat from * across row, ch 7, turn.

Repeat Rows 3 and 4 until desired length. End off.